JESUS CHRIST
YESTERDAY AND TODAY

JESUS CHRIST YESTERDAY AND TODAY

Introduction to Biblical Spirituality

JACQUES GUILLET, S.J.

Translated by
JOHN DUGGAN, S.J.

FRANCISCAN HERALD PRESS
Publishers of Franciscan Literature
Chicago, Illinois   60609

JESUS CHRIST YESTERDAY AND TODAY, TRANSLATED FROM THE FRENCH EDITION OF
DESCLÉE DE BROUWER, 76 BIS, RUE DES SAINTES-PERES, PARIS 7, FRANCE, WITH THE
TITLE *Jésus-Christ hier et aujourd'hui*. LIBRARY OF CONGRESS CATALOG CARD NUMBER:
65-18948. © TRANSLATION, 1964, GEOFFREY CHAPMAN LTD. PUBLISHED IN THE
UNITED STATES OF AMERICA BY FRANCISCAN HERALD PRESS, 1434 WEST 51ST STREET,
CHICAGO, ILLINOIS 60609.

IMPRIMI POTEST
DOMINIC LIMACHER, O.F.M.
Minister Provincial, Sacred Heart Province

NIHIL OBSTAT
MARK HEGENER, O.F.M.
Censor Deputatus

IMPRIMATUR
MOST REV. CLETUS F. O'DONNELL, D.D.
Vicar General, Archdiocese of Chicago

JANUARY 25, 1965

PRINTED IN GREAT BRITAIN

Contents

Translator's Note   ix

Introduction   1

I   *The Coming of Christ and the Expectation of Justice*   12

1. Justice in the mind of Israel. 2. Justice and the covenant. 3. The prophets against injustice. 4. The expectation of God's justice. 5. The paradox of Christmas. 6. The gospel idea of justice and the worship of God. 7. The gospel and the poor. 8. God poor, and God just.

II   *The Glory of the Lord*   26

1. Glory in the bible. 2. Moses on Mount Sinai. 3. Elijah on Sinai. 4. Isaiah in the temple. 5. Expectation of glory.

III   *The Baptism of Christ and the Blessed Trinity*   42

1. The baptism of John. 2. The Spirit and water. 3. The baptism of Christ. 4. Our Lord and the Holy Spirit.

IV   *The Holy Spirit in Our Lord*   53

    1. Jesus led by the Spirit to the devil. 2. Jesus overcoming the devil, in the Spirit. 3. The anointing of Christ by the Spirit. 4. The Holy Spirit and the poor.

V   *Our Lord in Conflict*   67

    1. The battle for man. 2. Conflict with Satan. 3. Struggle with God.

VI   *Our Lord's Poverty*   80

    1. Our Lord in poverty. 2. Jesus 'dispossessed himself'. 3. Our Lord's time limited for him. 4. A poor man among men. 5. The risen Christ still a poor man. 6. The unfathomable riches of Christ.

VII *Our Lord's Obedience*   93

    1. Doing God's will. 2. Obedience to men. 3. Obedience to events. 4. Obedience to the scriptures. 5. The obedience of the Son. 6. Obedience to God and obedience to creatures.

VIII *Prayer in the Gospel*   110

    1. Prayer for the kingdom of God. 2. Persistence in prayer. 3. Prayer in time of trial. 4. Prayer of thanksgiving. 5. Our Lord's priestly prayer.

IX   *The Son's Thanksgiving*   123

    1. 'Revealed to little ones.' 2. The raising of Lazarus. 3. The eucharist. 4. The priestly prayer. 5. The passion. 6. The resurrection.

X   *The Gospel and Bread*   139

    1. The multiplication of the loaves. 2. The last supper. 3. The meals taken by the risen Jesus.

XI *The Priesthood of the New Covenant*   152

    1. The covenant on Mount Sinai. 2. The new covenant. 3. The implications of the last supper. 4. The priest of the new covenant. 5. Priest and layman.

XII *The Gospel and the Mass*   170

    1. The longed-for paschal meal. 2. The gift of the Lord. 3. The sacramental gift. 4. The mystery of faith.

XIII *'Mary kept all these words'*   182

    1. The Church in the person of Mary. 2. 'All is consummated.' 3. The mother present in the Church.

XIV *The Gift of the Spirit*   190

    1. The baptism of the cross. 2. Pentecost.

XV *Christ the Life of the New-Born Church*   197

    1. The temptation to live in the past. 2. The impact of the Holy Spirit. 3. The Spirit, the presence of Christ. 4. The Spirit, the action of Christ. 5. 'Life means Christ.'

XVI *Christ's Prayer and Ours*   211

    1. The prayer of the Son in the gospel. 2. Our Lord's prayer a source of strength to the apostles. 3. Praying as sons in the Spirit of the Son.

XVII *Our Work in Life and the Expectation of God's Kingdom*   226

    1. 'Stay as you are.' 2. Duties as a man and duties as a Christian. 3. 'As though . . .' 4. Duties of state in the gospel.

Translator's Note

A WORD of explanation seems necessary on the version used for the texts of scripture, which form such an important element in the book. In principle one has aimed at using the *Revised Standard Version*,[1] at least in the extended extracts from the Old Testament, which feature largely in Chapters I and II. (However, it will be observed that 'justice' has been put instead of 'righteousness': this has been done without any theological implication, but simply in fairness to the author's subject as indicated in the title of the first chapter.) It so happened that the translator had already completed many of the New Testament chapters using the Knox translation[2] before it was agreed that Catholics could use the *Revised Standard Version*. It seemed unnecessary to go into reverse over this, especially as the Knox version seemed in itself such a help to an immediate understanding of the significance of texts, particularly in the epistles. Actually, in fairness to the author and his use of the texts, it was sometimes necessary just to translate his French version, taken from the *Jerusalem Bible* (which, incidentally, was not yet available in English at the time the translation was being done). In many cases the author's use of the texts is extremely personal and to a certain extent conditioned to his literary style. For instance, he is fond of free indirect speech—more so than is natural in English. Here it often seemed better to insert the actual text.

[1] Thomas Nelson and Sons, Ltd   [2] Burns & Oates Ltd

All one can say is that every effort has been made to do justice to the author's thought and use of scripture quotations, in a way that would most help English-speaking readers. A scripture specialist might feel that this varied use of different versions is somewhat inconsistent and unscientific, but the scope of the book is not meant to be rigorously critical or theological. In the publisher's note to the French edition, Père Guillet is described as an exegete leaving on one side (for the occasion) all technical preoccupation with biblical criticism—though of course he remains perfectly well aware of critical and historical questions, as can be seen in the Introduction.

Introduction

THE TITLE, *Jesus Christ, Yesterday and Today*, may seem rather pretentious for a collection of articles originally intended to be grouped with others and to throw light on particular aspects of Christian life.[1] A reader who might be expecting a broad synthesis on our Lord's personality and work, on his earthly life and his everlasting life in the glory of the Father, may be disappointed to find here a series of partial studies of our Lord. The justification for this collection is indicated in the two-fold title: *Jesus Christ* indicating the unity underlying these studies; *Yesterday and Today* implying the range of human life and the diversity of situations involved in it.

Jesus Christ is the subject of every chapter. All of them are based on the gospel and follow it in broad outline. Also, they seek, through the words and actions of the gospel, to discern the character of our Lord, the principles guiding his life, the secret of his personality and his influence on people. This knowledge can only come through the gospel, and this book aims primarily at helping people to read the gospel text. However, the real meaning of the gospel can only be grasped by

[1] Apart from 'Our Lord in Conflict', previously unpublished, and two articles from *Revue de l'Action Populaire*, viz. 'The Coming of Christ and the Expectation of Justice' (Dec. 1954) and 'The Gospel and Bread' (April 1956), all the articles gathered here have been published in the French spiritual review *Christus*. Some of them have been considerably recast.

faith, not just as a record of past history, but as the revelation
of him who became mortal man, died, and now lives for evermore. The Word was made flesh, and every feature of this flesh
is of interest to us, as revealing the glory of the only-begotten
Son, his work of the redemption, and the abiding power of
our Lord over his kingdom. So this book tries to co-ordinate
gospel memories and Christian experience, to 'get through to
our Lord' in the uniqueness of his earthly life and then in the
universal extension that his risen life assumes under the power
of the Holy Spirit. Our Lord's baptism is the prototype of
Christian baptism, his being tempted represents a key-
experience in Christian life, his conflicts are types of those
awaiting us, his prayer is the source of our prayer, his passion
and resurrection are perpetuated in the members of his
Church.

Since the Word was made flesh and now lives on in his risen
flesh, since his present life extends throughout the world his
actions of yesterday—if we wish 'to know him and the power of
his resurrection', we must return to his life-story and linger on
its details, so as to find in them in particular 'a sharing in his
sufferings'.[2] To live Christ's present life, the Church clings to
the contemplation of his life of yesterday, untiringly medi-
tating on the gospel. So in grouping these articles together we
have followed the gospel narrative from the baptism of Jesus
to the foundation of the Church.

It may be surprising to some readers that, in view of this
reference to the historical aspect of the text of the gospels, we
have kept that side of the question within modest limits. It is
true, we have not gone into his historical problem for its own
sake. No effort has been made to buttress the gospel narratives,
or to reconstruct the events they relate, as if these narratives
did not present any problems. The details of the baptism of
Jesus, for instance, are taken quite literally. We have not
examined the question of what Jesus really saw or heard in his
encounter with the tempter nor how the narrative came to be
recorded. We have followed indiscriminately the respective
accounts of our Lord's trials by the high priest, with no
concern for differences between the evangelists, or for the

[2] Phil. 3 : 10

historical probabilities of one as against another. We have presented our Lord from the start of his ministry in the full light of his divinity, as if the most primitive New Testament documents did not show that it required the resurrection and Pentecost for the disciples to recognize in him the Son of God as well as the Messiah. How then can we claim we are being faithful to history and referring to the Christ of the gospels?

This omission, or at least this carefully guarded discretion on the sequence of events, needs some explanation. It does not mean that we are failing to see the importance of these questions, nor that we are trying to put them 'in brackets' as being too difficult or too tricky. Far from ignoring them, we consider that these questions do arise and must be taken into account; but the only way to solve them is to put them in their right setting or perspective, that intended by the gospel accounts. This perspective is just what this book is trying to bring out, so by way of introduction we want to indicate what gives us the assurance, when we open the gospels to hear God's message, that we are on the firm ground of history and real facts.

For this we must start from our Lord's resurrection. That was the date that mattered, the time when the Church's faith took shape. This arose from the certainty that the risen Jesus was the Messiah sent by God, not just as a man like other men, that where he belonged, where he came from and had just returned to, was the zone of divinity, the glory of his Father. From then on Jesus was more than a much venerated master, a prophet without his like; he is God's anointed, the Lord of the world, coming from God and abiding in God. This discovery by the disciples marks a decisive stage in the development of their faith. This seems to have been up to then mainly a generous but passive fidelity to someone whose influence dominated them unaccountably. Now it becomes a final and fully justified allegiance to one of whom they know for certain what he is and what he came to do, the Lord Jesus.

This two-fold change, in our Lord's way of life and in his disciples' faith, raises a fundamental problem. Given that Jesus had now revealed himself to be different from what he appeared during his mortal life, and since their relationship to him was basically changed, is it possible—short of a constant

unnatural effort—to return to his past without distorting it?
Is it not an inevitable reaction to be for ever seeking to find, in
the life of our Lord before he died, features that only the
resurrection revealed? The mortal man tends to be eclipsed
by the risen Christ. He can only be restored to view artificially,
and to write his history would seem no longer possible.

A comparison may bring out this difficulty. When we go
back over the life of an outstanding personality, we normally
have the latter part of his life to throw light on and provide the
key to his whole life. In a sense this over-all interpretation is
really the truest, the nearest to the secret of the dead man, and
it is normal that we should begin with that to unravel the
meaning of a career now closed. Granted this approach is
indispensable, how careful you have to be if you are to avoid
distorting history! What a temptation it is, to try to recapture
in the early years a figure it took a lifetime to form! How
many saints' lives give their hero marks of consummate perfection from the cradle. If such an approach were completely
misleading, it could be scrapped *en bloc*. But there are grounds
for it and you cannot help doing it, for after all it is the same
person, and the continuity of a man's life is an essential reality
for a historian, but he needs special insight and subtlety to
grasp this continuity.

When we are treating of our Lord the problem becomes
complex to the point of being insoluble. Everything about him
is unique, having no common measure with ordinary experience. It is not only his death, in total dereliction by God and
with entire abandonment to his Father, that gives meaning to
his life. Still more, it is the resurrection, showing the unique
value of that death before God, and how privileged his Son is.
Now this resurrection sets up between Christ and his followers
an unprecedented kind of relationship, no mere faithful
following in the footsteps of a wonderful master, sharing his
ideas and his way of life, but the certain conviction of possessing him still, though absent, of being animated by his Spirit
and re-living his very actions. Shall we ever be able to turn
back and find the true picture of the 'son of the carpenter'
through this radical transformation of his image? How are we
to show in his human actions their secret fountainhead, the

Person of the Son of God? But how are we to bring this out as it was originally shown forth, when the witnesses were still incapable of recognizing it? To show him as the God he is, but as God not recognized, and to show him through the recollections and the gaze of men who saw him uncomprehendingly—this is a *tour de force* requiring genius.

But this is just what the gospels achieve, and apparently without effort. The Christian reading them with faith finds both Jesus of Nazareth as he appeared to the crowds and the Son of God such as he revealed himself to be. This achievement has two causes, one being the very Person of Christ our Lord and the way he revealed himself, the other the way the gospels record the revelation.

When we spoke of the transformation in our Lord brought about by his resurrection and the new relationship set up between him and the disciples, we were only giving one aspect of the truth, which requires completion. It is true that by raising him up, 'God has made him master and Christ',[3] so giving him as it were a new character, not merely a glorious recompense but the 'name that is above all names',[4] and his place at the centre and summit of the universe for all eternity. But it is equally true that this new position was our Lord's by right from the first moment of his human existence, that resurrection was built into his being, and that the apostles straightway realized that 'it was impossible that death should have the mastery over him'.[5] The resurrection was the experience of a new condition for our Lord in the glory of God, but by the same token it is the revelation of his permanent and eternal status as Son of God; 'Now, Father, do thou exalt me at thy own side, in that glory which I had with thee before the world began'.[6]

This revelation begins with the disciples' own experience of the resurrection. Admittedly, the accounts of the appearances of the risen Christ contain an element of composition and reconstruction. Hence it is impossible to make them coincide, or even to set them exactly side by side, some of their details being irreconcilable when taken literally. On a literal reading

[3] Acts 2:36
[5] Acts 2:24
[4] Phil. 2:9
[6] John 17:5

of chapter 24 of St Luke it would seem that the ascension took place on the evening of Easter Sunday, and there would seem no means of fitting in the apparitions in Galilee related by St John and St Matthew. Without going into an examination of the texts, one need only observe that on the fundamental facts they are in agreement, right from the earliest books of the New Testament. One of the basic facts is that the witnesses ate and drank with him after his rising from the dead.[7] This proves that he has a real body and is not a dream, and also that he does what he likes with it, quite unlike its condition before his death. Above all it proves that in his glory he continues to be in bodily relation to his disciples, and so is still a man, still the same man. He can appear or disappear, make himself known or change his appearance; but if he makes himself known, it is always under the simplest appearances, in familiar attitudes and with no trace of being distant or remote. Having risen and entered into the divine glory, he remains the man he was, as natural and approachable and spontaneously at his ease among his friends. This naturalness is a precious sign that the apparitions were not invented: they would have been imagined as more impressive, like the transfiguration, or on the lines of scenes that our Lord described himself before his death: 'You will see the Son of man again, seated at the right hand of God's power and coming on the clouds of heaven.'[8]

So faith discovers the divine stature of the risen Christ, and his sovereign grandeur, but it finds them in a person who is identical with the one they had known and followed. His face had not changed; he had not even come back to bring new instructions. He is content with brief encounters, just long enough to confirm by his presence the message he had given during his life and to entrust his disciples with carrying it to the whole world. All this shows that from the time of his mortal life he had been what the resurrection revealed him to be, the anointed Messiah of Israel, the Lord of the world, the Son of God. His true personality was already present and perfect when he toiled along the roads, when he tried to enlighten his hearers, when he was suffering and dying. It was the only-begotten Son of the Father that spoke and bled, but this secret

[7] Acts 10:41   [8] Matt. 26:64

was as yet unknown. To know him in truth there was only one way for the witnesses of his resurrection, namely to go back to the days of his earthly life. It was no use trying to imagine him in the world of glory, to seek to follow him by 'straining their eyes towards heaven';[9] in that world where God 'dwells in light inaccessible'[10] he is invisible. But given that on disappearing from this world he is still the same as in the days of his natural life, it is to these we must return to seek his glory. It is not a question of putting new life into memories or weaving a spell from a wonderful past, but only of finding in the words and actions of Jesus of Nazareth the glory displayed by his resurrection, the glory that remains for all eternity what it was for thirty years under a visible form, the glory of the only-begotten Son.[11]

Far from faith opposing history, in the case of our Lord, it puts us on the way to historical truth and wants to have it as accurate as possible. The more attentive one is to the facts, the more one can reproduce the exact shade of meaning in his thought and in his words and the more one can have insight into his true personality. In this reconstruction of the past, there are bound to be approximations, with recollections dimmed and accounts crystallized in different forms according to the people passing them on. These shortcomings are not the result of faith, but of human nature, which divine inspiration works with. Faith, in itself, makes for fidelity, not alteration.

Still, though faith is an incentive to restore Christ's doings with the maximum of accuracy, these doings cannot for the most part be separated from the reactions of the witnesses, and they only partly grasped the scope of all he said and did. To be strictly true to history, practically every time we relate anything about our Lord we should have to differentiate between the effect produced there and then and the ultimate meaning of his actions, the glory they were charged with and which only the resurrection would reveal. More than once St John's gospel brings out this double impact and two-fold understanding of our Lord's words,[12] and this is not a fleeting

---

[9] Acts 1 : 10   [10] 1 Tim. 6 : 16
[11] John 1 : 14   [12] John 2 : 22; 12 : 16; 14 : 20

characteristic, but one of the keys to this gospel, which shows
an acute sense of history.[13] On the other hand, our Lord's
actions on earth being the revelation of his glory and containing God's riches, were not destined only for the immediate
witnesses but for all mankind. They brought salvation to the
world, they founded the Church. How are we to express this
world-wide scope and fullness of meaning? A historian formed
on modern lines would no doubt answer: by accompanying
the objective account of the facts and the exact record of the
words by a commentary intended to bring out each time the
new scope and meaning they would take on with the resurrection and the foundation of the Church. On this point too St
John's gospel is the nearest to our way of thinking, whether he
interrupts the account to point out the significance of a
detail,[14] or whether, by a device that is more subtle and much
more frequent, he brings out the symbolic and sacramental
implications of the facts related. The other gospels are
generally more down to earth and seem not to go beyond the
simple facts. But they too give our Lord's words and actions
their full impact, for, though relating them just as they stand,
they present them as directly addressed to Christians and to
all men. It can happen that this addition of a universal
audience to the original audience of our Lord may lead to
including anachronisms and even details not likely to have
happened. But a little understanding should enable us to see
that the gospel would not be the gospel of our Lord addressed
to the world if it were reduced to just the words as actually
heard and understood by the original bystanders. The Holy
Spirit, making the Church go back over those words in the
light of the resurrection, and keeping it faithful to its mission
as the Church of Christ and faithful to those very words,
was bound, in several cases, to indicate their import by a basic
minimum of commentary.

An example may help to show that there can be certain
superficial inexactitudes in the gospels, without any damage to
the record; far from it. Our Lord's walking on the waters, the

[13] See X. Léon Dufour: 'Actualité du quatrième évangile' in
Nouvelle Revue Théologique, 1954, pp. 449–68
[14] John 11:51; 12:33

night following the multiplication of the loaves, is related by St Matthew and St Mark in quite different ways. The ending of the incident in particular seems to involve two incompatible versions. According to Mark (6:51) Jesus 'came to them on board the boat and thereupon the wind dropped. And they were astonished out of all measure; they had not grasped the lesson of the loaves, so dulled were their hearts.' By contrast, according to Matthew (14:32–3), 'they (Jesus and Peter) went on board the ship, and thereupon the wind dropped. And the ship's crew came and said, falling at his feet, Thou art indeed the Son of God.' It is clearly the same incident, but the reaction produced in the apostles is radically different in the two cases. Which are we to follow, and if we adopt one, how can we avoid discrediting the other?

This example, that appears at first sight to put us off reading the gospels with any serious attention to detail, since they involve such discrepancies, can actually help us to read them with the maximum of interest in the details. These two ways of relating the same episode serve to make us read them in depth, and there is no question of choosing the one that seems more likely, but seeking from both the truth they convey. Mark's account is certainly the more factually accurate: the apostles are portrayed very naturally with their slowness in taking in the faith and their silence born of fear. Matthew transforms this being seized with fear, and expresses it by the gesture of falling on their knees, a gesture no doubt borrowed from the worship of our Lord in the Church—clearly an anachronism. Both points of view have their truth. The first impression produced by this action of our Lord is the stupor and dismay of the disciples, swept off their feet and overwhelmed by an unaccountable happening. But this happening has another end to it, so to speak, and it is by this other end that Matthew approaches it. Unaccountable there and then, it belongs to the series of sayings and doings of Christ leading up to his resurrection and his full revealing. Each of these actions, each link in the series, looked at from the point of arrival, provides a positive contribution to this revealing, bringing out particular features of our Lord and particular effects of his action. The amazement striking the witnesses dumb already meant two things: it conveyed the incomprehension of man lost in the presence of God; but it also meant something positive, the recognition of divine power, an acknowledgment leading to faith, belonging to faith, though not yet the full expression of faith. In the disciples falling on their knees in the boat, as described by Matthew, we see the catechist's concern, in relating the gospel, to bring out its significance for the life of the Church and to foster in his hearers the Christian reflex of faith and adoration. This involves an anachronism, but no unfaithfulness to history or truth, for it expresses an essential aspect of this episode. Between the stupor of the twelve in their boat and the faith of the Church enlightened by the resurrection and by the Holy Ghost, there is real continuity. If the apostles were in that boat, it was because they had given themselves to our Lord who had called them and had responded to his teaching. They find it very hard to take in this teaching, which they find difficult, but they follow it, for, without knowing why, they believe in it with a glimmer of faith containing in germ the full light of Pentecost. Likewise, with the twelve around our Lord, the Church is there in the boat, the Church in embryo, slowly coming to the knowledge of the Lord. It was essential, in writing the story of Jesus, to indicate the divine fountainhead of his being, even when the eyewitnesses were unaware of it. In the same way, so that the Christians for whom this story is intended should find in it the source of their faith, they must discover in the original witnesses all the stages in the development of faith, from the first almost blind and passive acknowledgment to the full luminous certainty of one who knows him to whom he has entrusted himself.

All the gospels unfold their story between these two poles —at one end the initial material facts, sometimes picturesque and original, sometimes banal and insignificant; at the other end the spiritual and supernatural context of these events, constituting the history and action of the Son of God made man. The Christian reading the gospels does not have to opt between these two poles, or choose one gospel rather than another. He may certainly prefer one gospel or one version of a scene in the gospels. He may even, provided he is suitably qualified to do so, submit the gospels to critical investigation, discerning the most primitive form of the text and the transformations due to transmission in the Church. Such studies are neither superfluous nor sterile, and this book owes a good deal to them. Still, our viewpoint is normally that of the faith as such, the simplest and most profound, for which all the gospels with all their minor variations conspire to yield to us the inexhaustible riches of Christ.

The riches of Christ, which he receives from his Father and of which he makes us a present, are the Holy Spirit. The Holy Spirit is the secret of our Lord and his life, and must be the source of our life too—such is the concept envisaged by this book. It tries to throw light on the Christian way of life by showing it reproducing our Lord's life, by means of an inward continuity, the living presence of the Spirit of the only-begotten Son in the hearts of the children of God. The Christian lives by the Holy Spirit and by his power within us; he lives by Jesus Christ and models his own life on his. But because Jesus and the Spirit are one, these two endeavours merge, these two lives are one. Given that Christ in the flesh has lived the fullness of the Spirit, and that he gives us this Spirit in the sacrament of his flesh, allegiance to Christ and docility to the Spirit become inseparable; the life of the Spirit and life according to the gospel are one and the same thing.

I

The Coming of Christ and the
Expectation of Justice

'RORATE CAELI DESUPER!'—'Shower down, O heavens, justice from above!' The expectation of justice in Isaiah fills the liturgy of Advent; can we say it is fulfilled by the coming of our Lord? Is it really justice that our Lord brings on earth?—the justice the prophets dreamed of and which men still need, justice to put an end to the injustices afflicting them. At first sight it seems a far cry from the indignation of Amos or even Jeremiah to the sermon on the Mount which says: 'If a man strike thee on the right cheek, turn the other cheek also towards him.'[1] It is understandable that superficial observers should take their stand on this change of attitude, either to praise Christianity for transforming revolutionary anarchy into praiseworthy submission, or to accuse it of substituting resignation for a noble spirit of rebellion. A closer look at the texts will enable us to correct such hasty impressions and to have a better idea of the justice our Lord brings to the world.

Before approaching the gospel, and so as to appreciate better the newness of its message, it will be useful to look at the Old Testament.

1. Justice in the mind of Israel

The idea of justice was basic to the mind of Israel. It had much in common with our present-day idea of justice, but it

---

[1] Matt. 5:39

did not quite coincide with it. Three essential elements seem involved: justice was a state of the social community, a state in which it lived comfortably in prosperity and peace; this justice, belonging to all the members of the community, supposes that each of them sees his right recognized and respected; this in turn supposes in the hearts of all an awareness of their duty of loyalty and fraternal solidarity towards all the others.

The definition of justice was not based upon each one receiving his due, but upon the prosperity and harmony of the community. Hence the relation between justice and peace was direct: peace was not only the consequence and sign of justice, it was its achievement, its normal and spontaneous development. If the leaders of Israel were called judges, it was not merely that one of the main prerogatives was to execute justice and settle law suits; their whole task consisted in establishing justice, defending the peace of their people from internal violence and foreign menace.

Justice and peace required that each man should see his right recognized. The way the Old Testament speaks of right is very significant. It only uses the word in connection with the poor and the unfortunate. Admittedly it does recognize the owner's right to his private property, since the ten commandments, its basic laws, condemn theft and even covetousness.[2] However, in the concrete, when the bible invokes anybody's right, it is always the right, threatened or violated, of the poor. The widow, the orphan, the poor man, the stranger, these are the people whose right has to be upheld—people not in a position to assert it themselves. If these rights are violated, it is a sign that society is resting on an injustice.[3] Even a wrong-doer is entitled to recover this right, when he is reduced to misery, perhaps through his own wrong-doing. So too Israel, the victim of her enemies and chastised by God, finally regains her right to appeal to God, a right recovered by suffering hardships.[4]

For the right of the poor to be upheld and for justice to prevail, the turmoil of business and pleasure must not dominate the voice of those who count on their own strength to

---

[2] Ex. 20:15-17   [3] Is. 1:17; 5:23; 10:2   [4] Ex. 22:26-7

assert their right. This requires, in the members of the social community, a constant reaction against their natural selfishness, and unremitting attention to others and their needs. The people of Israel had a firm conviction of the attitude and dispositions people need if they are to practise social justice. No one word in Hebrew or English can convey them all, but from different expressions a clearly defined ideal emerges, composed of loyalty to others, fidelity to the bonds of kindred, friends, countrymen, fellows in work or adversity, even the alien seeking refuge, and it is based on a conscience that is ever attentive to treating the humblest folk not only with respect but with trust. Among the great figures of its history, this people always held in veneration the memory of David. What won their heart and made them see in King David the model of the expected Messiah, was that neither power nor passion spoiled the spontaneous instincts of a noble heart. David mourning the death of Saul, his enemy; David refusing to drink the water that nearly cost the lives of his soldiers; David indignant that anyone should deprive a poor neighbour of his ewe-lamb; David smitten by the death of Absalom, his rebellious son—in all these very human reactions of loyalty and solidarity, in the reflexes of a 'heart in the right place', whose natural bonds triumph over considerations of state, the people of Israel for ever recognized the peak of its moral ideal.

2. Justice and the covenant

The justice Israel dreamed of, and the feeling for other people it involves, is something very human, the natural outcome of a 'heart in the right place', and also the result of God's intervention. The Israelite ideal of justice is that of a human community among others, dwelling in its own land in a social condition resulting from human history and experience, but it is likewise that of a people owing its origin to God's action and destined to achieve God's purpose. Every human community rests on an ideal of justice. In Israel, natural qualities and acquired characteristics, and God's own tuition, all combined to give the feeling for justice a very special character.

The special situation of Israel was summed up in the word

'covenant'. All peoples have at their origin, if not a social contract of the Rousseau type, at least some *de facto* situation accepted by the community and providing the foundation of their rights. At the origin of the existence of Israel there also exists a juridical foundation, a contract, but of a unique kind: the covenant between God and his people. God, by a sovereign free initiative, undertook to take charge of the life and future of the people and to guarantee them the justice that their neighbours then expected from their 'judges', as they called their chiefs and princes. It was a magnificent promise: if God took charge of Israel, who could do them any harm? No natural forces or human powers could prevail against them, provided they remained faithful to the covenant of their God.

This God is a God of justice. He possessed to the full the feeling for mankind that made David such a wonderful figure. Peoples have always dreamed of a prince capable of sensing their miseries, coming into a wretched cottage and bringing happiness there. This is only a charming plot for fairy tales. But in Israel it was a sure belief, based on the best authenticated incidents. The God of Israel it is whose ear catches voices not heard by men, absorbed by their business and their pursuits, the murmuring that rises from the lips of the poor. The world in its turmoil passes by this misery without looking, too busy to listen and in too much of a hurry to stop. But God does listen to these cries of distress.

This is not just a pious hope, and the proof is that the texts describing God attentive to human misery are not 'uplift', but those most free from sentimental exaltation, namely legislation and articles of the code of laws. And the proof that this belief in God's feeling for justice was taken seriously was that this belief formed the basis on which the Law relied. Let Israel listen to the voice of the poor, for God will not let it go unheard, and he will make any man pay for his selfishness, if he has not listened to it.

'You shall not wrong a stranger or oppress him, for you were strangers in the land of Egypt. . . . If you do afflict them, and thy cry out to me, I will surely hear their cry. . . .'[4]

This just God undertakes to provide his people with justice

[4] Ex. 22:26–7

measuring up to his own, a state of harmony and peace that no political régime can produce. Such are the promises of Deuteronomy. In spite of appearances, they are not fanciful, but they presuppose the conditions of the covenant. They presuppose that an unshakable sense of justice reigns in the hearts of the people, and a conscience unwavering in trial. The Law aimed at fostering such a conscience: that was what it was for.

3. The prophets against injustice

The Law, unfortunately, was constantly being violated. The task of the prophets was to recall the terms of the covenant to a people always tempted to forget them. To consider themselves the people of God without obeying his Law, to pride themselves on the wonders of Sinai without practising the commandments received there, this was Israel's mistake. If God has chosen a people apart, it is because he expects a lot from them. Woe betide them if God's expectation is disappointed:

'You only have I known of all the families of the earth: therefore I will punish you for all your iniquities.'[5]

Another mistake was to trust to outward worship of God in order to find him. There is no valid sacrifice for Israel apart from the observance of the covenant, and no way of consecrating their life to God other than by being faithful to the Law. How could the just God agree to take upon himself the injustices of men? The prophets are forever warning the multitudes thronging the altars:

Take away from me the noise of your songs; to the melody
    of your harps I will not listen.
But let justice roll down like waters;
and righteousness like an everflowing stream.[6]

'What to me is the multitude of your sacrifices?' says the
    Lord;
'I have had enough of burnt offerings of rams and the fat
    of fed beasts. . . .
When you come to appear before me, who requires of you
    this trampling of my courts? . . .

[5] Amos 3:2   [6] Amos 5:23-4

Your new moons and sabbath and calling of assemblies—
I cannot endure iniquity and solemn assembly.
When you spread forth your hands, I will hide my eyes
    from you.
Even though you make many prayers, I will not listen;
your hands are full of blood.
Wash yourselves; make yourselves clean. . . .'[7]

The downfall of the chosen people, the capture of the holy
city, the deportation of Israel into a pagan land, were the proof
that the prophets had spoken the truth: their injustices would
come down upon them. Any state built on injustice is condemned to perish, but a people that betrays the covenant of the
God of justice is condemned to terrifying destruction. The
chastisement of Israel was unparalleled. For all time the captivity of Babylon remains the formidable proof that God takes
injustice seriously.

4. *The expectation of God's justice*

The God of justice cannot be content with destroying injustice. If he is to see his work through, he must make justice
prevail. The prophets, while repeating to Israel that its injustice would be its undoing, always announced that, on the
ruins of the old city, God would set up a new Jerusalem, with
a new name, 'Justice-Town, Faithful City'.[8] In the distress of
exile, when God seems to have abandoned it, Israel goes over
its wrong-doings and feels the lesson of the prophets sinking in.
The conviction is strengthened that God is preparing for some
unprecedented intervention in the world, but consistent with
God's way of acting, a revelation of justice to come.

In this expectation of new justice there are many elements,
some inherited from the past or from recent experiences,
others only vaguely imagined. It will be justice rendered to
Israel. True, its wrong-doings have merited its misfortune,
but this in its turn gives it a claim on God. It will be a case of
God rendering justice to himself, for his honour is involved in
the fate of his people. He insisted on showing he would not
tolerate injustice, but he was to complete his triumph over

[7] Is. 1 : 11–16   [8] Is. 1 : 26

injustice by showing that justice could exist and prevail. It will be God's justice, for men have shown themselves incapable of ensuring justice. But it will be human justice, to be achieved on earth, in town and country, in homes and courts. It will be a justice establishing peace in a regenerated city, and a justice penetrating men's hearts and renewing them with inward faithfulness. For this justice to be established here below, God must change men's hearts, planting in them, deeper than selfishness, a spring of unselfishness and kindness, an outpouring of God's generosity, the fertile gift of the Spirit. Such is the topmost pinnacle of the expectation of justice in the Old Testament. It is expressed in the purest notes that the Church echoes at the approach of Christmas, in the last days of Advent.

> Shower, O heavens, from above and let the skies rain down justice; let the earth open, that salvation may sprout forth, and let it cause justice to spring up also; I the Lord will see to it.[9]

> Let me hear what God the Lord will speak, for he will speak peace to his people, to his saints, to those who turn to him in their hearts.

> Surely his salvation is at hand for those who fear him, that glory may dwell in our land.
> Steadfast love and faithfulness will meet; justice and peace will kiss each other.
> Faithfulness will spring up from the ground, and justice will look down from the sky.[10]

5. *The paradox of Christmas*

Christmas is the accomplishment of this expectation, the coming of the justice promised by God. Unhesitatingly the Church bursts into wonderment to see the prophecy fulfilled:

> For to us a child is born, to us a son is given; and the government will be upon his shoulder,
> and his name will be called
> 'Wonderful, Counsellor, Mighty God, Everlasting Father, Prince of Peace'.

[9] Is. 45:8   [10] Ps. 85 (86): 8–12

Of the increase of his government and of peace there will
   be no end,
upon the throne of David and over his kingdom,
to establish it, and to uphold it with justice and with
   righteousness
from this time forth and for evermore.[11]

This wonderment raises a problem. The contrast between
the splendour of the hope and the smallness of the fulfilment
raises once again the paradox of the gospel. It is not easy to see
how Christmas answers the great expectations of justice raised
by the Old Testament. Far from marking the establishment of
justice on earth, Christmas seems to represent a permanent
acceptance of injustice. Rarely can the rights of the unfortunate, so keenly sought for by the conscience of Israel, have
been more callously disregarded. That our Lady in her condition should not have found room in Bethlehem, the home-
town, surpasses the normal level of human hard-heartedness.
The angels singing in the heavens 'Peace on earth' may recall
splendidly the vision of Psalm 85, but it only makes the
question more challenging: can we say that on that night
there came the dawn of the justice that had been promised?
   The paradox of Christmas is the stumbling-block of the
gospel. To many sincere seekers of justice, Christmas, like the
beatitudes, seems to mark an illusion, an evasion. The strong-
minded expectation of the Old Testament seems to peter out
in a too easy willingness to accept things. For centuries legis-
lators and prophets rose up against injustice, stood up against
the rich and powerful, lived in the assurance that one day God
would put an end to all these wrongs. Is our Lord their true
successor? John the Baptist fits the part better, dying for his
attack on the sins of Herod's court. But our Lord is of another
spirit. No one doubts his sincerity and nobility of character,
but must we not admit that his gospel accepts injustice and
has no message for man dedicated to the achievement of justice
among men?
   Such a reaction is obviously not right, but do we always
know how to guard against it? It rests on a real difficulty: it is

[11] Is. 9:6–7

quite true that some of the expressions of passionate indignation in the prophets are largely soft-pedalled in the gospels.
Are we to consider them as primitive attitudes to be suspended,
only remote preparation for the hungering and thirsting after
justice in a perfect, interior sense, as envisaged in the beatitudes? Or are we to interpret the gospel texts, softened by
centuries of watering down, with the passionate ardour of the
prophets and with their determination to see the beatitudes
achieved on earth?

The truth cannot be a happy mean, avoiding extremes and
reducing the risks of both positions. It is to be found, as in all
really Christian solutions, in the integral acceptance of all the
factors, both Old Testament and New. Here, as in all else, our
Lord come not to destroy but to fulfil. Two examples may be
chosen to illustrate the correlation of Old and New Testament: the gospel idea of justice as connected with worship,
and in its relation to the poor.

6. The gospel idea of justice and the worship of God

'If your justice does not give fuller measure than the justice
of the scribes and pharisees, you shall not enter into the kingdom of heaven.'[12] The justice of the scribes consisted primarily
in observing the Law in all its rigour. The examples chosen
by our Lord to show the full implications of the Law are not
taken from the details of casuistry, but from the main commandments of the Law, in particular those concerning our
relations with others: Thou shall not kill, Thou shalt not
commit adultery. So it is evident that our Lord did not intend
to reduce the requirements of the Law concerning justice and
regard for the poor. To try to make the gospel less exacting in
these matters than the Law would be to betray the gospel. The
whole gospel message goes to prove that the essence of the Law
is joint attention to God and man. 'Be ye perfect as your
heavenly Father is perfect'[13] is significantly made more explicit
in the words 'Be merciful as your Father is merciful'.[14] Even
the expression 'merciful' needs to be rightly understood. It
too easily suggests pity aroused by sad cases. It needs supple-
menting by the biblical tradition, involving deep concern for

[12] Matt. 5:20   [13] Matt. 5:48   [14] Luke 6:36

other people, much wider than mercy, making us feel personally their sufferings and joys, as if everybody were our own kith and kin. True, the gospel does not speak of justice here, but it has it in mind and, following the Old Testament tradition, is conscious that justice can only be achieved where there is the right attitude in the heart.

The gospel not only presupposes the Law and its requirements in the matter of justice, it explicitly reaffirms them: 'Woe upon you, scribes and pharisees, you hypocrites that will award to God his tithe, though it be of mint or dill or cummin, and have forgotten the weightier commandments of the law, justice, mercy and honour! '[15]

This is just how the prophets spoke: practices are vain if the essence of the law is lacking. If the description of scourges called down upon a guilty people sounds more impressive than the simple language of the gospel, it is only because we forget that all the horror of the chastisements described by the Old Testament can mean nothing so terrible as a 'Woe!' from the lips of Christ.

So too we need to recall the prophets to discover the extraordinarily strong meaning of an apparently harmless sentence in the sermon on the Mount: 'If thou art bringing thy gift before the altar, and rememberest there that thy brother has some ground of complaint against thee, leave thy gift lying there before the altar, and go home; be reconciled with thy brother first, and then come back to offer thy gift.'[16] This sounds mild compared with the vindictive sayings of Amos and Isaiah dismissing from the sacrifice prominent people guilty of injustice. But if we look into it, the gospel statement, without raising the voice but with inflexible firmness, goes further than all the prophets. It is not merely that instead of actual injustice, it considers a man against whom a brother has some ground of complaint, whatever it may be. But it needs to be noticed that this is not just a counsel to apply in an emergency, preferring brotherly love to sacrifice. Just as in the situation described by the prophets, it is a case of being 'warned off' from divine worship. Under the covenant there could be no intercourse with God for all who lived in injustice in contempt

[15] Matt. 23:23   [16] Matt. 5:23-4

of the Law. Whatever they did before the altar was an outrage hateful to God. The gospel message here repeated that of the prophets explicitly and even more strictly. It is useless claiming to come near to God in worship while at loggerheads with a fellow man. It is no accident nor is it a mere detail that St Matthew twice puts on the lips of our Lord the words of Hosea: 'I desire mercy and not sacrifice'.[17]

The sermon on the Mount looks to the Old Testament and constantly refers to its way of speaking, adding our Lord's own interpretation. But the heart of the gospel is the new covenant by which our Lord, just before he died, taught his disciples the meaning of his passion and of all Christian life. This new covenant, like that on Sinai, has its own terms and obligations, put in new language with no counterpart in the old: 'Have love for one another as I have loved you'. The temptation of Israel had been to rely on its history, as if the wonders God had worked for his people guaranteed their salvation, and to rely on the temple and its worship as divine institutions providing infallible access to their God. But neither history nor worship carried any weight without faithfulness to the Law and to the justice it enjoined. So too with the Christian. He is tempted to rely on the gospel and the Church and the wonders of God's generosity. He may think he is sure of finding the grace of God and salvation thanks to the sacramental system. He is mistaken if he disregards the charter of the covenant he has entered into: 'have love for one another'. Neither the role of Christ, nor the effect of the sacraments, can dispense him from this obligation. Woe upon him, if he thinks he is justified just because he has inherited a tradition and a set of practices! Christians led on by ardent desire for human solidarity and thinking to find charity without the sacraments of Christ are indeed misguided; but so too is anyone who thinks he is living the life of the sacraments while violating the law of charity. There can be no Christian charity that is not fed on the eucharist and fostered in the eucharist, the thanksgiving of the assembled Church. But to venture to approach the eucharist while setting aside the claims of charity is to profane our Lord's sacrifice.

[17] Hos. 6:6; Matt. 9:13; 12:7

7. *The gospel and the poor*

Christianity means charity. So once again we are up against
the common reproach. 'What have you made of justice, the
justice the prophets died for? You may be following the
gospel, but you are confirming the objection: by saying the
poor are blessed you are letting down the poor.' To see the
right answer to this difficulty—a very real one and exemplified
only too often—we must examine the gospel closely in its
relation to the Old Testament. The latter based justice on
attention to the poor. Where the cry of the poor goes un-
heeded, the community lives in injustice. The gospel upholds
this claim in full. It is true it proclaims the blessings of the
poor and hungry, whose misery is reduced to appeals for help.
But this is because the kingdom of God is at hand, and God
whose ear heeds every such appeal is going to manifest himself.
God is to acknowledge his own, those whose voice he listens
for, hitherto lost in the madding crowd. In declaring them
blessed, our Lord means their cry has been heard and the
response is on the way.

Does this mean the world has changed? Yes and no. No, in
that misery and injustice were to remain and often grow more
overwhelming many centuries after the gospel. Yes, on the
other hand, inasmuch as the kingdom of God is at work, in so
far as the love of God in Christ Jesus shines through Christian
people. The beatitudes are only fulfilled in the gospel context
and where the gospel is taken literally. Where God does not
reign, the poor man falls by the wayside. But in the realm of
action of Christ's love—and only God knows the frontiers of it
—the poor are happy, for they can realize, by the way men
treat them, how God loves his children. The poor to whom the
helping hand brings no joy have not the kingdom of God
within them. Conversely, we may well follow this criterion,
that if there are in the world poor and unfortunate people who
have found joy in seeing others come to their aid, it is indeed
the charity of Christ that has found its way to them.

We must be clear about this: the poor are not blessed
because of their hunger, but because of the love of Christ in
their helpers. So the beatitudes give the Christian no right to

B

resign himself to human misery. They call upon him to make a constant effort to prove they are true, by giving people an idea of God's generosity. When our Lord pronounced the beatitudes he cured the sick and multiplied the loaves to show them being accomplished. We Christians entrusted with the beatitudes only show them forth if our charity shines in the world as a sign of God's presence. We keep on saying the poor man represents Christ, but we must weigh well what we say. The poor man only represents Christ for the Christian if he resolves to feed him, to clothe him and to visit him. To invoke the gospel in support of leaving the poor in misery is a terrible illusion. True, the poor man left naked and hungry is still Christ, but Christ calling down upon injustice the indignation of the poor and the weight of divine anger.

8. God poor, and God just

The God of Sinai and the prophets is the God of the poor. The God born at Christmas is God poor. This encounter between God and poverty is neither caprice nor pure compassion. In so far as we may explore the secrets of God's heart, we must recognize that there is a mysterious bond between God and poverty. The poor form on earth one of the most expressive revelations of God's character, and we have every reason to think that God, who opens to men the riches of his grace, preserves amid all the splendour something of kinship with the poor. This is basic to bible and gospel.

But it would be a distortion of this truth to separate it however little from the equally divine and imperious claim of justice. God poor is also God just, the God of justice. It is manifest in the Old Testament: God is just because he is close to the poor, sensitive to all distress, angered by all forms of injustice. The gospel is equally clear: the Son of God is born in a manger. He dies a victim of an unjust sentence, but he has no intention of excusing injustice or tolerating it for one moment. Rather he has come to let men see to what depths their injustice has made them sink and to what crimes the lust for money and power can lead—to betray the Son of God, innocence itself. At the heart of all injustice and of all ill-gotten riches, there is the blood-stained face of Christ crucified.

Any man who has really seen this once cannot consent to injustice any more, but must find therein untiring energy to fight against injustice. Far from allowing us to lose sight of the God of justice, the God born in the stable obliges us to put to the service of justice all the powers of love. If Christmas is the coming of justice, it is because through his Son Jesus Christ, the Father gives us the Son of man who makes us for ever attentive to the appeal of human misery, and his Holy Spirit who alone can give us the grace to listen and to respond.

II

The Glory of the Lord

G OD'S GLORY is contained in the features of his only-
begotten Son Jesus Christ: 'The Word was made flesh
and came to dwell among us; and we had sight of his
glory, glory such as belongs to the Father's only-begotten Son,
full of grace and truth.'[1] But the better to recognize in Christ
the glory of the Father, it is good to contemplate him in the
light of the great revelations of God to his people, the solemn
'theophanies'. Moses on the mountain, and Isaiah in the
temple—in studying these scenes we shall not be getting away
from Christ. Rather we are calling upon those who came
closest to God in their faithful waiting for the Messiah, to
help us to see Christ with their faith and hope, the better to
grasp what he is: the visible showing forth of the invisible
God.

1. Glory in the bible

In the bible 'glory' is something very human and in fact very
earthly. In a Greek environment glory meant renown, the stir
made by great personalities. Among the Hebrews, more positive and down to earth, glory is the weight a man carries in
the world, the authority of his words, the influence and impact
of his way of acting. Riches form one element of it, but much
more important is the position he occupies and the strength of
his personality. As influence and renown normally go together,

[1] John 1:14

'glory' often went with the same situations among Greeks and Jews. But in all the Bible uses of the word 'glory' we need to remember the elements of substance and authority implied. The glory of a man is what he is worth and what he can achieve: its brightness is in proportion to the guns he carries. When Joseph reveals his identity to his brothers and invites them to bring their father Jacob to see him in Egypt, he tells them the position he occupies, and it is one of glory. 'Tell my father all the glory I have in Egypt. . . .'[2] A power that spoke for itself, which they could see with their own eyes, a strength that was sure of its rights and its ability to do good, the product of uncontested greatness: such was glory.

Such visible impact was bound to draw attention to itself by obvious manifestations, but to be real glory it had to be based on massive and solid substance. Kings knew this and to show forth their glory, that is the reality of their power, they surrounded themselves with such things as gold and ivory, materials of weight and splendour. We may notice incidentally another royal glory, of far greater substance and purity, the 'Tower of Ivory', the 'House of Gold'.

But glory is not just a shining accessory, nor is it a ceremonial garment for state occasions; it is the direct radiant expression of the true worth of a person. Van Gogh wrote: 'I want to paint men and women with something eternal about them: primitive painters gave them a halo; we try to achieve it by the vibration of colour.' What Van Gogh saw in people he met, and tried to convey by colour, was these people's true glory, their very being appearing in its beauty. The glory of God is his secret being revealing itself.

The Old Testament is never tired of telling about the glory of God. The psalms rejoice to see it radiate upon the universe and call upon all creation to sing about it. The Laws given to Israel are meant to display before other peoples the glory of its God. The prophets call for its revelation and foresee it unfolding over Jerusalem and the whole world in the days of the Messiah. The great fear of Israel, when guilty of misdeeds, and the great hope of Israel, when it has been faithful, is to see God appear in all his glory. There is hardly a book in the Old

[2] Gen. 45:13

Testament where this mingled hope and fear does not appear, more or less consciously and ardently. But there are, in the course of this long-drawn-out desire, some moments of almost consummate fulfilment, when glory appears close at hand, when it seems that God wants to break through the heavens and come down to his creature.[3] Fleeting moments covering only a few verses throughout the bible, but for centuries generations lived on these lightning experiences, conveyed in words of great power. The most outstanding of these experiences, used also in the New Testament, are those of Moses and Elijah on Sinai and Isaiah in the temple of Jerusalem. From these rare summits we may glimpse precious rays of God's glory, if we look up with faith.

2. *Moses on Mount Sinai*

On the morning of the third day there were thunders and lightnings, and a thick cloud upon the mountain, and a very loud trumpet blast, so that all the people who were in the camp trembled. Then Moses brought the people out of the camp to meet God; and they took their stand at the foot of the mountain. And Mount Sinai was wrapped in smoke, because the Lord descended upon it in fire; and the smoke of it went up like the smoke of a kiln, and the whole mountain quaked greatly. And as the sound of the trumpet grew louder and louder, Moses spoke, and God answered him in thunder. And the Lord came down upon Mount Sinai, to the top of the mountain; and the Lord called Moses to the top of the mountain. . . . 'Come up to me on the mountain, and wait there; and I will give you the tables of stone, with the law and the commandments, which I have written for their instruction . . .' and the cloud covered the mountain. The glory of the Lord settled on Mount Sinai, and the cloud covered it six days; and on the seventh day he called to Moses out of the midst of the cloud. Now the appearance of the glory of the Lord was like a devouring fire on the top of the mountain, and in the sight of the people of Israel. And Moses entered the cloud, and went up on the mountain. And Moses was on the mountain forty days and forty nights.[4]

[3] Is. 64 : 1   [4] Ex. 19 : 16–20; 24 : 12–18

This first manifestation of God's glory is one of power: power making itself seen and felt through natural phenomena, earthquakes, mountain storms re-echoing from summit to summit across the valleys, the rocks thunder-struck. To be sure, God's glory has no need of such extraordinary signs. It is no less actively present in the day-by-day unfolding of the marvels of the universe. The heavens with their light and harmony and immensity are a transparent screen reflecting God's glory.

> The heavens are telling the glory of God
> and the firmament proclaims his handiwork.
> Day to day pours forth speech,
> and night to night declares knowledge.
> There is no speech, nor are there words;
> their voice is not heard;
> yet their voice goes out through all the earth,
> and their words to the end of the world.[5]

As the sun's rays light up the whole earth, so the glory of the Lord shines through all his creation.[6] But the phenomenon that seemed to bring God's glory closest was the thunder-storm. The crash of thunder seemed to be the very voice of God, the unleashing of the storm seemed to release upon the earth the blast of his almighty power, and the blinding flash of the lightning spoke of his fearful presence. Psalm 29 is a hymn to the Lord of the storm:

> Ascribe to the Lord, O heavenly beings
> ascribe to the Lord glory and strength.
> Ascribe to the Lord the glory of his name;
> worship the Lord in holy array.
> The voice of the Lord is upon the waters;
> the God of glory thunders,
> the Lord, upon many waters.
> The voice of the Lord is powerful
> the voice of the Lord is full of majesty . . .[7]

In this way of presenting God as speaking in thunder, there was of course a risk of idolatry, as though natural phenomena

<hr />

[5] Ps. 18 (19): 1–4   [6] Ecclus. 42: 16   [7] Ps. 28 (29): 1–4

were God's own actions. Some pagan gods were merely deified
thunderstorms. All around Israel, in Syria and Canaan, the
god Hadad in the kingdom of Damascus, and the god Baal
invoked by the false prophets of Carmel challenged by Elijah,
were gods of thunder and lightning, and had been set up to
lend human form and sentiment to nameless forces threaten-
ing human life. There could be no harvest in these countries
without rain, and no rain without storms. So Hadad and Baal
were thought indispensable as sources of life and fertility, but
they were as blind and capricious as storms, driven about at
the whim of the winds. Man might try to assuage their cruelty,
forestall their caprices, flatter their manias, even exalt their
generosity, but there was one thing man could not even think
of enquiring—what they wanted and what purpose they
achieved. Season after season, they came again, driving on
the clouds, fertilizing or ravaging the soil. They did both good
and evil, both good and harm to men. They brought terror
and joy with perfectly heartless indifference and with the
utter impartiality of a power operating with no conceivable
purpose.

The true God alone has his purpose in pursuing his work,
and his full glory will not appear till his work is accomplished
in his risen Son at the head of redeemed humanity. But his
work has nature for its framework and base, and his glory is
bound to begin to show itself in nature. There is in nature an
all-pervading and overwhelming power, an immediate living
presence, an unconscious kinship ('Mother Nature'), arousing
in man the awareness of a personal force and bringing him
face to face with God, listening to him and ready to respond.
There is an initial revelation of God's glory in creation which
the bible frequently recognizes and records. In the Old Testament thunderstorm was one of the great moments of this
revelation, when nature said God's name most loud and clear.
It was likewise bound to be pounced on by idolatry, eager to
seize on the voices of nature, not heeding who was their true
cause. So to preserve his people from worshipping Hadad and
Baal, Yahweh must needs reveal himself in thunder and
lightning, but as their lord and master.

The God of Israel therefore manifested himself in this way,

laying bare the emptiness of Baal by plunging lightning on
the very spot where he was worshipped, on Mount Carmel,
after his false prophets had vainly invoked him for hours.[8]
Baal was the storm-god pure and simple, but for the true God
storm-language is only one of many and the storm on Sinai has
nothing to do with a dramatic moment in the cycle of the
seasons. Whatever be the place of storms in nature, their meaning here was different. This storm belonged to the history of
the tribes of Israel when, fleeing from bondage in Egypt, they
camped about the mountain. This storm was not to bring rain
or devastation on the land. In the bible account it was to show
the 'baseless fabric' of the world fading at the approach of
glory. Solid mountain masses and unshakable pillars of the
world sway to and fro, granite splits, and the hardest rock
melts: nothing to support them, gulfs open on all sides; the
world rests on the void. The great symbols of the true God,
best expressing his sovereignty and absolute freedom, are not
the regular natural phenomena, but the exceptional ones
breaking the course of nature and revealing its essential frailty.

These things are not God's glory itself but only its outer
surface and defences. Even the lightning that rends the clouds
and lights up the darkness in a flash is only a spark from the
divine furnace. Above and beyond cloud and lightning, God's
glory is an incandescent source of light. Only Moses came near
to it, and from the radiance his countenance was so bright that
his brethren could not gaze at it.[9] Yet Moses did not see God's
glory face to face. He had prayed to God to let him contemplate
his glory. But this Yahweh could not do. 'My face thou canst
not see; mortal man cannot see my face and live to tell of it.
There is a place here, close by me, where thou mayest stand on
a rock; there I will station thee in a cleft of the rock, while my
glory passes by, and cover thee with my right hand till I have
gone past. So, when I take my hand away, thou shalt follow
me with thy eyes, but my face thou canst not see.'[10] Naïvely
told, this is a story with divine depth to it. It sounds as if God
has a face and hands, but at the moment he passes an infinite
distance appears: none can see him and live.

[8] 1 Kings (3 Kings) 18:38   [9] Ex. 34:29–35
[10] Ex. 33:18–23

But divine glory does not destroy or lay waste: it has no rivalry against all else that lives and has being. The earth trembles at its presence, because it has not its own means of subsistence, and all creation is hollow, but it does subsist as God's own handiwork. The people at the foot of Sinai are all trembling, but it is not an hour of death; it is the hour of their birth as God's people.[11] At the approach of divine glory man is seized with panic, but he cannot avert his gaze from this sacred fire. Its flame devours, but does not destroy. It attacks and transforms, it consumes and consecrates. While the people, terrified and fascinated, gazed after him, Moses climbed the mountain, disappeared into the cloud and pierced the lightning barrier. Forty days and forty nights he stood before the Lord. What was he doing there in the full blaze of glory? He was hearing God's words, receiving the Law and the promises, which were to be the life of his people and would make them blessed among all nations, the sacred centre of humanity. In the heart of God's glory was the divine voice proclaiming the all-important command: 'Be ye holy because I am holy.'[12] It is the will of a person, giving a command, meaning to be obeyed, a holiness that will not tolerate contamination but means to radiate and win all hearts.

Feeling himself the object and target of this divine will releases terror in man. It would not be so bad to see the earth tremble about him and the heavens fall, if it were not his own existence he felt endangered. He feels so sure of himself and his power, his culture and his discoveries. Then God suddenly reveals the 'insubstantial pageant' of all he relies on most. What use are his efforts, how can his actions stand up to God's infinite urgency and greatness, his passionate interest in men? Desperately, like Adam hiding in the trees, men seek shelter against God.

Man, alas, is above all frightened of God. He is afraid of being burned at his touch, like the Israelites who touched the Ark. That adds subtlety to his denials, cunning to his attempted escapes, and makes the pious inventive in devotional tricks to deaden the shock. . . . Whether incredu-

[11] Ex. 19:5   [12] Lev. 20:26; Ex. 19:6

lous, indifferent or believers, we compete with one another in ingeniously guarding ourselves against God.[13]

Even proximity with some outstanding man is enough to shake us. How mean our ordinary concerns seem by comparison. The mere fact of such a person's presence, without a word being said, is enough to dissolve everyday illusions. It is a disturbing experience to live in contact with a great man, or with a saint. What must it be like in the presence of God? 'Who shall survive this devouring flame, the near presence of fire that burns unceasingly?'[14]

Disturbing and formidable as they are by their mere contact, the great man and the saint are the honour of our race, and just to have seen one in our midst is enough to enlighten and inspire us for years on end. So also, at a quite different level, with God's glory. It is a devouring flame, but man needs it to live on. So Moses discovered on Sinai. His people had been unfaithful to God. They had 'exchanged the glory that dwelt among them for the semblance of a bullock at grass'.[15] They had worshipped the golden calf. Moses straightway grasped that all was lost if Yahweh abandoned Israel, and he besought him, with the offer of his life: 'If thy face come not with us, rather abandon us where we are!'[16] Let the divine glory remain in the midst of Israel, or else they would fall into a worse bondage than Egypt. The only treasure of this people, hidden behind the thundering cloud and God's secret designs, was the radiant glory and holiness of their God. The only danger for them was to abandon this glory and its claims on them for the glint of gold and indulgent idols. Man's everlasting sin: 'They have exchanged the glory of the imperishable God for a vain image . . .',[17] knowing death is the fruit: 'with the just decree of God before their minds'.[18] To lose God's glory is to lose everything, for it is all our treasure. It may take the form of the burning appeal of a secret voice, lost among distant memories and worldly cares, but always there and ready to burst into flame. It may be a light leading us on

[13] H. de Lubac, *The Discovery of God*, London, 1960, p. 157
[14] Is. 33:14   [15] Ps. 106:26   [16] Ex. 33:15
[17] Rom. 1:23   [18] Rom. 1:32

and giving our life a meaning in spite of waywardness and set-
backs. It is always a will that is stronger than our failings, a
holiness that makes its demands even in the depth of our
moral failures; it is the 'ever-fixed mark' of our conscience and
our life.

Ruthless towards sin, uncompromising, God's glory brings
mercy and pardon. This was Moses' final experience. Beseeching God to forgive Israel, he begs God to give him 'sight of thy
glory',[19] and when it passes before his eyes, Moses hears a voice
yielding up a secret that is the very mystery of God: 'Yahweh,
Yahweh, God of mercy and pity, slow to take vengeance, rich
in kindness, faithful to his promises.'[20] The holy God is the
God who forgives, he forgives because he is holy. His glory,
his holiness radiant and inviolable, relentless to unrepentant
sin, has the power to penetrate to the inmost heart of fallen
men and give them new life. Before the burning bush Moses
had heard God reveal his name: 'I am the God who is',[21] and
he realized that the imperishable God of Abraham would
never let down the children of Abraham. Like an inextinguish-
able flame, his will had seized upon his people and would
achieve his purpose with it. Then sin had come, Israel had
betrayed its God, what then would Yahweh do? Would he put
up with their failings and settle for a compromise? Impossible:
as God he could never do that. His holiness remained absolute
and his claims are paramount. But in the very heart of his
holiness he reveals the secret that enables him to make sinners
holy, a generosity that forgives all infidelities, a faithfulness
that is incapable of ever going back, the tenderness of a mother
for her child.

3. Elijah on Sinai

He arose, and ate and drank, and went in the strength of
that food forty days and forty nights to Horeb the mount of
God. And there he came to a cave, and lodged there. . . .
And behold, the Lord passed by, and a great and strong wind
rent the mountains and broke in pieces the rocks before the
Lord, but the Lord was not in the wind; and after the wind
an earthquake, but the Lord was not in the earthquake; and

[19] Ex. 33:18   [20] Ex. 34:6   [21] Ex. 3:14

after the earthquake a fire, but the Lord was not in the fire; and after the fire a still small voice (the whisper of a gentle breeze). And when Elijah heard it, he wrapped his face in his mantle, and went out and stood in front of the cave. And behold there came a voice to him and said, 'What are you doing here, Elijah?' He said, 'I have been very jealous for the Lord, the God of Hosts; for the people of Israel have forgotten thy covenant, thrown down thy altars, and slain thy prophets with the sword; and I, even I only, am left; and they seek my life, to take it away.' And the Lord said to him, 'Go, return on your way to the wilderness of Damascus; and when you arrive, you shall anoint Hazael to be king. . . .'[22]

Elijah makes his way up to the mountain, like Moses before him, and in very similar circumstances, after the apostasy of God's people falling into idolatry. He too is alone and unaided, even more so than Moses, who had already felt God's glory close to him and could remind him, to obtain his forgiveness, that he had been chosen and marked out for his favour. 'If indeed thou dost look upon me with favour', he makes bold to say.[23] But Elijah can only say: 'I am no better than my fathers . . . I can bear no more, Lord: put an end to my life.'[24]

But, strengthened by the food provided by the angel, Elijah went on till he reached God's mountain. There he also experienced the scenes that terrified Israel, the hurricane, the earthquake and the fire. But the Lord was in none of these. Such fearful things were only the preludes, the outer fringe of his glory. This is suddenly revealed in 'the whisper of a gentle breeze'. This silence is more pregnant, more charged with weight of meaning, than all the preceding turmoil. Moses had seen the radiance of God's glory when he passed through the ring of storms surrounding the summit. For Elijah there is nothing at all to be seen, and yet he had to veil his face and could not sustain the divine presence. Yahweh spoke and gave the prophet his mission. Glory on this occasion was no outward phenomenon, and Elijah's face bore no trace of the encounter.

[22] 1 Kings (3 Kings) 19:8–15   [23] Ex. 33:13
[24] 1 Kings (3 Kings) 19:4

But the nucleus, so to speak, of his experience was identical with that of Moses: it was God expressing his will and achieving his purpose. Moses had been sent to bring Israel the Law and the promises. Elijah was sent 'back the same way' to the scene of his previous endeavours, to resume the struggle, with no sign of change, no outward appearance of his encounter. But he carried within him the almighty impact of divine glory. This strength was not visible, as in the case of Moses, nor was it that of a miracle-worker with the authority of a leader dominating his people. Elijah had only the strength of his message, but his message was God's. By it the glory of the Lord was to radiate over Israel, penetrating to the secret of their hearts, 'reaching the very division between soul and spirit'[25] pursuing its task of purification and consecration.

4. Isaiah in the Temple

I saw the Lord sitting upon a throne, high and lifted up; and his train filled the temple. Above him stood the seraphim; each had six wings: with two he covered his face, and with two he covered his feet, and with two he flew. And one called to another and said: 'Holy, holy, holy is the Lord of Hosts; and the whole earth is full of his glory'. And the foundations of the thresholds shook at the voice of him who called, and the house was filled with smoke. And I said, 'Woe is me! For I am lost: for I am a man of unclean lips, and I dwell in the midst of a people of unclean lips, for my eyes have seen the King, the Lord of hosts!'

Then flew one of the seraphim to me, having in his hand a burning coal which he had taken with tongs from the altar. And he touched my mouth, and said: 'Behold, this has touched your lips, your guilt is taken away, and your sin forgiven.' And I heard the voice of the Lord saying, 'Whom shall I send, and who will go for us?' Then I said, 'Here am I! Send me.' And he said, 'Go and say to this people. . . .'[26]

We are no longer on God's mountain but in God's temple. But now, in the heart of the promised land, brooding over Sion, it was still the glory revealed on Sinai. God who pledged

[25] Heb. 4:12   [26] Is. 6:1–8

his word and his honour to Israel, entrusted his glory to Israel too. They are not really two different gifts: glory is the outward sign of God's word and its almighty power. When Moses had engraved on the tablets the Law and the promises received on Sinai and placed them in the tabernacle, the sanctuary for the chosen people on the march, 'a cloud covered the tabernacle and it was filled with the brightness of the Lord's presence; nor could Moses enter the tabernacle that bore the record of the covenant, so thick the cloud that spread all about it, so radiant was the Lord's majesty'.[27] Yahweh, who had manifested his holiness and faithfulness on Sinai, set out with his people: 'The divine cloud by day, the divine fire by night, still brooded over the tabernacle for all Israel to see it, wherever they halted on their journey.'[28] God keeps his word; he does not let it become an 'empty echo'[29] but sees to it that it is accomplished in full. Judgment on sin, forgiveness of the sinner, consecration of a holy people, the message within the ark will be carried out because it is surrounded with the glory of the Lord. God advances in conquest at the head of his people; it is his kingdom that is on the march. He leads them into Palestine, presents the land to Israel, takes up his abode at Jerusalem, the city of David, and when Solomon builds him a sanctuary in freestone and cedarwood to replace the mobile tabernacle, God consecrates his new dwelling as he had the old. As soon as the priests had placed in the holy of holies the ark containing God's words, 'the Lord's house was wreathed in cloud; lost in that cloud the priests could not wait upon the Lord with his accustomed service; his own glory was there, filling his own house. 'Where the cloud is', cried Solomon, 'the Lord has promised to be; it is true, then, the house I have built is to be thy dwelling, thy throne for ever immovable.'[30]

For Israel, from then on, the temple of Jerusalem was 'the dwelling place of thy glory'. Every time a child of Israel saw the house of Yahweh over the roof-tops of the city, he could relive the experience of his fathers at Sinai, their terror at the passing of God's sovereign power, the triumphant certainty of having God with them and the fascinating manifestation of

---

[27] Ex. 40:32   [28] Ex. 40:36
[29] Is. 55:11   [30] 1 Kings (3 Kings) 8:10–13

the mystery of God's holy presence. For pilgrims on the roads up to Jerusalem, for the faithful Jew reciting in his heart the psalms of his people, the highest prayer and the purest hope was a repetition of Moses' prayer on Sinai. 'In the holy place may I contemplate thee, ready for the revelation of thy greatness, thy glory.'[31] 'It is thy face, Lord, I long for; do not hide thy face from me.'[32] The sons of Israel who repeated these prayers down the centuries never claimed to attain something that Moses himself could not attain. Still, in the presence of the sanctuary the faith of each could feed upon the experience of Moses and rest secure on what he had seen.

Such was the faith of Isaiah the day he was in the temple gazing upon the holy of holies. Suddenly his faith was borne up on a wave of divine power, as Moses, at the call of God, had gone up into the cloud. Isaiah then saw what he had been trying to make out amid the darkness: he saw the Lord. He could only describe his throne and his royal train, but he saw his glory and he was stricken with terror. The seraphim veiled their faces in this holy spot, and there was he breathing out his sinful breath, and he felt going out with it all the corruption of his heart, all his load of sin. He had profaned the glory, he felt he must perish. To his amazement, the glory destroyed his sinfulness. It had brought Moses forgiveness for his people; its burning contact brought Isaiah a new lease of holy life. Moreover, he was conscious of glory filling the earth, spreading out from its temple in Jerusalem, with himself as the instrument of this outpouring. He saw what God would enable him to do: to bring to the people the words of Yahweh. His power of destruction and judgment upon all pride and arrogance,[33] his power to purify,[34] his power to sanctify and renew.[35]

This was to be Isaiah's life-work, and the Church for all time was to echo the triple 'Sanctus!' and contemplate the glory of the Lord through the eyes of the prophet. This glory is holiness itself: it is destructive of sin, but life to the sinner. Infinitely superior to all human greatness, it lets nothing escape its flame, which must needs consume the earth.

The prophets and servants of God are those whom this flame

---

[31] Ps. 62 (63): 3   [32] Ps. 26 (27): 8–9   [33] Is. 2:10–11; 6:11
[34] Is. 1:25; 4:4   [35] Is. 5:16; 6:12

has caught and will never relinquish. Whether they have, like
Isaiah and Moses, seen it in dazzling light; or, like Elijah,
sensed it in the stillness of all creation: or whether, like Jeremiah, they have felt it gripping their vitals like a burning
passion: they have all been seized upon by God's glory and
can live for nothing else. It is not merely that they work for it:
it works on them and in them. Their sole concern and their
whole attention is to find out where its driving force would
lead them, to follow its impulses with all the strength and voice
they have, and in all fidelity display the power of God's glory.

The more they live on and for this glory, the more ardently
they long to see it revealed—not as a consolation to them
personally, but as the fulfilment of the promise made to the
people. To discover God's glory means to be seized upon by
it and sent to bring to Israel and the world the infinite power
of this glory. How else could they think of this glory, save
encircling the world and filling it with its splendour? What
other interest or expectation could they have in the world,
save to see it enkindled with this flame and transformed in
the glory of God?

5. *Expectation of glory*

Arise, shine; for your light has come,
and the glory of the Lord has risen upon you.
For behold, darkness shall cover the earth,
and thick darkness the peoples;
but the Lord will rise upon you,
and his glory will be seen upon you.
And nations shall come to your light,
and kings to the brightness of your rising.[36]

A voice cries:

In the wilderness prepare the way for the Lord
and make straight in the desert a highway for our God.
Every valley shall be lifted up,
and every mountain and hill be made low;
the uneven ground shall become level,
and the rough places a plain.

[36] Is. 60:1–3

And the glory of the Lord shall be revealed,
and all flesh shall see it together . . .[37]

Show us thy steadfast love, O Lord,
and grant us thy salvation. . . .
Surely his salvation is at hand for those who fear him,
that glory may dwell in our land.
Steadfast love and faithfulness will meet;
justice and peace will kiss each other.
Faithfulness will spring up from the ground
and justice will look down from the sky.[38]

The purest vision of divine glory in the Old Testament was
seen with the eyes of faith, during Israel's exile in Babylon,
when the glory of the Lord had deserted the temple and God
seemed to have abandoned his people to their sins. Then in
the presence of the gods of Babylon in all their glory and the
pomp of their shrines, in the heart of a great empire and an
imposing civilization, amid a guilty and stricken people of
Israel, crushed in shame and decadence, there arose a prophetic
affirmation. Israel had despised the word of God, violated his
Law and spurned his promises; it had damaged his glory and
been scorched by the flame of his holiness: Israel had provoked God's anger, it was about to perish.

Then the miracle happened again: the glory that strikes to
the ground is the glory that can raise up again. Banishing this
people from its own land and way of life, it lit up in their
midst a new faith. The object of this faith was still the glory
of God, but no longer just on Sinai or at Jerusalem. Faith saw
glory revealing itself to the whole world and drawing all men
to itself. What form this glory should take the prophet was
not concerned to describe, nor could he imagine. Before his
eyes there was the glory of Babylon, its temples and its empire,
spreading from sea to sea, from Egypt to the Indies, but he
knew that all this was a mere bubble compared with the glory
of the Lord. The glory of God would have the power of an
empire and the splendour of a kingdom. It would cover the
whole earth and reach to every creature. But it would need

[37] Is. 40: 3–5   [38] Ps. 84 (85): 7, 10–11

no force of arms, it would be truth and goodness, justice and peace, the splendour of God's countenance upon the world.

Like the Babylonian empire, God's glory would have its servants. In their vision of the glory of the Lord invading the whole world, the prophets of the exile, inspired by the Spirit, caught sight of the mysterious figure of the suffering servant of Yahweh, entrusted by him with the task of establishing his glory. Though left with no majesty, no beauty and despoiled even of human appearance,[39] it is he who, by his suffering and death, will draw all the splendour of God's glory on his face and reflect it to the uttermost ends of the earth: 'Thou art my servant, in thee I shall reveal my glory.'[40]

[39] Is. 52:14   [40] Is. 49:3

III

The Baptism of Christ and the Blessed Trinity

'I BAPTIZE THEE in the name of the Father, and of the Son, and of the Holy Ghost.' This is the most important thing the Church does on earth, the most urgent of all her tasks—one that she allows even a pagan to do in her name, if he intends to do what the Church does. Yet this rite does not speak of the Church, but only of the three divine Persons. It is the Church that baptizes, and the sacrament gives her new children, Christians. But a Christian, though belonging to the Church, is primarily a man belonging to the Blessed Trinity, bearing the name of the Father, Son and Holy Ghost.

What are we to understand by this 'belonging' to the Trinity, and what does it do to the baptized person? What does it tell us about God who binds himself in this way to his creatures?

1. The baptism of John

'I am baptizing you with water for your repentance; but one is to come after me who is mightier than I. . . . He will baptize you with the Holy Ghost and with fire.'[1] The last of the prophets and greater than they, John the Baptist and precursor came to baptize. The kingdom of God is nigh, and the Lord is at hand: with God coming there is not a moment to lose, the hour to repent has struck. The Lord is a holy God; he does not tolerate sin. 'He sounds men's hearts and reins'; the

[1] Matt. 3:11

42

sinner cannot stand before him. True, it is not his nature or instinct to destroy. He is a living God and gives life to creatures, and he wants them to live and not perish, but he cannot abide iniquity, and evil in his presence must be blotted out.

So John proclaims two things: one depending on him, to which he invites all men of goodwill—baptism in water; the other he is only to announce, for God has reserved it for another, greater than he—baptism with the Holy Spirit and with fire. This formidable baptism is to set the world afire so that God may appear in it: this fire is to consume all stain and impurity, so that God may establish his kingdom and radiate his glory over all his creation. This is no human task, but divine, a work of God's holiness and power, so John attributes it to the Holy Spirit. Unaware as yet that he is a divine Person, John nevertheless knows by experience and the teaching of the prophets that the Holy Spirit is the mysterious all-pervading force by which God comes upon his elect and dedicates them to his service.

John cannot approach this fire himself; it belongs to the one who is to come after him and whose coming will change the face of the earth. All that John can do is not to touch the fire but to take water in his hands and sprinkle it over those ready to repent, to pour the wave of repentance and purification over men, so as to prepare them as far as possible for the passing of the searing flame. This is all he could do and all he was meant to do, all he could ask of the excited crowds that flocked to him. He saw sharply the sinfulness of God's people against God's claims and he knew with certainty that the hour of their fulfilment was at hand. Like Moses in the presence of the burning bush, John could see no further than this burning horizon. His task was to call the people to repent and be baptized in water. The rest was for him that was to come.

All of a sudden, standing before him, there he was—he that was to bring flame and light the fire of holiness was standing in the Jordan water alongside sinners. Could John have been misled? Could the fire foretold be only a hallucination? But Jesus did not gainsay or modify anything John had said. He gave his support to the genuineness of John's mission by asking to receive John's baptism, and he, bowing to this supreme accent of authority, confers on Jesus the only baptism he can give, the baptism of water.

2. *The Spirit and water*

There is a symbolic relationship between water and the spirit, based on nature and richly expressed in scripture. Like wind and fire and light and everything not weighed down to earth and to 'flesh and blood', water is a symbol of God's activity. Water, liquid and transparent, pure and purifying, water falling from heaven to refresh, revive and fertilize things withered, inert and sterile—water seems a natural symbol for an activity whose secret working is beyond man and his tools, an inner-life-giving activity, such as God's must be. Rain is the source of life more visibly in Palestine than elsewhere, and in the Old Testament it formed one of the most favoured comparisons for God's free giving.[2] Faced with the downfall of Israel under its sins, impotent to rise and live again, the prophets announce its conversion as a renewal of the earth after the rainy season:

> I will sprinkle clean water upon you, and you shall be clean from all your uncleannesses, and from all your idols I will cleanse you. A new heart I will give you, and a new spirit I will put within you; and I will take out of your flesh the heart of stone and give you a heart of flesh. And I will put my Spirit within you, and cause you to walk in my laws. . . .[3]

> For I will pour water on the thirsty land,
> and streams on the dry ground;
> I will pour my Spirit upon your descendants,
> and my blessing on your offspring.[4]

> I will pour out my Spirit on all flesh;
> your sons and your daughters shall prophesy,
> your old men shall dream dreams,
> and your young men shall see visions.

[2] Deut. 11:11; 28:12; Is. 5:6; 45:8; 55:10, etc   [3] Ez. 36:25-27
[4] Is. 44:3

Even upon the menservants and maidservants
in those days, I will pour out my Spirit.[5]

It is natural that our Lord, following this tradition, should
speak of the Spirit he had come to give the world as an inexhaustible spring of living water: 'If any man is thirsty, let
him come to me and drink; yes, if a man believes in me, as
the scripture says, fountains of living water shall flow from his
bosom. He was speaking here of the Spirit which was to be
received by those who learned to believe in him.'[6]

If we pressed these comparisons too far, in the effort to see
the relation between water and the Holy Spirit, we might
make the mistake of thinking of the Spirit not as a Person but
as a divine atmosphere or medium we are plunged into at our
initiation as Christians. Receiving the Spirit is not simply
drinking in as deeply as possible, as our lungs breathe in
deeply the mountain air, some radiance of purity, light and
freshness; still less is it yielding to some divine harmony. It is
an illusion to identify the Spirit with religious experience of
any kind.

True, man's experience of air and water can help to lead
him to a grasp of what the Spirit means, and the bible images
have a special value. But they are only comparisons, and it
would be a mistake to transpose them too naturally to the
spiritual life. It would be reducing the Spirit to a natural
element, however subtle and pure, belonging to the natural
order, subject to our experience and analysis. Whatever the
prophets say of raining down dew and springs of living water,
it must be understood alongside the actual facts that are the
essence of their message. Then their way of speaking is as
matter of fact as could be: 'I will put my Spirit within you,
so that you will follow in the path of my law, remember and
carry out my decrees.'[7] 'Whoever calls upon the name of the
Lord shall be saved.'[8] 'I belong to Yahweh.'[9] What could be
simpler or more matter-of-fact? Nothing about passivity
whereby the individual welcoming the Spirit in him must
surrender his personality. The great biblical images of water

---

[5] Joel 2:28-9   [6] John 7:37   [7] Ez. 36:27
[8] Joel 2:32   [9] Is. 44:5

do still have their value. They serve to stir up in the soul the instinct of acceptance without reserve, passivity not rising from inertia but from readiness to respond; then God is able to enter in and transform the soul. But images and comparisons must fade away in contact with actual experience of the Spirit, which leads to interior renewal and real newness of life.

The New Testament sets aside even more firmly any illusion claiming Old Testament support to identify the Spirit of God with any human experience however exceptional. The New Testament does not link the Spirit with water as a natural element, but with baptism as a sacramental action in which water is given a new status from being in contact with an action of Christ. So to grasp the action of the Spirit, we need think no more of any natural waters, but only of what Christian baptism meant for our Lord and the apostles.

3. The baptism of Christ

Out of John's baptism, something human in concept and execution, God produced an event that revealed realities that surpass human imagination. Only John seems to have taken in this revelation, but it contained the whole secret of Christ and his work on earth, and all the richness of Christian baptism: 'Even as he came up out of the water he saw the heavens opened, and the Spirit, like a dove, coming down and resting upon him. There was a voice, too, out of heaven. "Thou art my beloved Son; in thee I am well pleased." '[10]

We must be wary of over-stressing the objective features in this scene, but on the other hand we must not reduce it to mere symbolism. If the gospels say our Lord saw 'a bodily form like a dove',[11] they do not mean to describe an external objective form in the atmosphere, but rather a spiritual experience, a vision similar to that received by those who receive revelations. It is not a case of a physical miracle, but neither is it a purely imaginary description to inform the reader who our Lord is. It is an inner experience of our Lord seeing the Holy Spirit and hearing the Father's voice; but this seeing and hearing affects him in his human nature, as from outside him. The account speaks, as mystics do, of sight and hearing, to signify

[10] Mark 1:10–11   [11] Luke 3:22

that they are in the presence of realities that are distinct from them and come to them from outside.

Our Lord 'saw the heavens opened'—this we understand as seeing God. The narrative does not say that God made himself visible. It is true, of course, that our Lord never left the presence of his Father and lived permanently in his immediate presence. But it is also true that he lived this immediate presence in the condition that St Paul described as 'emptying himself'. The human nature he shared with us was not transformed by the presence of the divine nature, and it remained subject to the conditions affecting human beings in this fallen world. 'The heavens opened': between God and our Lord there is no barrier and the Son is in direct contact with the Father. But he remained on earth in the midst of sinful men. He did not cross the threshold of glory and, like us, he was a pilgrim on his way to the Father and his home.

'The heavens opened': the age-long wait of humanity, since sinful man was shut out of paradise and cut off from God, was fulfilled at that moment. Between God and man 'his cherubim, with a sword of fire'[12] were less of a barrier than the mass of human sin. They really symbolize the forces of divine wrath falling upon human sin. Hence also our fear in the presence of God and our resistance to his love, as well as his anger and disappointment with men. It was impossible for us to escape from this situation and ever to enjoy the sweetness of God's friendship.

It was impossible also ever to lose the memory or nostalgia for this friendship. From Adam mankind inherited and kept up its refusal of God, an immediate reflex of distrust towards his initiative, and also the undying desire to find him again and surrender to his love. The Old Testament heightens the painful awareness of sin holding us in thrall, and the passionate eagerness for deliverance when the breach should be made in the wall of our prison. One of the last prophecies in the Book of Isaiah beseeches the God of Israel:

O that thou wouldst rend the heavens and come down,
that the mountains might quake at thy presence. . . .

[12] Gen. 3:24

We have all become like one who is unclean,
and all our righteous deeds are like a polluted garment. . . .
Thou hast delivered us into the hand of our iniquities.
Yet, O Lord, thou art our Father;
we are the clay, and thou art our potter;
we are all the works of thy hand.[13]

The baptism of our Lord is the moment this breach in the prison wall was made. Heaven, shut up ever since the first sin, was now opened. This was done, just as the prophet had prayed, by the Father. If God saves, it is because he is the Father; and it was the Father primarily who revealed himself at the baptism of our Lord. He revealed himself in the mysterious way that is peculiar to him, with nothing of him appearing, for he remains: 'He that dwells in light inaccessible: no human eye has seen or can ever see him.'[14] But it is from him every gift and all grace must descend, for he is generosity pure and simple. From him there came to our Lord the perfect gift, wherein God is given in all his fullness, the Holy Spirit.

4. Our Lord and the Holy Spirit

Between persons every encounter is at least partly spiritual, in so far as it goes beyond merely mechanical or instinctive contact and makes people conscious of each other's presence. Every human encounter involves a degree of fellow-feeling for another, even if only to tell a stranger the way to some place. To be present to someone else, to understand him and be understood by him, one must be a spirit and act as such. For such an encounter to be perfect, the presence must be complete, and we must somehow, while remaining ourselves, dwell entirely in and identify ourselves perfectly with the other person. This is what love dreams about, what gives it all its strength and greatness, and it can only come from the spirit and be achieved between spiritual beings.

This aspiration, that is always uplifting mankind and filling it with joy when achieved, however modestly, and causing inevitable disappointment by its limitations, does have its

[13] Is. 64:1–8   [14] I Tim. 6:16

fulfilment somewhere. In God love is unalloyed and unlimited, and the Spirit is a person. The Father dwells in his Son by the Spirit, and the Son dwells in the Father by the same Spirit. In this mutual ecstasy and embrace, which is the Holy Spirit, the Father and the Son find their union.

The Spirit John was awaiting was a consuming fire; but he was manifested to our Lord under a divinely simple form, with the depths of the heavens opened, the mysterious wind and the ordinary dove. But in this simple framework it is the whole almighty power from on high that the Spirit brings home to our Lord, the fullness of God.

This fullness was in the words: 'Thou art my beloved Son; in thee I am well pleased.' The words were expressed by the Father, but it was the Spirit that brought them home to the Son. The Father bends down over his Son with the pride and joy that parents find in their children being like them, with the unique joy of God finding in a creature his own perfect likeness, in a man who is his own eternal Son. At last here is the one he has been preparing for ever since the first morning of creation, and whom he had foretold by the prophets; the man who would do all his will, who would accept all his love and return it with all his heart, with his whole soul and with all his strength. And being the pride and joy of God the Father is our Lord's whole joy and strength. This is the food he lives on, to please his Father and know he is wholly about his Father's business.

This joy and strength were given to our Lord by the Holy Spirit: that is the part he was taking in this incident and the meaning of his presence. It was not like inspiration coming to the prophets, to dictate some special action, to take over from the human being and endow it with new and abnormal power. He came to bring home to our Lord as man his own true personality, to enable him to hear from within what the Father says, telling him what he is, the beloved only Son of the Father. The Spirit does not say this of himself, it is the Father's utterance, but it is the Spirit that makes it heard in the depths of the heart of the Son. By the Spirit, our Lord knew and welcomed his Father's voice. The narrative makes it clear that, for Christ, seeing the Spirit descend upon him and hearing the voice were not two distinct moments, but two inseparable experiences, or two components with one resultant experience. Without the Spirit's inner assurance to our Lord and the resulting attitude of filial acceptance and surrender, the Father might seem to be a sovereign almighty power but external and almost a stranger to him. This supposition is obviously unthinkable, for the Trinity cannot allow of any encounter between Father and Son without the intervention of the Holy Spirit, but the presence of the Third Person does show how fully the Trinity is an interior reality of encounter and communion.

We feel some inkling of the need for this mystery of the Trinity, as a result of our own incompleteness. The painful experience is with us at all times. It is not enough for a father or mother to have children in order to see the full achievement of this relationship. How much resistance they encounter in them, and what shortcomings they feel in themselves! It is rare for children to fulfil the aspirations parents have for them. If they do, it requires an exceptional convergence of circumstances and influences, in which parents may play a large part, but other factors must certainly intervene. The most successful upbringing is no doubt one where the child owes most to his parents, but it will also be one where he absorbs the maximum of gifts from outside, gifts his family cannot teach him. There cannot be, among men, any father who merits the title with absolute right: 'You are not to call any man on earth your father; you have but one Father, and he is in heaven.'[15]

Corresponding to these shortcomings on the part of parents there are limits also on the children's side. Wherever the fault lies, it is a fact that there is frequent and painful lack of understanding. Parents do not recognize themselves in their children, nor do the children find in their parents quite the image they vaguely hope to see. The disappointment is mutual, and it forms a harsh wall between them, preventing parents from exercising their authority and sons and daughters from acting as such. In numerous homes nowadays this wall is so thick that the father-son relationship is a mockery, only involving casual encounters of no significance, unfortunately

[15] Matt. 23:9

inevitable. For a child to know that he is his parents' son, it is not enough to know he is their offspring, to share their home and their way of life, even to submit willingly and unreservedly to their authority; he must feel within him that all his powers and will to live and all his confidence towards others come to him from his parents, from their strength, their presence and their love.

Between human beings, between father and son on earth, however close their intimacy, this communion itself remains necessarily limited. To try to make it total and exclusive would be a foolish and fatal illusion. But between our Lord and his Father, this ideal was realized in its entirety, the communion between them is wholly complete, with no trace of shadow or reserve. Because he is the only-begotten Son of God from all eternity, our Lord lives constantly before his Father, receiving all his being from him, doing and saying all he does in conjunction with him, not with passive and servile imitation, as a child might, but with full self-possession, with the awareness of a perfect exchange whereby he gives the Father just as much as he receives from him. But he is also flesh of our flesh in the human nature given him by his mother. He needed, just as we do, to acquire from the world around him—the earth and its fruits, his people and their culture—the gifts of human experience needed for growth and life. So he lived the life of our humanity as the only-begotten Son. He assimilated all creation and learned all human life by experience. In all that he received from men, the food he ate, the skills that he learned with wood or on the land, in the wisdom acquired from the elders or from the scriptures he heard read, in every moment and each detail of what is for us ordinary everyday life, our Lord never ceased to feel himself carried and fashioned by the creative hand of his Father, responding to it by consecrating his whole being to his service, living his whole human life as his beloved son.

All this required the presence and action of the Holy Spirit. In order to realize their sonship and react accordingly, all children need to feel far more than a look of affection and attention. Every child needs an inner certainty of their father's relationship, with the force and the implications involved, and a realization that true fatherhood calls for mutual understanding. In the same way, but in a uniquely unprecedented form —for in the Trinity there is not just mutual presence, but an actual Person involved—the Father does not give himself to the Son without their mutual Spirit, not only as a necessary witness or a confidant, but as the medium of their encounter and the seal of their union.

So it was that, at the moment of his baptism, as an echo to the voice coming down from heaven in which Christ recognized the Father from whom he receives his being, his life, and his mission, there was an inner response or presence, the witness of the Spirit dwelling in him, conveying the message of the Father, making it for ever efficacious, and making every fibre of his being as a man the incarnation and expression of the only-begotten Son.

IV

The Holy Spirit in Our Lord

IN VIOLENT and deliberate contrast to the scene of the baptism of our Lord, the gospels pass straight to his temptations. The sight of the heavens opened yields place to the desolate horizon of the desert; the expression of the Father's good pleasure and pride, to the sinister figure of Satan; the strengthening peace of the Spirit, to the suggestions and threats of the tempter. But here, as before, it is the same Spirit who conducts all. Though silent, it was he that re-echoed the word of the Father in the mind of our Lord; and it is the same Spirit who now leads him to face the devil, exposing him to his propositions and his challenges.

1. Jesus led by the Spirit to the devil

There is a paradox in this, the stumbling-block of the gospel and the scandal of the cross. The Spirit that manifested himself upon Jesus, bringing him the Father's love and joy; the Spirit who is God's strength and acts in Christ as in himself, with no resistance to his power or light, led Jesus, not to the glory of the Father, but to Satan in the wilderness. No doubt it was to enable our Lord to triumph over Satan, but by passing through temptation. It was to reveal to our Lord his power over sin, by letting him feel its contact and its suggestions. In our Lord's first move in the public life can be seen the rule that is to govern it all: God yields him to the power of his enemies, the power of sin—apparently weakness and folly, in

53

reality the strength and wisdom of God. For the temptation, like the whole public life for which it provided the overture and the keynote, was to confirm the depths of the Trinity-communion we caught sight of at our Lord's baptism.

The three divine Persons were present in the desert, each in the role proclaimed at the baptism of Jesus, but a new actor came upon the scene, whose role was to bring out the parts played by the three principals. So the devil, who imagines he is the lead, was condemned to reveal, all unwittingly, the infinite riches and wisdom and love of God.

In attacking our Lord the devil is gambling to find out if he is the Son of God: 'If thou art the Son of God, bid these stones turn into loaves of bread. . . . If thou art the Son of God, cast thyself down. . . .'[1] Whatever meaning Satan may have given to 'Son of God', and even supposing he was aware of the existence of the three Persons, he could not grasp the bond of love between them. He was certainly enlightened enough in his hatred to see that in Jesus God had raised a faithful servant such as had never appeared among men, and to sense that between God and him there was the closest of bonds. But Satan would no longer be Satan if it were possible for him to appreciate such a mutual bond of union and to realize the meaning and generosity of such mutual love. So, naïvely, ingenuously almost, he asked the question which he imagined was decisive —and in fact it is, in a sense far deeper than Satan could imagine, for it goes to the depth of our Lord's being—'If thou are the Son of God . . .'. For Satan it is simple logic: the Son of God cannot allow himself to die, it would be the ruin of his mission in life. So let him do this simple thing and agree to change the stones into bread, so as to eat and live for God his Father.

It was indeed essential for our Lord to live, to be what he was meant to be and to accomplish his mission. But to live, for him, was to be nourished on the word of God. This word or message from God is the one he heard from the Father at his baptism and which the Spirit re-echoes in his heart: 'Thou art my beloved Son, in thee I am well pleased'. A message, which like all divine messages, carries categorical demands as well as

---

[1] Matt. 4 : 3, 6

absolute assurance. Given that he is the beloved Son, how could there be any question of ever being anything but pleasing to the Father? Other men belong to this world and have roots in this world to support them, and so are capable of knowing the joys this world can give. Our Lord can have no other support, no other joy comparable to that of looking into his Father's face and seeing his pride and joy at recognizing his own Son in this man, though a prey to hunger and tempted by Satan. If the assurance of this message and the demands involved were to fail, our Lord would have been no more than a sinful man, like the rest of us. The hypothesis is unthinkable: our Lord could never cease to be the only-begotten Son, divine love could never fail, God could never stop being love. The outcome of the temptation could only be the defeat of Satan: but it would only be a real defeat if the conflict was real, if our Lord really and truly felt hunger and need, if he actually looked at the nations of this world and the means Satan could offer him to win them. With lucid insight, our Lord summed up this world and the power of sin in it, the vast potential of evil that could be loosed on the world—a terrible insight that we cannot even envisage without shuddering. Did he, at this early date, experience the terror and anguish of his agony in the garden? The gospel says nothing of this: only that Jesus looked Satan in the face and put him to flight: 'Back, Satan!'

2. *Jesus overcoming the devil, in the Spirit*

The spiritual life means basically sharing in the relation of Father and Son in the Spirit, but this sharing is to be lived out in a sinful world by creatures subject to sin. Sin is not only an obstacle or series of obstacles on the way to this sharing of life, which have to be negotiated one after the other, as a commander gradually silences the defences of an enemy position. In the spiritual life sin is an ever-present opponent, something present that is constantly needing to be overcome. Sin would not be sin—separation from God with loss of the life of grace—if it did not aim at inserting itself just where man finds access to God, if it did not seek to destroy this sharing, by frustrating it or distorting it. So it is, by a strange but natural

C

coincidence, that the intentions of the Spirit and the machinations of Satan seem to converge on the same point. The Spirit
that brings our Lord the Father's voice and joy leads him to
Satan to make the tempter taste defeat and show him that his
powers are powerless to separate Father and Son. The tempter
seeing in human flesh a creature for whom God is really and
truly the only Lord, the only God, the only Father, cannot but
attack Jesus to thwart his unparalleled pretension. That Jesus
is the Son of God is the one vital point, both for the Holy Spirit
and for the evil one, the supreme treasure at stake between
them. If Jesus is the Son of God, the devil must not miss the
opportunity of exploiting this unique potential and utilizing
for his own ends the unique privileges vested in him, the
personal protection of God and the destiny God works out for
him. 'Thou art the only-begotten Son', echoes the Holy Spirit
in the heart of Jesus, and the tempter re-echoes: 'If thou art
the Son of God. . . .'

The spiritual life, like the life of our Lord in the Spirit, is
not a life sheltered from evil, with no awareness or concern
about sin. It involves a clear insight into the world and the
power of sin. From the pinnacle of the temple, contemplating
Jerusalem (whether with the eyes or with the imagination, it
matters little, and the evangelists are not concerned to settle
this question, any more than St Paul explains his extraordinary experiences), our Lord saw the hearts of that people,
the aspirations of the busy folk in the streets and of those going
up to the temple. He fully realized the effect that could be
produced on human weakness by a performance of great
strength, the enthusiasm that would be touched off in Israel
by a demonstration of power, with signs appearing in the
heavens, upon the appearance of a dazzling personality. At the
tempter's side, he looked down on the nations of the world and
saw, more clearly than the devil, his hold upon them and the
part he played in the world. How men are dominated by
money, hate, fear, envy, pursuit of pleasure and lust for power
—our Lord had no need for Satan to tell him: the Spirit
dwelling in him reveals it all with far greater insight.

But our Lord's insight into the world given over to sin,
because it was inspired by the Holy Spirit, was a saving look

that was to set the world free from sin. Because of our Lord's indwelling Spirit and his living communion with the Father, because he possessed the life of the Spirit in its fullness giving him the Father and giving him to the Father, our Lord grasped with an unerring eye the deadly disorder of sin, the mad claim of the creature to live as a law unto itself, to be its own support and happiness. But because our Lord lived this sharing of life with the Father in flesh and blood like ours, sensitive to pain and fear, he experienced the temptation, not of the madness which he saw into so clearly, but of how sin can be seductive, imperious and spell-binding. He knew through hunger and thirst how much men need earthly food, and how much they must endure to prefer heavenly food, the support that comes from God. He knows, having lived among men in constant touch with the crowds, how dependent we are on success and the approval of those about us, and what courage it takes never to flatter or curry favour, always to tell the truth and to re-nounce all attempts to exert pressure or force on the frailty of man. He knows, for nothing can escape him that in any way offends God, all the resources that sin can command in this world, all the cruelty, perfidy and baseness it can muster, and how the innocent man is always defenceless against sin. Know-ing all this by the light of the Spirit, our Lord overcame all these temptations, defied all these threats and, in the strength of the Spirit, repulsed the tempter. Satan was not deprived of his weapons, and he would use them again; but he was already overcome, for they had no power over our Lord.

The Holy Spirit is the light guiding our Lord in all these suggestions of Satan, to see instantaneously the wrong that must not be, coming between him and the Father. With this light, our Lord unmasked, behind the tempting images, the terrifying face that no one before him had ever gazed on, the formidable, grotesque face of Satan. The strength of our Lord is the Spirit bringing the infallible certainty that all must be endured rather than that the slightest lack of regard should be shown to the Father; bringing the inward assurance that he can face all threats once his Father's honour is at stake; bringing the joy of consecrating every moment of existence to the Father up to the supreme testimony of total sacrifice and

absolute love. To confront the powers of evil, Jesus possessed
nothing, name, riches, power—not even the power he held to
cure and save others which he must not turn to his own use.
He offered himself, famished, disarmed and naked to the most
terrible of all enemies, the prince of this world. He had but
one source of strength, the inner witness of the Spirit, the
voice telling him that nothing, neither life nor death, neither
present nor future, neither man nor devil, could ever separate
him from the love of his father.[2]

The triumph of our Lord is also that of God: 'The Lord thy
God shalt thou adore.' This outcome makes us realize why the
Spirit led Jesus to this sinister encounter with Satan. It shows
that the Father found in Jesus the preordained servant, ready
for all sacrifices, unhesitating in all that involves God's honour,
the one who can only live in the joyful sight of the Father, the
only-begotten Son. This encounter also shows that a creature
of flesh and blood, liable to hunger and desire and fear, is
capable, though still belonging to our race, of being the
humanity of the Son of God and expressing his obedience and
love. This means that the presence of the Spirit in Christ
manifested at his baptism is perfect and efficacious in the
highest degree, wholly possessing his human soul. That a
human heart can love God in this way, that a body of flesh
should find the strength to serve him in this way, that a child
of a sinful race in a world dominated by violence and cunning
and money should have the courage to choose weakness, and
poverty and innocence—all this is a proof that Satan is not, as
he claims, the lord and master of mankind, and that the Spirit
of God remains paramount, able to transform and sanctify the
heart of man.

The temptations in the desert are thus the proof that our
Lord's baptism is not a fleeting moment of light cast upon him,
but an abiding and inexhaustible source of strength for him.
But they show also that this strength is involved in a never-
ending struggle, breaking out in the desert; that the salvation
of the world is a sure prize for the man advancing to meet this
struggle with no other weapons than those of God.

Such, too, is the real meaning of our own baptism as Chris-

[2] Rom. 8 : 38–9

tians. It is not a passing event. It is an initiation of a man's life into the divine life of the three Persons, an initiation to be worked out in this world of flesh and blood. In his whole bodily life, in all the work of his hands and his mind, in the development of his skill and culture, in the whole world he is helping to build, the baptized Christian is called to live as a son of the Father animated by the Holy Spirit.

This bodily nature is a fallen nature, prone to rebel against God, and this world is a prey to Satan, at the mercy of violence and scandals and systematic corruption. But this world has been redeemed and the Christian should find himself at home in it as in his Father's kingdom, keeping his heart pure and his hands clean, seeking justice rather than fortune, fidelity rather than pleasure, the service of his brethren rather than what he can get out of them. This he can do only in the strength of his baptism, in the faith of the Lord Jesus and in welcome response to the Holy Spirit, in lucid resistance to the devil and all his workings, in acceptance of hardship and effort. Baptism means renouncing Satan and allegiance to Christ. This renunciation and this allegiance are worked out day by day in contact with the world and temptation. Confronted with the devil, amid the demands of his body and senses, bewildered almost to the point of dizziness by the fascination of human success and enjoyment, daily encountering the power of sin in the world, the Christian is master of it all by his baptism. He possesses within him the name and the strength of those who are stronger than all sin—the name of the Father, who has them all in his hand so securely that Satan cannot make them his prey; the name of the Son, living and dying in his own flesh for his Father's sake; the name of the Holy Spirit, poured out in our hearts and making a new-born creation spring into being in a world of corruption.

3. The anointing of Christ by the Spirit

Hearing the Father uttering his love for him in the Holy Spirit did not lull our Lord into a feeling of certainty and calm, nor for one moment cause him to forget the world and yield to the happy feeling of relaxation. If our Lord's joy and strength consist in welcoming the Spirit of his Father and in

knowing he is his Son, this presence immediately brings with
it a mission to accomplish, a life to live. Coming soon after the
scene of the baptism, where the Father speaks and our Lord
seems only to listen and hear the message, there is another
scene, closely related to it especially in St Luke's account,
where Jesus inaugurates his ministry in the synagogue at
Nazareth. No longer is it the Father speaking, but our Lord
himself, and he introduces himself thus: 'The Spirit of the
Lord is upon me; he has anointed me, he has sent me.'[3] The
interior strength dictating his words and guiding his action is
again the Holy Spirit, as at the baptism. Acting in one
continuous movement, the Spirit defines both what Christ is
and what he is to do, his status as Son of God and the Lord's
anointed. These two are inseparable: if he is the Son of God,
it is to share this sonship with man, to be their Saviour, the
Christ. Conversely, being the Christ awaited by Israel and
coming to save men, given that the only salvation God has for
them is to be his sons, the Christ must be the Son of God, and
the salvation God calls us to is 'the fellowship of his Son, Jesus
Christ.'[4]

These refinements bring out a basic truth about our Lord
and also about our spiritual life. We are constantly inclined
to separate, or at least find it hard to integrate, the spiritual
life and everyday life, prayer and action, living for God and
living for others. The spiritual life of which Christ is the
unique model as he lives it in its fullness, not only being dwelt
in and possessed by the Spirit, but being also wholly his
achievement—'incarnatus est de Spiritu Sancto'—life in the
Holy Spirit knows of no such divisions. True, it does not fall
into the popular fallacy on charity of putting God and man on
the same level, but it will have no separation between the first
and greatest commandment, the love of God, and the second,
the love of our neighbour, which is of the same order and
without which the first is an illusion. For us, as for our Lord,
to live in the Spirit is to stand before God and hear him tell
us he is our Father and welcomes our love, but it also means,
by the same movement of the Spirit, to grasp and achieve our
consecration to a sacred task, the service of the kingdom of

[3] Luke 4:18   [4] 1 Cor. 1:9

God. The same Spirit that enables us to cry 'Abba, Father!' also enables us to dedicate our lives to the service of our brother men.

The presence and unique action of the Holy Spirit in our Lord explain two characteristics that one would consider irreconcilable, and which are very rarely found together except in the most holy souls. On the one hand, our Lord seems possessed by an unshakable certainty, the awareness out of reach of all forms of doubt or temptation, of being exactly in the right place, in the full possession of himself and his powers, reacting absolutely rightly to all that occurs, never having any problems. This certainty does not arise, as in fanatics or '*illuminati*' or people of dominant will-power, from a one-track momentum brushing aside all objections, or a force polarizing all energies and determining all reactions. Our Lord, on the contrary, is constantly free, always responding to the whole world of creatures, and his most decisive choices and clear-cut decisions never seem preordained or predetermined. This sense of assurance combined with ease in self-possession express the awareness of the only-begotten Son, who knows 'whence he has come and whence he is going',[5] as also do his free access and full possession of the Spirit—though *we* know nothing of the way it comes or the way it goes[6]—his certainty of never being alone[7] and of always being a source of honour to his Father.[8]

But on the other hand this sovereign freedom and assurrance combine in our Lord, by a paradox arising from the very mystery of Christ, with the permanent awareness of a stern rule to be carried out, a destiny to be fulfilled at all costs. This realization of the imperative dominating his whole life is particularly acute in his approach to his passion, not only as a fatal event that he must accept and undergo, because such is the Father's will, but as the event whereby his own personal destiny is achieved, and in which the deepest meaning of his life is consummated and revealed. Not only does our Lord speak of his passion as an event that is certain and inescapable, not only does he foresee it as a necessity both

[5] John 8:14; cf. 13:3   [6] John 3:8
[7] John 8:16, 29   [8] John 8:49

intrinsically and extrinsically—Jerusalem must be the only place for a prophet to perish,[9] the seed must die,[10] it was fitting that Christ should suffer.[11] But, what is more remarkable still, is his way of speaking of his fate and the passion in particular as the accomplishment of his destiny as the Son of man.

Our Lord is the Son of man, and constantly he speaks of himself as such in the third person. 'The Son of man has nowhere to lay his head',[12] 'the Son of man has authority to forgive sins',[13] 'the Son of man will be given up into the hands of the chief priests',[14] 'the Son of man did not come to have service done to him; he came to serve others',[15] 'you will see the Son of man again, when he is seated at the right hand of God's power, and comes on the clouds of heaven'.[16] This way of speaking is not only a way of stressing that he really belongs to the human race, the descendant of Adam, as really as he comes from the Father and is the Son of God. Nowhere in the gospels do we find 'the Son of man' put alongside 'the Son of God' to complete the title. 'Son of man' is not a common noun, applicable to any one at all. Jesus was not just 'a son of man'; he was of all the children of men, 'the Son of man', the one foretold by the prophet Daniel[17] whose coming was to mark, for the Jews, the coming of the kingdom of God. Introducing himself as 'the Son of man' was for our Lord one way of proclaiming that he was the Messiah awaited by Israel, the Saviour of the world.

It was a very special way of proclaiming this. On the one hand it inspired the highest hopes, for this Son of man was to come on the clouds of heaven and judge the world with the power and glory of God; on the other hand, this title was laden with a sinister fate and death. What gives this fate its absolutely irrevocable character is that our Lord identified it with the figure of the Son of man whom he came to embody; so much so, one might almost say, that he would not be the Son of man if he escaped this fate. Not only must our Lord undergo the suffering, but he had to do so because he was the Son of man, in order to be what he is by being born into this world, but

---

[9] Luke 13:33
[10] John 12:24
[11] Luke 24:46
[12] Matt. 8:20
[13] Matt. 9;6
[14] Matt. 20:18
[15] Matt. 20:28
[16] Matt. 26:64
[17] Daniel 7:13

would not fully be until he had lived out the life fixed for the Son of man by God in the scriptures. If, *per impossibile*, our Lord had evaded a part of his mission by not reproducing by his every deed every line of his 'image' as expected by God, he would not be the Son of man, Israel would not have had its Messiah, mankind would not have been redeemed.

If this supposition is unthinkable, as it is, and if God can be sure of his Son incarnate in our kind of life—if our salvation was indeed to be accomplished, it was because our Lord was invested with the Holy Spirit. It was the Spirit that, consecrating his human flesh and all his human nature, made it capable of taking up the superhuman task laid down for him by God. It was the Spirit that, out of a frail creature born of woman, made the Son of man, able to carry the sins of the world, to love men unto death and to love God above all else. It was the Spirit that led Jesus all his life long, making his every action the perfect response to the expectation of God, to God's supreme appeal.

What the Spirit accomplished uniquely in Christ the Holy Spirit also reproduces in the hearts of all holy souls. Those who are led by the Spirit of God have no need for an external law;[18] it is not that they do not have a law, but that it is a wholly interior and infinitely more rigorous one, the very law of their being. As the Lord could not fail to accomplish all that is said of the Son of man to the last iota, if he was to be indeed the Son of God filled with the Spirit, so too the Christian living according to the Spirit cannot be unfaithful to God's will without being false to himself and his true being. The new creation born in him of the Spirit is no strange or unaccountable figure, but the one that expresses his deepest personality, the likeness that God creates in him to gaze on with love.

4. The Holy Spirit and the poor

Strong personalities with considerable influence are felt to be dominated by great aspirations and preoccupied by concerns of great moment. It is as though a keen wind bears them

----

[18] Gal. 5:18

along, sweeping aside all mean considerations and trivialities. This wind need not of course be that of the Holy Spirit, it may be born of flesh and blood, it may be ambition of a noble kind, though very self-centred, or the spirit of revolution, strong and lucid, within its own limited hopes of achievement. The Holy Spirit likewise picks on some of us for certain tasks, concentrates our energies, shakes up our defences and scatters our idols, not to set up another in their place, but to have us consecrated to the service of the one, true, living God.

To enable us to check that it was the Holy Spirit putting before him the way of life and the demands he had for him, our Lord gives us this sign: the Spirit of God consecrates him to the poor and unfortunate, sends him to bring them the joy of salvation. This link between the presence of the Spirit and the gift of salvation to the poor is a constant factor in the gospel, and its source is in Christ himself, who does not reveal his whole personality and essential relation to the Spirit except in contact with human distress and misfortune.

In the synagogue at Nazareth, explaining who he was and what he was to do, our Lord refers to the prophecy of Isaiah:[19] 'The Spirit of the Lord is upon me; he has anointed me and sent me out to preach the gospel to the poor . . . to bid the prisoners go free. . . .'[20] The poor and the prisoners the prophet in exile was thinking of were the Jews in captivity in Babylon, crushed under slavery in a pagan enemy country. Our Lord appearing among men finds them subjected to worse misfortune, to a more ruthless slavery. In the sick flocking to him, in men's infirmities and disabilities, in human suffering and death, Christ sees the sinister traces of sin and the hatred of Satan, the liar and the murderer.[21] Just as, under the unerring guidance of the Spirit, Jesus was led out into the desert to experience the diabolic power of Satan face to face, so at every step he takes along our roads our Lord discovers, in the miseries revealed or concealed as he passes, new forms of our shame, new evidence of the powerful prince holding this world captive. As he had vanquished Satan by the Holy Spirit, he now made the demons feel the power of his holiness,[22] 'through the

[19] Is. 61:1   [20] Luke 4:18
[21] John 8:44   [22] Mark 1:24

Spirit of God'.[23] He was conscious, each time he restored life or health, that he was dealing another blow on his enemy.[24] That is why, when John from prison sent to ask if he was 'he that is to come',[25] our Lord replied by referring to his works for human misery—'how the blind see, and the lame walk, how the lepers are made clean, and the deaf hear, how the dead are raised to life, and the poor have the gospel preached to them'.[26] If there is no mention of the Spirit in this, his presence is manifest in just the effects that Jesus foretold in the synagogue at Nazareth. It was the Holy Spirit leading him to men in need.

Different in atmosphere but very close in meaning and scope is the episode in which 'Jesus was filled with gladness by the Holy Spirit' and gave thanks to his Father for having hidden all this from the wise and prudent and revealed his wonderful plans to little ones.[27] This way of acting God's part, this inversion of the world's usual scale of values, did not only arouse in our Lord a keen sense of wonder, it tapped the deepest source and current of love uniting him to the Father, that is none other than the Holy Spirit: 'Be it so, Lord, since this finds favour in thy sight. My Father has entrusted everything into my hands; none knows what the Son is, except the Father, and none knows what the Father is, except the Son, and those to whom it is the Son's good pleasure to reveal him.'[28]

In seeking 'little ones' and those out of favour in men's eyes, in bringing the poor the riches of God, and God's joy to those suffering and mourning, our Lord is not just being instinctively sensitive to human misery, he is fulfilling the deepest need of his nature, abandoning himself body and soul to the movement of the Spirit, to the love of the Father and his response thereto. Only the poor, with no treasure on earth, are capable of receiving the riches our Lord brings, the only riches he has, the Spirit given from the Father. To those who already find in this world, in themselves or outside, their source of happiness, to those who have chosen to seek their own happiness, our Lord has nothing to give. He is a stranger for them, an intruder of no consequence, since he has nothing of what

---

[23] Matt. 12:28   [24] Luke 13:16   [25] Matt. 11:3

[26] Matt. 11:5   [27] Luke 10:21   [28] Luke 10:21-2

they seek, and they do not need the one thing that he does possess, the joy brought to him by the Spirit of God. By contrast, to those who hunger and thirst, who feel their wretchedness and the emptiness of life, our Lord can display all his power, he can bring them what the Holy Spirit supplies him in unending stream, the certainty of belonging to God and being able to do without all else, to possess him as all their riches.

God is love, and so he can only give his infinite riches as a gift, and one can only possess him as a gift, that is in the Holy Spirit. We can only possess the Holy Spirit as a gift if we are poor in spirit. The absolute poverty of Christ, the earthly manifestation of the total allegiance of the Son to the Father, is the condition and sign of his infinite riches, the perfect possession of the Spirit. Thus, possessing nothing on earth and having no human support or means of influence, our Lord, because he has nothing to give but the Spirit, goes straight to the heart of man in his acceptance of poverty, he brings the good news to the poor; opening to them his own unique treasure, he gives them the gift of his Spirit.

V

Our Lord in Conflict

D ID CHRIST bring us war or peace? Is the Christian life a relentless struggle against enemies to be overcome, or is it a stubborn refusal of violence in any form? Does it mean a perpetual state of siege, or being ever more deeply involved in life and events? Is it a harsh and exhausting war, or a victorious peace? In support of each of these ideas one could multiply texts, apparently in opposition, setting up a series of contradictions: 'Do not imagine that I have come to bring peace to the earth',[1] 'Peace is my bequest to you',[2] 'The kingdom of heaven is open to violence . . .',[3] 'Blessed are the peace-makers',[4] 'Behold thy king is coming to thee, humbly, riding on an ass',[5] 'Then, in my vision, heaven opened, and I saw a white horse appear. Its rider . . . goes to battle for the cause of right'.[6]

Rather than prolong the list, and without trying just now to see how these texts can be co-ordinated and integrated, we must first study our Lord himself. To grasp the meaning of his words we must see him in action. His way of speaking has many different aspects, but in his actions and reactions to others he reveals himself with absolute spontaneity and asserts himself with unerring sureness and freedom, which enables us not only to discover the coherence of his message but also to see better its spiritual depth and divine richness.

[1] Matt. 10:34   [2] John 14:27   [3] Matt. 11:12
[4] Matt. 5:9   [5] Matt. 21:5   [6] Apoc. 19:11

67

Going through his life we find mysterious contrasts underlying his words and making them strange to our minds. It is clearly not enough to refer to the over-simplification of oriental parlance or the implications of speaking in symbols. As we watch him and listen to him we realize that we must consider conflicts in his life, really seeing that it involved a daily struggle; and yet in this we must avoid misunderstanding and trace the very real and varied aspects of this struggle with great care.

1. The battle for man

From his birth, well before ever taking any initiative himself, our Lord is up against the hostility of men. The gospels of the infancy stress this from the very beginning, a feature that will be with him all his life. His birth indeed brings 'peace on earth to men that are God's friends',[7] but 'this child is destined . . . to be a sign which men will refuse to acknowledge'.[8] Magi come and adore him, but Herod and all Jerusalem, 'all the chief priests and learned men among the people',[9] already acting as they would in the passion, remained blind to this kingship that they read about in the scriptures. The opening episodes in St Mark, and the very first miracles, show our Lord being watched by men who never relaxed their vigilance, whose heart was carefully barricaded against him. Jesus, seeing the faith of the paralytic and the bearers who had lowered him down through the roof, spontaneously tells him he is freed: 'Thy sins are forgiven thee.'[10] 'He is talking blasphemy' is the immediate reaction of the scribes. He goes into a synagogue and finds there a man with a withered hand, 'and they were watching him, to see whether he would do a work of healing on the sabbath, so that they might have a charge to bring against him'.[11] They had guessed right: Jesus did cure him, but not without making it clear he was conscious of their sharp opposition: 'he looked round on them in anger, grieved at the hardness of their hearts'.[12] Not less than the miracle itself, our Lord's justification of it—'to do good on the sabbath day, or to do harm?'—and the firm stand he took

---

[7] Luke 2:14   [8] Luke 2:34   [9] Matt. 2:4
[10] Mark 2:6   [11] Mark 3:2   [12] Mark 3:5

against them, provoked the pharisees' reaction: 'the pharisees went out, and at once began plotting with those of Herod's party to make away with him'.[13]

No doubt we should not always consider the order of events in the gospels strictly chronological, and the fact that the opposition of the adversaries of our Lord is recorded in the earliest chapters would not in itself be enough to prove that their determination dates from the first days of the public life. However, it is clear that the gospels do present our Lord face to face with implacable opposition from the beginning of his teaching and from his first miracles. Similarly, the sermon on the Mount that inaugurates the preaching of the gospel pre-supposes in the beatitudes persecution and calumny,[14] and also enemies and 'those who persecute you'.[15]

It would be a false reading of the gospels to overlook or tone down this permanent and essential feature of the public life of Jesus. The admiration of the crowds, the acclamations on his path, are matched by an even more assiduous escort, the relentless troop of silent observers, commissioned to take it all down, and clever individuals forearmed for controversy. Day and night, our Lord, whose life was indeed a 'public life', with no home, 'nowhere to lay his head',[16] no means of livelihood for himself, was confronted with suspicion and hate, his words more or less deliberately falsified and his intentions travestied. A day-by-day, unremitting conflict with stupidity, blindness and spiteful and contemptuous antipathy. Such was our Lord's life; an exhausting strain on a man, normally leading either to contempt for others or to being reduced to collapse. Our Lord was not impervious to this strain; he sometimes showed his anger or weariness: 'Ah, faithless and misguided generation, how long must I be with you, how long must I bear with you?';[17] 'Jerusalem, Jerusalem, still murdering the prophets . . . how often have I been willing to gather thy children together, as a hen gathers her chickens under her wings, and thou didst refuse it!'[18]

Our Lord's struggle against human sin was no mere friendly bout or piece of play-acting, but a fierce encounter with no

[13] Mark 3:6   [14] Matt. 5:11   [15] Matt. 5:44
[16] Matt. 8:20   [17] Matt. 17:17   [18] Matt. 23:37

quarter. Our Lord did not record men's failings as a detached observer, regretfully. He stripped them of their masks and pursued them wherever they took refuge. Friend or foe, fickle crowds or wavering disciples, none escaped the earnest gaze of Christ weighing them in the balance. When the time of the passion came, they would all be found grouped together against their adversary! Judas and his money, the Sanhedrin and their hate, Pilate with his eye to the main chance, Peter afraid for his skin, all Jerusalem yelling fiercely or cowardly silent. All the sin challenged by Christ seized the chance to hit back, fastened on to him and only let go when his death was certain.

Cruel as it was, this mortal combat did not raise an insurmountable barrier between the two sides. Far from it: dying at their hands, our Lord reconciles them to his Father. Between his enemies and himself, he managed to set up, at the very moment they prevailed over him, a solidarity that was stronger than their hate. They could put him to death but they could not stop him laying down his life for them. They turned on him the hideous face of sin, but loving them to his last breath he proved that it was still worth while to care for them; they were not beyond redemption, and love could still prevail over sin in their hearts.

Our Lord's conflict among men is not against them, but for them. He committed himself, and commits his followers, to an unrelenting struggle: 'If any man has a mind to come my way, let him renounce himself and take up his cross and follow me.'[19] But this struggle is not waged against man or any human values. Our Lord's attitude to human values and human nature is in no way negative, still less aggressive. Man is always for him someone who matters. The poor cripple woman is a 'daughter of Abraham', and if her affliction can be shortened our Lord would hear of no delay, even on the sabbath.[20] He makes men's worries his own: if he urges us to trust them to God, it is not that he does not take them seriously, but rather that God alone, knowing what we are worth— infinitely more than the birds of the air—is capable of devoting to his children the care they deserve. For the blind to see, for

[19] Matt. 16:24   [20] Luke 13:16

the lame to be able to walk, that housewives should find missing money and fathers their lost children, that a wedding feast should have nothing to mar its joy, these are for our Lord most legitimate human desires, and such happy outcomes appealed to him and occurred wherever he went. Though he said: 'I have come to set a man at variance with his father, and the daughter with her mother',[21] this was not because he despised family ties. On the three occasions when the gospels relate that he raised people from the dead he was moved with sympathy with the widowed mother,[22] with the parents of the twelve-year-old girl,[23] and with the sisters of Lazarus.[24] The closest human ties must yield to the claims of the kingdom of God and the love of our Lord, but in this they lose none of their value.

This double aspect of our Lord's conflict among men—on the side of mankind to be saved, but attacked by sinful men—reappears in parallel form in the twofold aspect of mankind as seen by him. In the gospels, mankind means the world; and the world, in the traditional Christian way of speaking, as in the gospels, also bears this twofold aspect. 'God so loved the world that he gave up his only-begotten Son' for it.[25] 'I have come to save the world'[26] and to 'give life to the whole world':[27] his flesh is also 'given for the life of the world'.[28] 'God was in Christ, reconciling the world to himself',[29] and so it is a 'world reconciled to God'.[30] But 'the world treated him as a stranger',[31] hating our Lord[32] and finding no room for the Spirit of God, because it cannot see or recognize him.[33] In this sense the world is not the object of our Lord's prayer,[34] and he says 'I have overcome the world'.[35] It is no mere chance that 'the world' means two such different things, it is in the nature of things. The world means mankind and the universe it lives in. On the one hand, mankind inevitably tends to set itself up against God and build its universe in opposition to the gospel; so, faced with this reaction, the Christian must keep his distance and freedom of action. On the other hand, mankind is God's creation, designed for unity in that all its members belong to the same race and God has sent them a Saviour of their own race. It is for this human kind that our Lord was born, it is to them he sends his disciples; and the Christian owes mankind, owes this world, all his attention, his prayer, his endeavour and his charity.

2. Conflict with Satan

Our Lord's battle to reach men and convert them is a never-ending struggle. It filled his life, and since his departure his disciples have to go on with it and pursue it unceasingly until he comes again. It is not merely that as the generations follow each other they each have to win their own battles, but rather that the heart of man is always the scene of keen fighting. The gospels show us this battle fluctuating about our Lord, in the crowds wavering between enthusiasm and rejection, in minds torn between allegiance and doubt or disappointment, even among the disciples, whose faith had large gaps, with constant lack of understanding and serious failures at times. 'To keep his own in the truth', to enlighten and forewarn them, to train and correct them, to keep up their courage; all this formed a task that our Lord constantly had to start again, and to which he had to give his undivided attention at all times.

Christ's conflict with Satan seems very different. It is related in the gospels as forming a single incident, the temptation in the desert, a rapid passage at arms in which with three dazzling counter-thrusts our Lord unmasks the perversity of the tempter and the emptiness of his challenge. We must not be too literal in interpreting an incident unique of its kind. We must indeed take it as it stands, not neglecting a word, for every word is significant. We must remember that the encounter is not presented as the recollection of witnesses relating what they saw or heard. Nor is it quite like a diplomat reporting on conversations he has had. Still, this scene is no invention of the evangelists or the disciples, nor is it an imaginary reconstruction of the state of mind our Lord was in. The incident clearly bears the mark of our Lord's own experience, his skill in avoiding snares and in revealing wonderful light in a word of scripture, his unerring promptness in detecting falsehood, and his assurance in taking up his position at God's side and showing forth God's truth. It would be fruitless to speculate just how the gospels did reconstruct this experience, but it is quite certain they tell us of a real experience of our Lord's.

It is not stated that this experience, related at the outset of our Lord's public life and action, was an isolated incident and only happened once. It is stated that Christ's first move after his baptism and on being accredited by the Holy Spirit was to go into the desert to be tempted by the devil, as the gospels surprisingly put it,[36] because this encounter was to settle once and for all our Lord's orientation, the nature and scope of his work. It is a decisive battle, but not necessarily without any sequel, not an action 'without trace'. Far from it: though the devil, 'the prince of this world', who claims to exercise over the universe a dominion stolen from God and so is our Lord's personal adversary, retreated after his defeat; yet our Lord in the course of his public life stirs up and puts to flight the diabolic host, the manifold and sinister power bent on doing evil and ruining men. There is a close connection between the paramount mastery of Christ over the demons and his initial victory over Satan. The evil spirits are stricken with terror at his approach,[37] for they recognize him who was to make an end of the kingdom of Satan. The disciples found the devils made subject to them at the very name of Jesus,[38] for he had come to have Satan 'cast down like a lightning-flash from heaven'. Our Lord's conflict with the prince of this world, begun after his baptism, was to come to an end only when, the Son of man being lifted up from the earth and set upon the cross, his adversary was to be thrown down from his throne and bereft of all his power.

So there is a close link between our Lord's conflict with Satan and his struggle in the midst of men. There is really only one conflict and one adversary, the same under every disguise, whatever he may be called. The Apocalypse calls him 'the great dragon, serpent of the primal age . . . the devil, or Satan, the whole world's seducer'.[39] Our Lord called him 'a

[36] Matt. 4:17   [37] Mark 1:23, 5:6
[38] Luke 10:17   [39] Apoc. 12:9

murderer from the first', 'liar and the father of lies'.[40] In the
hostile looks about him and the mounting hatred, in the bitter
prejudice of men shunning him, our Lord recognized the
hereditary hold their 'father', the devil, has over them. For it
is Satan that our Lord is conscious of and aiming at in all the
obstacles that stand in the way of his search for men's hearts.

So the first thing in our Lord's conflict with Satan was to
discern the presence of the enemy, to cast his light on him
whatever false appearance or tricks he may have. Of the woman
suffering for eighteen years he says that it was 'Satan had kept
her bound'.[41] Of the cockle that grew in the Father's field
along with the wheat of the kingdom: 'the enemy has done
it.'[42] When Peter was indignant at the suggestion that the Son
of man might meet with defeat and death, it was Satan putting
the words into his mouth.[43] When Judas betrayed him, it was
'Satan finding his way into his heart'.[44] The desertion of the
apostles at his passion was because 'Satan claimed power over
them . . . to sift them like wheat'.[45] In the same way he had
claimed and obtained the right to torment Job, thinking to
confound both the Lord and his servant, but unconsciously
bringing credit on both.[46]

It was, of course, the scene in the desert that most showed
our Lord's ability to unmask Satan. There he spoke to him and
met him face to face. It would be idle curiosity, not encouraged
by the gospel, to seek a possible outward form for the devil's
appearance to Christ. It is not necessary that our Lord should
have actually seen or heard any particular thing or word, for
him to know infallibly that he was confronted with God's
adversary, Satan, in his highest form, the most personal and
the most fearful. If we seek to know how he recognized this
presence, we need no more than what the gospels tell us, the
words and the nature of the devil's suggestions. Where an
ordinary man would only have seen natural and reasonable
suggestions, at the most ideas that needed checking, our Lord
immediately grasped the hidden malice, pin-points the subtle
evil spirit secreting it, and replies with the most telling

[40] John 8:44   [41] Luke 13:16   [42] Matt. 13:28
[43] Matt. 16:23   [44] Luke 22:3   [45] Luke 22:31
[46] Job 2:6 and 10

counter-thrust. To thwart Satan it is not necessary to see him in all the troubles we encounter. Seeing the devil everywhere is the surest way of not seeing him where he really is, perhaps in the way we think to serve God, when we are only seeking to satisfy our own instincts, to display our talents and to lord it over the world we live in.

To detect the presence of Satan and foil his efforts there is no need to set up a state of siege, fostering an atmosphere of suspicion and anxiety, ever afraid of being deceived or led astray. Our Lord's insight into Satan comes solely from his attachment to his Father; his calm rebuttal of Satan owes all its strength to the Father alone. Given his attachment and allegiance to the Father, he has no need to scrutinize alternatives and beware of traps. For Satan to suggest to our Lord feeding himself, in body or heart or mind, on anything but God; for Satan to suggest his taking the initiative over the Father's plans, even by a skilful move and with the certainty of winning the whole world—any such idea finds our Lord forearmed and brings down the crushing rejoinder: 'God alone shalt thou worship'.

The effortless mastery of Jesus in the presence of Satan, so simple and almost childish, clearly belongs to the only-begotten Son and no one else: in fact it is a most striking mark of his divinity. Satan, by urging the claim of 'Son of God', expected that this Son, like anyone else, would make the most of his privileged origin and surround himself with power and pomp. Instead he found a man unarmed, alone and unaided; confronted with this absolute poverty, the refusal of any riches or success or victory that are not a gift of God to his Son, Satan is reduced to impotence. He can have no purchase on him, for he has absolutely nothing of his own and holds all that he is in constant dependence upon his Father.

Such too must be the armour of the Christian: 'Draw your strength from the Lord, from that mastery which his power supplies', says St Paul to the Ephesians; 'you must wear all the weapons in God's armoury, if you would find strength to resist the cunning of the devil'.[47] On hearing such language one might imagine actual preparations for fighting, and St

[47] Eph. 6:10–11

Paul enters into the spirit of it: he speaks of the soldier's equipment, belt and breastplate, shield and helmet and sword.[48] But he explains: the belt is truth, the breastplate is justice; our feet must be 'shod in readiness to publish the gospel of peace'; the shield is faith, the helmet is salvation, and 'the sword of the spirit, God's word'. All these things are spiritual weapons. They are not pacifist, in the sense too many people associate with the gospel and the Christian spirit passive protest against force in the world, but truly spiritual, deriving all their strength from the power of the Holy Spirit. Those who count only upon faith, hope and charity, embark on a vast enterprise, nothing less than the kingdom of God, but they need have no fear, they are armed with the strength of Christ and assured of the victory of his Spirit.

A sign of this victory is the accent of authority, almost of calm detachment, that our Lord assumes in addressing the diabolic powers. They are well aware of him and tremble at his approach: 'Why dost thou meddle with us. . . . Hast thou come to make an end of us? I recognize thee for what thou art, the Holy One of God.'[49] Our Lord cuts him off: 'Silence!' he said; 'come out of him'. What a difference there is between this sovereign disdain, this peremptory cutting off of any relation with the devil, and the endless trouble he would take with his followers for their instruction. Untiringly he keeps going over his instructions, finding comparisons and parables, explaining them in detail,[50] multiplying his miracles, as though they would never learn: 'How is it that you still do not understand?'[51] He spends whole nights in prayer, 'that their faith might not fail', and yet he only just succeeds, with Peter himself succumbing to temptation.[52] The devil is beaten, and always treated as such by our Lord, but the struggle of Christ for the sons of men would go on to his last breath on the cross.

3. Struggle with God

This struggle was, in a sense, between Christ and God. Christ began his public life with a temptation, when the Spirit

---

[48] Eph. 6:13–17   [49] Mark 1:23   [50] Mark 4:34
[51] Mark 8:21   [52] Luke 22:32

led him to the encounter with Satan. He ended his life with another temptation, far more terrible, far more exhausting, the agony of Gethsemani. In the desert Jesus experienced hunger: in the garden he experienced prostration, fear, repugnance. In the desert with three phrases he silenced three challenges and scored three victories. In the garden he could only repeat the same thing over and over again: 'Let this chalice pass from me . . . thy will be done', and yet the chalice did not pass and he seemed not to command the strength to drink it. In the desert he spoke with mastery: now he was begging and his prayer was being refused. Then he spoke of God with triumphant assurance, feeding on his word alone, content with his Father and nought else for his comfort. On the night of the agony he turned to his disciples in search of a little strength and friendship. In the desert he had Satan for adversary; in his agony his struggle was with God.

True, not only God: Satan had found his way into the heart of Judas, the prince of this world was ready for the kill, it was the hour when all the enemies of Jesus were gathering, time for the powers of darkness to prevail.[53] But all of them would have no power at all, and the prince of this world himself could do nothing against Jesus,[54] if the Father had not 'given up' his Son.[55] Just as Job, given up to Satan and tormented without respite, suffered much less from all his misfortunes than from the silence of God and the unaccountable ill-treatment God had condemned him to,[56] treating him as an enemy;[57] so Jesus, beyond the tortures, the hate, the cruelty, the unrelieved baseness revealed in the passion, was finally crushed by the indescribable abandonment by his Father: 'My God, why hast thou forsaken me?'[58] He is still his God, sole source of strength and nourishment to him, and so this cruel experience is not hell, the refusal of God invading the whole being and turning it against itself. On the contrary, more than ever our Lord remained solely dedicated to the service of his Father, only anxious to live by the words of his lips, but no answer comes to this love. God is silent, as if hostile, seeming

[53] Luke 22:53
[55] Rom. 8:32; John 3:16
[57] Ibid. 13:24; 19:11
[54] John 14:30
[56] Job 16:12
[58] Mark 15:34

infinitely remote. It was the horror of this agony that God
seemed to be withdrawing himself from him who could not
live without him, who could only live on the certainty of his
favour, wrapt in his love, for ever his joy. In the passion this
divine countenance seemed charged with nothing but anger.

For 'Christ never knew sin, and God made him into sin
for us'.[59] Bluntly St Paul here recalls a fearful mystery. It is
not a case of any failing of Christ in his attachment to his
Father; nor of any condemnation of Jesus cut off even
momentarily from God. Our Lord's passion is a mystery of
holiness and love. But the Father's love for the Son takes a
form that seems incomprehensible to us, afflicting our Lord
himself to the point of death. 'God made him into sin', God
made the all-Holy and Just One bear the weight of horror and
shame that drags down our guilty humanity; God made him
espouse and, as it were, sink to our level of decadence and
abandonment. Only the cruellest trials of great Christian
mystics give us a little insight into this abyss of suffering. The
unfolding of the passion as minutely laid down by God and
understood by the gospels, shows that it is the hour when the
Father 'did not spare his Son, but gave him up for us all'.[60]

The worst thing about the passion was not the hatred of
the Sanhedrin, nor the cruelty of the executioners, nor the
cowardice of the good men, nor even the treachery of Judas.
The worst is that God seemed to come down on the side of all
these people whose sin amalgamated them against Christ.
Before the authorities and before his people, Jesus solemnly
asserted his belonging to God alone: neither he nor his kingdom was of this world: he had but one Father, in heaven; he
is a king, but his only glory is that of the Almighty; he counted
on the help of no creature on earth, he relied on God alone.
Could God refuse to pronounce in his favour, without coming
down on the side of his enemies? Before all Jerusalem and the
whole world Jesus proclaimed that God alone was his support:
if God did not manifest his support, it could only go to show
that he was impotent to intervene or that Jesus was an impostor. God being almighty, the only explanation would seem
that Jesus was not his Son—'If thou art the Son of God, come

[59] 2 Cor. 5:21   [60] Rom. 8:32; cf. John 3:16; Acts 2:23

down from that cross.'[61] True 'they do not know what it is that they are doing'[62] or saying: but they are just saying what they see. When they heard our Lord utter the cry of distress: 'My God, why hast thou forsaken me?'[63] it was natural for them to take it as an admission, escaping from a dying man, of the failure of his claims: God no longer with him, no longer his Father.

The victory of Christ was that he could say 'Why hast thou forsaken me?' and, in the same breath, 'My God!'—keeping intact and inviolate to the end the mysterious communion between him and his Father, the determination to drain the fearful chalice to the very dregs, the certainty of accomplishing to the last iota what was written in the scriptures, of being absolutely faithful to the mind of the Father as he looked at the world and to the inscrutable plan he was carrying out in the passion. For our Lord to cling to God in this abandonment, to forgive men just as they were revealing the depth of the iniquity in their hearts, to go on calling 'Father!' him from whom he received sentence of death and to commend his soul into his hands; all this proves that there still was in Christ, stronger than sin and stronger than death, the everlasting love that unites Father and Son, their mutual gift, the Holy Spirit.

This is the victory of Christ, and it is the victory shared by the three Persons of the Trinity. This victory provides the final explanation of our Lord's mysterious struggle with the Father, of his agony at Gethsemani, of the abandonment on the cross, of the years spent battling against the wickedness, avarice and hypocrisy of men, and the temptations and assaults of Satan. It finally explains how God could allow human sin, and justifies the creation of a human race free and able to reject him. At this hour on Calvary, the Father accepts from the lips of his dying Son the 'Yes!' for which mankind was born. The conflict of love between God and man is consummated in the resurrection. For this joy to come to pass, for God and for us, it was worth while that this world should be created and that it should be the scene of such conflict.

[61] Matt. 27:40   [62] Luke 23:34   [63] Matt. 27:46

VI

Our Lord's Poverty

OUR LORD'S poverty, as indeed everything about him, is a mystery of God. Just to use it as an argument or an appeal to sentiment is to profane it; and to claim to bring it into line with our human reckoning is to explain it away altogether. One can only put oneself before our Lord and as simply—in fact 'poorly'—as possibly, contemplate him and ask for the grace to listen and understand.

1. Our Lord in poverty

Jesus was born poor, lived poor and died poor. His poverty was not spectacular, but of a kind that classed him with those 'without means', living at the mercy of circumstances, liable to destitution at short notice. An administrative measure caused him to be born away from home, the modest condition of his parents failed to secure accommodation, and his cradle was a manger in a stable. Such was the sign by which he would be recognized by those who found him first, themselves poor: 'a child still in swaddling clothes and lying in a manger'.[1] For years at Nazareth he was a workman like any other. When he made himself known among men, he lived as a poor man, without any pretence. With nothing of his own, no house or income, he lived on work and alms combined, partly on the fishing of his disciples, partly also on the generosity of a few women who ministered to him. He lived a hard life, knew

[1] Luke 2:12

80

hunger and thirst and fatigue, finding sometimes friendly
hosts and at other times hostility.

Though open to all and counting among his close friends
men who were well off, he was not dazzled by riches and
devoted the bulk of his time and interest to poor people, the
sick and people of no consequence. He did not live in any
privileged class of humanity, where rank and fortune put
people out of reach of human misery. Day after day, wherever
he went, the same sights awaited him, the same cries surrounded him, the distress of the wretched, the wounds and
the infirmities, the flotsam and jetsam of humanity.

But as he made no display of his poverty, so our Lord never
found any satisfaction in human misery. He proclaimed the
blessings of the poor, the hungry, the distressed, but he would
not stand by and see a mother mourn her son, and he multiplied the loaves to save a multitude from suffering hunger. He
attributed no value to privation or destitution in themselves;
he did not exalt the poor for possessing nothing, but for being
able to receive all things. He personally had no scruple in
accepting hospitality and being generously treated, staying at
times in the houses of friends, and having devoted helpers for
him and his disciples. He died with nothing to leave, but was
buried in a rich man's grave. Poverty for him is not a rule of
thumb, not a programme never to be modified. He sat lightly
to his poverty, but it was absolute, for it was part of his very
life.

2. *Jesus 'dispossessed himself'*

Our Lord was poor interiorly: it was not, as often happens,
a case of managing to profit by the good things of this world
while professing to despise them. He was ready to accept them
and appreciate them, but without the slightest fear of losing
them, without ever being preoccupied to amass them or keep
them. He was poor absolutely, not just detached from material
goods, but also free and divested of all the supports that men
depend on in their lives. Nothing belonged to him, not his
friends nor his own future or his plans, not even his own
ideas or his own work.

Our Lord's way of speaking is significant. One of his

favourite ways of saying things is to say what he has not got,
what he does not do, what he is not: 'I cannot do anything on
my own authority';[2] 'I seek not my own will';[3] 'I am not looking to my own reputation';[4] 'The learning which I impart is
not my own';[5] 'I do not belong to this world';[6] 'It is not on my
own authority I have spoken'.[7] His disciples are not so much
his own; they have been entrusted to him by the Father.[8] This
reluctance to claim possession is not hesitation on his part nor
is it fear of committing himself or taking action. On the contrary, no one could be more aware of what he is, with a full
and unique awareness of his identity: 'I, who speak to thee,
am the Christ';[9] 'It is I who am the bread of life';[10] 'I am the
light of the world';[11] 'It is I who am the door of the sheep-
fold';[12] 'I am the good shepherd';[13] 'I am the resurrection and
life';[14] 'I am the Master and the Lord';[15] 'I am the way; I am
truth and life';[16] 'I am the true vine';[17] finally, quite simply,
'Jesus said . . . I am'.[18] There is no contradiction or gap
between these two ways of speaking. Sure as he is of himself
and what he is doing, he is equally conscious that his assurance
comes from another, him whom he hears and sees at all times,
his Father.

The depth of his being, the secret he reveals to his own, is
summed up in the words, 'I am', and 'I do not do anything on
my own authority'.[19] We are inclined to see a paradox in this.
To be, we think, must mean to assert oneself as an independent
person, not needing someone else, possessing all one needs to
exist. Our Lord is, in that sense, and does assert his existence,
as only God can do, without beginning and without decline,
with no risk of accident or failure. But all that he has and is
he owes to the Father, and never ceases to receive from him.
Co-equal Son of the Father, endowed with all the riches of
God, he holds none of it as his own; his infinite riches he

[2] John 5:30; cf. John 5:19, 8:28   [3] John 5:30; cf. 6:38
[4] John 8:50; cf. 7:18   [5] John 7:16
[6] John 8:23   [7] John 12:49
[8] John 6:37-44; 10:29; 17:6   [9] John 4:26
[10] John 6:48-50   [11] John 9:5
[12] John 10:7   [13] John 10:11
[14] John 11:25   [15] John 13:13
[16] John 14:6   [17] John 15:1
[18] John 8:58   [19] John 8.28

receives eternally from the plenitude of God. So it is that 'His nature is, from the first, divine, and yet he did not see, in the rank of Godhead, a prize to be coveted; he dispossessed himself, and took the nature of a slave'.[20] This was no caprice of a satiated potentate weary of his treasures, but the spontaneous instinct of God's Son coming to share with man the filial joy of receiving all one could wish for and yet possessing nothing. Who among men can receive all things in this way, except the man who is poor? Our Lord, in order to live our human situation as the Son, chose to do so in absolute poverty.

3. Our Lord's time limited for him

What we have heard our Lord saying is not so many fine words; these words, long meditated by St John, convey and explain our Lord's normal conduct, noticeable in all the gospels. Our Lord did not belong to himself and one of the signs of this was his way of living in time and making use of time.

One of the forms of wealth is to have time to look around, to be master of your own time, to use it as you please, to take time off as and when you like, to pick the time you want to do things. Not to be master of one's own time, to feel oneself from morning to night controlled by the workshop hooter, the factory shift, the times of buses and shops, rising and meals, is one of the harsh forms of privation that people have to undergo nowadays. To be able to adjust one's hours of work, even though longer and busier than other people's, is now a privilege and a luxury. In a different civilization which often appreciated leisure more, our Lord found his whole life absorbed and sacrificed. Not absorbed in the pursuit of grandiose schemes, but sacrificed to the demands of the immediate present and the needs of others. Not a moment of his own, no time 'to play about with'. The moment he arrived anywhere, they hurried to him with the sick and the lame. From morn till night, he had to be talking, healing, listening, explaining, defending himself, to the point of 'not having time to eat'.[21] Even when the sun had gone down, they brought sick people to him, and 'at very early dawn', after hours of

[20] Phil. 2:6–7　　　　　　[21] Mark 6:31

solitary prayer, he already pressed on, for he must needs go on
to the next place.[22] Once only the evangelist mentions that he
planned to take a rest for a time, for his exhausted disciples to
relax, and the plan fell through when Jesus saw the multitude
like sheep without a shepherd.[23] A typical example: the only
quiet spell our Lord counted on escaped him because his time
did not belong to him, but was wholly given over to the Father
and his work. Amid this life, taken up with urgent tasks, even
prayer was not a time of freedom and oblivion, no mere 'quiet
time'. On the contrary, it was a time when our Lord gathered
and concentrated all his strength to obtain from the Father
the success of his work and the coming of God's kingdom.

With his time limited and with never a moment to waste,
our Lord was never tense or hustled. He was short of time, but
never a miser with it. It can often be a sign of wealth to be, or
appear to be, extremely busy. The would-be rich man counts
the minutes like profits slipping away. Our Lord never seemed
impatient or in a hurry to have done with anything. This
showed his self-possession and above all his absolute devotedness to other people. His time was no more precious than that
of the wretched folk that besieged him. His time, in all truth,
was not his own; it belonged to all who needed him. A very
instructive episode is the meeting with and healing of the
woman with the issue of blood.[24] The woman, who had suffered from it for twelve years, and who made her way through
the crowd and managed to touch the hem of our Lord's
garment, thought only, in her faith, of the Lord's power, and
hoped modestly to save him trouble and waste of time. Her
idea did in fact seem opportune at such a moment, when the
ruler of the synagogue was beseeching Jesus to hurry to the
assistance of his daughter, now at the point of death. Just
before, Jesus had followed him immediately, but now he
stopped, as if not realizing the child's condition, and the
father's anxiety. He could not refuse a look of understanding
to a faith such as this woman's was. He stopped, asked questions, wanted to hear the answers. It seemed time wasted, the
time spent on this woman; but it was time that he recovered,
for time, like the rest of creation, really belonged to him, and

[22] Mark 1:32-8   [23] Mark 6:31-44   [24] Mark 5:21-43

Jairus, by reason of these wasted minutes, would have made a further step in faith. So Jesus could dispose of time, but he always did so as a poor man, only in the service of God's kingdom.

Our Lord was equally a poor man with regard to the future. When you study him in action you see he could not freely dispose of future time. True, he knew perfectly what was in store for him, and he had none of the uncertainty and hesitation that we have. But this did not mean that he was the master of the future: he received it from his Father, not as a treasure to dispose of at will, but as a trust of which he had to give an account. 'While daylight lasts, I must work in the service of him that sent me; the night is coming when there is no working any more. As long as I am in the world, I am the light of the world.'[25] Here is a mystery of dependence and poverty: the Light of the World, such as no darkness can master, and he is obliged to give his light before darkness comes on! Jesus always knew what he was going to do, he was never taken unawares by events, but you never see him planning a programme or a time-table. Such things are necessary for us, in our efforts to save and utilize time as it escapes us. For us all time is equally good,[26] the stuff life is made of and available for any purpose. But our Lord did not have such a choice: at any one time he could only do what the Father asked of him. Constantly on the alert, he let no moment escape that the Father had given him. When he spoke of the future, he spoke of it as a necessity: 'Behold today and tomorrow I am to continue casting out devils and doing works of healing; it is on the third day I am to reach my consummation.'[27] The predictions he made about himself were all about the passion, about the hour when, delivered to the machinations of sin, he was to breathe his last in the hands of the Father. This hour, when 'darkness has its will',[28] is 'his hour', the one for which he came into the world. 'How impatient I am for its accomplishment!'[29] He had 'longed and longed' for it.[30]

[25] John 9:4-5
[26] Cf. John 7:6
[27] Luke 13:32
[28] Luke 13:53
[29] Luke 12:50
[30] Luke 22:15

4. A poor man among men

The man who is poor does not have power over people.
Having no prestige and no means of pressure or intimidation,
he has to rely on their generosity and pity. If that is denied
him it will go hard with him. He may as well fade out; no one
will greatly mind. Such was the fate of Jesus and such did he
seem to the world at large.

Because he was a poor man among men, he always realized
they had something to offer him, every one of them. Not one
but had an interest for him: the sick, down-and-outs coming
to him, tiresome beggars the apostles wanted to silence, insignificant children they tried to set aside; he welcomed them
all and looked at them all. All of them had a value for him, all
had their secret. He needed them all. The rich and powerful,
who pride themselves on running other people, expect nothing
from them except the correct reaction. They have nothing
more to learn about people: they know all about them and
could not care less. Our Lord's knowledge of people was from
the heart. His gaze could see into their past, their secret
motives, their fate. He could on occasion be exasperated by
them. He could be wearied or overwhelmed by them, disappointed in them, but he always cared greatly.

Before his gaze the woman of Samaria found all her defences
crumble, but at the same time she discovered a new freedom
and independence in the recognition of the Messiah. A
supremely gifted teacher, our Lord was never like a 'trainer'
calculating the correct reflex to produce. From each person he
expected a choice, a choice that meant something to him,
either for joy or for distress. He waited for the response of the
rich young man, as he waited for the reaction of the apostles
to his question: 'Will you also go away?'[31] He was thrilled at
the profession of Peter: 'Blessed art thou, Simon son of
Jona.'[32] The faith of the centurion and the Canaanite woman
filled him with wonder. To every man he met he offered a
priceless treasure, the love of the Father, for he is infinitely
rich in this. But from all he expected, patiently, and silently, a

[31] John 6:68   [32] Matt. 16:17

gift that has priceless value for him, faith; for this he made himself poor.

His death brought out his poverty. At the foot of the cross his mother and a few other women could only help him with their tears. His disciples had let him down, denied him, betrayed him. His enemies had never dared to hope for such a complete triumph. Not one demonstration in the town in his favour, not one protest. God, whose Son he claimed to be, had shown by his silence what side truth was on: God had let him do some miracles for a time, but at the vital time he had just abandoned him. Whether Jesus had been an impostor or deluded, it mattered little; it was clear that evening that God was not with him. It would have been enough to let him come down from the cross, everyone would have been convinced, and his judges would have been the first to applaud this unhoped-for victory. But all was now over. God had been silent to the very end, Jesus had died bereft of everything—not only in the poverty of a man who dies with nothing to leave, but like a man dying bankrupt in the instant when the truth appears to show up the emptiness of his enterprise.

This appearance of bankruptcy was all of a piece with the rest of his life. Our Lord always refused to exert any pressure on the hearts of men or to dictate their ideas. He refused to impose himself by surprise, by craft or intimidation. He did indeed have at his disposal legions of angels, the powers of matter and of spirit; but he came among us with nothing but the strength of poverty: 'I am a king. . . . What I was born for, what I came into the world for, is to bear witness of the truth. Whoever belongs to the truth, listens to my voice.'[33]

But who does belong to the truth? Do not men belong to the devil, the murderer, the liar and the father of lies?[34] Our Lord had experience of that. Men were impressed by his way of speaking about God, and filled with wonder at his miracles. But from this wonderment to faith, from the enthusiasm of the crowd miraculously fed to the allegiance required for belief in the bread of heaven, there is a gap that seems unbridgeable, and Jesus saw his followers depart one after the other. Only the apostles remained, and what pressure could he

[33] John 18:37 [34] Cf. John 8:44

D

exert to keep them? How strong was their faith? 'Will you
also go away?'[35] If they wanted to, how would he stop them?
When faced with refusal to believe, he was literally disarmed,
to the point of being 'unable to do any miracles'.[36] It was in no
way prejudice on his part or judgment formed in advance, for
'he was astonished at their unbelief'.[37] He missed no opportunity of trying to win hearts; 'Jerusalem, Jerusalem . . .
how often have I been ready to gather thy children together,
as a hen gathers her brood under her wings, and thou didst
refuse it.'[38] He gave everything he had, self-sacrifice, generosity, every effort to explain; but with how little effect when
men's hearts were closed!

He was disarmed and poor, in the way that the father of
the prodigal son was, for all his wealth, when he saw him go
away. He gave him half of all he possessed and would have
given him much more, but what was the use, since, with all
he gave him, he could not keep him? So much is God's love
also poor and disarmed, subject to every form of betrayal, poor
indeed as long as deprived of the one thing it seeks, the faith
of the man it is offered to. So too with our Lord: he preached
and worked miracles, he warned his hearers and taught them
all they needed, he spent nights in prayer for them, only to see
them abandon him at the end. If only he had been willing to
restore the kingdom of Israel, with the trump cards he held,
how easy it would have been to win everything!

5. The risen Christ still a poor man

Christ rose again, the Son of God entered into his glory, and
so, we might think, all would be different. The time of trial
over, things would resume their normal course. Here is the
point where human wisdom found itself surpassed and con-
founded by the power of God. That Jesus should be born and
live and die a poor man was something of which human
understanding could sense the natural attraction and grandeur. The vanity of riches, the folly of baseness they so often
bring to their devotees, such things have long been familiar to
men. Many civilizations, when not wholly corrupt, have

---

[35] John 6:68   [36] Mark 6:5
[37] Ibid.   [38] Luke 13:34

realized the grandeur of human distress in its appeal. Not only the bible with its semitic and 'anarchic' tendencies, but also the Greece of Aeschylus recognized in the appeal of human misery 'the anger of Zeus in supplication: there is no more lofty object of awe for mortal men'.[39] But in Athens as in Jerusalem, perhaps even more so in Jerusalem than in Athens, poverty is ultimately only a time of trial, destined to be ended in riches and glory. What the risen Christ represented was something absolutely unprecedented, something strictly divine.

Jesus Christ rose again in the glory of his Father, and this glory filled heaven and earth. All the riches of creation were now his. Beyond the reach of pain or weakness or death, he had the whole world in his hand, he could dispose of the future until the consummation of the world. Gathering his disciples on a high mountain, like the one on which Satan had shown him the kingdoms of the world, he now took up the devil's lying claim on his own account: 'All power has been given to me in heaven and on earth.'[40] Yet this power is not the power of riches. The risen Christ brought his followers neither fortune nor any improvement in their kind of life. By a paradox that puzzles our simple minds, he drew from the statement, 'All power has been given to me', the conclusion whose logic escapes us: 'Go, therefore, and make disciples of all nations. . . .' In this he was warning them that their life would go on being just the same as the one they had led while he lived among them, trudging dusty roads, uncertain of any welcome, at the mercy of indifference or hostility, bearing a message of vital import and with no human means of imposing their ideas. Was that all that the risen Christ brought his followers?

Stranger still, did our Lord become rich? It was natural he should do without earthly riches, now that all creation was at his disposal. But the deeper poverty that was his, his way of dependence on men and events and the Father's guidance, was not that just the same after the resurrection? What difference was there in this respect? We should have thought that now he was risen he should make his presence felt in Jeru-

[39] *The Suppliants*, 478–79   [40] Matt. 28:18; cf. Luke 4:6

salem and so win those who, just before, were defying him to
come down from the cross. They would be the first to acclaim
him, and his resurrection would really have been a triumph. It
would have been much more than a personal triumph, it
would mean the capitulation of a whole city and a whole
people, the conversion of Israel and the triumph of God. However, the triumph of our Lord was reduced to a few appearances to chosen witnesses. Jerusalem remained divided, stirred
to some extent, but basically hostile and often persecuting;
and the conversion of the Jewish people, only partially
achieved, was to become and remain for Christians only an
assured hope, living on in the poverty of expectation. The
risen Christ did not assert himself any more than before, and
he remained the Son wholly dependent on the Father, who was
to 'go up to his Father's side',[41] who was to send to his followers
'the fulfilment of the Father's promise',[42] who entrusted them
to 'the time fixed by the Father's own authority'.[43] The risen
Christ remained the poor man of Bethlehem and Calvary,
who chose the poor and little ones for his friends, and, now
that he was entering upon his glory, kept the same familiar ease
with them, the same simple humanity.

His followers are still the poor, and it is in them that he
remains present for us, now that we cannot see him personally: in the poor, the sick, those in prison, those who in his
lifetime formed his usual company and who, until the end of
time, are to be the prolonging of his presence among us. The
risen Christ is still the poor man, the neglected person we find
embarrassing and 'pass by on the other side'.

6. The unfathomable riches of Christ

A great change has taken place in our Lord's poverty. It is
not now poverty in need, but poverty finding fulfilment.
Christ remains as he was, as wholly dependent on his Father
and close neighbour to human wretchedness, but now he is
the one who has received all things and gives all he receives to
his followers. Power over all creation is given to him; from
the lowest to the highest 'God has put everything under his
dominion', as the head of the Church.[44] By enabling him freely

---

[41] John 20:17   [42] Acts 1:4   [43] Acts 1:7   [44] Eph. 1:22

to bestow the Holy Spirit,[45] the Father enables him to reach all hearts and sanctify the whole world.

The deepest conviction of the early Christians was of being endowed by Christ with an inexhaustible treasure. 'Silver and gold are not mine to give,' said Peter to the paralytic begging alms at the temple gate, 'I give thee what I can: in the name of Jesus Christ of Nazareth, rise up and walk';[46] and as he lifted him up he was cured and leaped for joy. In truth the followers of Christ had received a heritage of untold richness, and the generous lot befalling them was all the more keenly felt for living in poverty and without means of their own. Because he knew himself to be a 'vessel of clay' of common and frail material, Paul realized he was the carrier and trustee of an extraordinary treasure, 'the gospel of the glory of Christ'.[47] Because Paul found himself for ever hustled, persecuted, stricken down or in constant danger; because, in spite of his labours and successes and wonderful graces received from God, the apostle always came up against his inherent frailty, the personal shortcomings that every man experiences as a source of humiliation and suffering, he exulted in the gifts of God, in the strength given to him to labour and proclaim the gospel, not forgetting his frailties but always acutely aware of them.

In the Church and in each one of us this mystery of Christ's poverty is at work: 'He impoverished himself for your sakes, when he was so rich, so that you might become rich through his poverty.'[48] Poverty in itself is not a good thing; by depriving us and leaving us without what we need, it prevents us making use of the riches of creation which are good and desirable things. God did not promise his chosen people poverty; if they were faithful, he promised them an abundance of good things and length of days in a land blessed with dew from heaven and the fat of the land. To those who gave up all for his sake our Lord promised a hundred-fold; and the blessing in store for the poor was not to possess nothing but to have the joy and wonder of discovering God's generosity and entering into possession of God's kingdom.

[45] Acts 2:33
[46] Acts 3:5
[47] 2 Cor. 4:5
[48] 2 Cor. 8:9

But the sinfulness of man prevents God giving himself to them, for sin in man means he is incapable of accepting. Mistrustful of God, mistrustful of others—such as parents, when he is coming to man's estate—he must be for ever 'getting and spending'. How can God open his treasures to hands for ever jealously clutching their prey? How can God give himself to human beings eaten up with envy? His generosity is spent in vain if it cannot arouse men's hearts to feelings of gratitude.

God has found the solution to this apparently hopeless impasse. He has someone whom he can count on, a person free from all envy and mistrust, to whom from all eternity he has given all his riches, for he sees in him only willing acceptance and gratitude, his only-begotten Son. If anyone is able to resolve the complex of fear and anxiety that keeps human beings tied to their poor riches, it is he. 'The Word was made flesh. . . . We have all received something out of his abundance.'[49] 'His nature is, from the first, divine, and yet he did not see, in the rank of godhead, a prize to be coveted; he dispossessed himself, and took the nature of a slave.'[50] So that man could be rich in the end, so that his hands and his heart should be open to God's treasures, so that he should see the overflowing generosity of the Father in the superabundance of creation, Jesus made himself a poor man and, in the midst of privation and lack of all things, lived out in human life the grateful response of God's own Son.

[49] John 1 : 14–16   [50] Phil. 2 : 6–7

VII

Our Lord's Obedience

'OBEDIENT UNTO DEATH, even to the death of the cross';[1] such, in outline, was the whole life of Christ. There can be no insight into the soul of our Lord, no way of understanding its reactions, unless one grasps the secret of them, and this secret is obedience.

If we are to forestall superficial objections and wrong interpretations, it is vital to study faithfully and exactly what our Lord's obedience was, the model of Christian obedience and of religious obedience.

1. Doing God's will

To obey is basically something very concrete and material: doing the will of someone else. Such was our Lord's way of understanding it, and such was the purpose he saw in his life on earth: 'I come down from heaven not to do my own will, but the will of him who sent me';[2] 'I come to do thy will, O my God'.[3] The actual word 'obey' is only recorded once from his lips, and it simply means carrying out the order given: 'If you had faith . . . you might say to this mulberry tree, "uproot thyself and plant thyself in the sea", and it would obey you.'[4] Our Lord does not seem to have put before himself or others a virtue called obedience as such. For him, to obey was always a definite thing to do, the one that the Father called for

[1] Phil. 2:8; cf. Rom. 5:19; Heb. 5:8   [2] John 6:38
[3] Heb. 10:7   [4] Luke 17:6

at any given moment—these words to say, or silence to be
kept, this sinner to be admonished or welcomed back, such a
sign to be refused or such a miracle to be worked, to wash
this man's feet or to kiss that man's face. It was not a disposition of soul, it was the most matter-of-fact kind of thing:
the action of a servant given a job to do, who is not judged on
his protestations of devotion to duty or on his intentions, but
on the way he carries out his task. Ruthless realism this, and
without it obedience is a mere word; any title of virtue it
might claim would be only an illusion. The night before the
passion, wishing to leave his disciples a last image of himself,
he took on the garb and functions and posture of a slave: 'He
laid his garments aside, took a towel and put it about him; and
then he poured water into the basin, and began to wash the
feet of his disciples, wiping them with the towel.'[5] An act of
humility and charity, an act of obedience also; it was the act
of a servant who is at the disposal of his master to carry out
his orders. Reviewing his life in the sight of his Father, our
Lord sums it up in the same way, in terms of work done: 'I
have finished the work thou gavest me to do.'[6]

2. *Obedience to men*

The commonest form of obedience is submission to the
different authorities exercising power. Our Lord practised this
obedience; he lived in submission to men. If, on occasion, he
needed to indicate, with regard to his parents or the temple
tax, the priority of belonging to his heavenly Father, such
quite exceptional statements only stressed more markedly his
ordinary obedience—so ordinary and constant that it could
be taken for granted, and even his mother was surprised at
his first independent act. His obedience was so entire and
unfailing that it made him just like all the other children
around him, just like anyone else in his home town or country.
When the time came for him to emerge from the general
mass of people, his obedience became even more marked.
Most of the people with whom he rubbed shoulders along the
roads or in the villages only had remote relations with the
powers that be, through tax-paying and conforming to police

[5] John 13:4-5   [6] John 17:4

and administrative arrangements. Because his life and his
message were to be such a challenge, Jesus was called upon to
take up an attitude towards the chief Jewish and Roman
authorities. He certainly had no sort of superstitious cult of
authority: he spoke with outspoken frankness of men in power
—of Herod, 'that fox';[7] likewise of the scribes and pharisees,
the legitimate successors of Moses.[8] He had no illusions about
the motives and the ways and means used by kings and princes,
who 'win the name of benefactors',[9] but 'lord it over their
people and make the most of the power they have'.[10] Never,
however, did Jesus preach or practise rebellion, even against
the most unworthy authorities. It seemed natural to him to
obey them, so much so that he hardly ever spoke about it. His
apostles, Peter and Paul, would have to inculcate obedience
to the higher powers, but he, living it as he did day by day, had
not a lot to say about it. They had to force him to give an
answer about it for him to take his position: 'Give back to
Caesar what is Caesar's, and to God what is God's.'[11] Did this
mean it was a point of minor importance? Not at all, but it
was one on which he did not claim to say anything new. Obedience to parents or to the state is not something that origi-
nated from the gospel; it rests upon the natural condition of
man. Having accepted this condition with all it involved,
Jesus lived as a son 'subject to them', then as a loyal citizen,
without fanaticism, not afraid of anyone, but not afraid to
speak out.

Admittedly, this obedience was not the only element in our
Lord's life. He obeyed a great deal more than many people do,
but also, more than anyone else, he took his own initiatives. He
adopted a way of life and customs that many people objected
to; he attached disciples to himself by his own authority;
without reference to anybody he infringed customs considered
sacrosanct. By this freedom of action he intended to manifest
his sovereignty, the unlimited power entrusted to the Son of
man,[12] but he also gave examples that are valid for all men.
It is as a man, in the name of the liberty that God gives his

[7] Luke 13:32
[9] Luke 22:25
[11] Mark 12:17

[8] Matt. 23:2; cf. Matt. 23:13ff.
[10] Mark 10:42
[12] Mark 2:10–27

children, that he proclaimed his right, in case of need, to pass
over the strictest legal prescriptions.[13] Independence of judgment and character were constantly breaking through.

This independence remained intact till his last hour. This
'hour' for which he was born and which was to reveal the secret
of his heart, was one of supreme obedience. 'The world must
be convinced that I love the Father, and act only as the Father
has commanded me to act. Rise up, we must be going on our
way.'[14] It is in obedience to men that the Father's command
would come to him, in the action taken by Judas and the
measures taken by the government authorities. Jesus was going
to submit, but he intended first to show that he did so freely,
that is that he was obeying. His last words before being appre-
hended brought out exactly how he was obeying: 'Rise up, let
us go on our way; already he that is to betray me is close at
hand.'[15] Judas and his band must not catch him unawares and
think they are holding him against his will. He would refuse to
take defensive action, but it would not be due to inertia or
fatalism: he insisted on keeping the initiative, placing himself
freely under arrest. If he had been constrained by force, how
could he bear witness that he had come into this world to obey?

Having thus asserted his freedom, Jesus yielded himself
into the hands of him that betrayed him, accomplishing what
he had long since prophesied: 'The Son of man is to be given
up into the hands of men';[16] 'given up into the hands of the
chief priests and scribes . . . into the hands of the gentiles'.[17]
Of all the ignominies of the passion, the one our Lord seems
to have felt most keenly was that of being handed over to his
enemies by one of his own disciples, and handed over to
heathens by his own fellow countrymen. All the evangelists
have recorded in the passion narrative the inexorable process
of being handed over time and time again. Judas hands him
over the high priests,[18] who hand him over to Pilate,[19] who,
after trying to unload him on to Herod, hands him over to the
Jews to have him crucified.[20] Jesus is passed on from hand to

[13] Mark 2:25; 3:4
[15] Matt. 26:46
[17] Mark 10:33
[19] Mark 15:1

[14] John 14:31
[16] Mark 9:30
[18] Mark 14:10
[20] Mark 15:15

hand, a plaything at the mercy of all the cruelties that could be invented by the 'power of darkness', to which his Father, even more than Judas or Pilate, gave him up first: 'He did not even spare his own Son, but gave him up for us all.'[21]

The obedience of our Lord in his passion had something quite unusual about it, for the authorities condemning him, though legitimate, were perpetrating an injustice. Our Lord did not contest the authority of the high priest or of Pilate; their power over him was legitimate, though the case was abnormal.[22] He submitted to their legal formalities, answered their questionings, and went to his death for giving a straight answer to the high priest when he solemnly put the question to him: 'Art thou the Son of God?' But though he recognized the validity of their courts, his docile acceptance only demonstrated the iniquity of their verdicts. By obeying them, he, the accused, took on the position of judge, and his death as an innocent man condemned all abuses of power. Without altogether understanding or meaning all that was involved, but knowing and meaning quite enough to make them responsible, his judges and their accomplices crucified the Son of God. The divine plan willed that Caiaphas and Pilate should confront him on that day, but behind them all of us are there, all who prefer injustice rather than the voice of conscience.

By obeying his judges and his executioners, our Lord did not in any way disguise their ignominous guilt; and his forgiveness, though it was ready to efface their sin, also revealed the baseness behind it. His submission had no trace of resigned spinelessness imagining it can appease evil by letting it prevail, and it gives no justification for any form of injustice. It only shows how far the Son of God wanted to carry obedience— down to the worst of the conditions sin has given rise to, slavery. Our Lord willed to experience the deepest distress

---

[21] Rom. 8:32

[22] It does not seem that his answer to Pilate: 'Thou wouldst not have any power over me at all, if it had not been given thee from above' (John 19:11), is about the origin of political authority. 'It concerns the precise case in question. Pilate imagined he could do what he pleased about Jesus. In point of fact, the only power he had over him was by divine concession' (D. Mollat, *L'Evangile selon Saint Jean, Bible de Jérusalem*, Paris 1953, in loc.)

from the harshest fate humanity knows, the appalling feeling
of being handed over defenceless to all the whims of hatred
and cruelty. In this way he triumphed over the crime that
killed him, and in this way he gave his followers and all the
victims of crime the grace to unite their sufferings to his
passion, and to transform their slavery into obedience.

This supreme form of obedience plays a capital part in our
Lord's life, but it does not form the whole of it, and it would
be rash to try to make such dependence the permanent rule
of Christian life. Necessary as it is for Christians to seek the
right attitude by keeping their gaze on the Saviour reduced to
the submission of a slave, it would none the less be wrong to
think of that as the only aspect of obedience in his life.

3. *Obedience to events*

Christ's obedience was always perfect and without limitations, but his submission with regard to men had many
different degrees. These differences did not come from our
Lord choosing between forms of obedience of varying strict-
ness. His unwavering choice was that of the most absolute
dependence with regard to his Father. He found this in submission to various human authorities, from the gentlest to the
most brutal, from his mother to Pontius Pilate. He did not
pick and choose between them; he took them all at the time
they presented themselves, when his Father sent them.

How did he recognize this time? By direct inspirations from
his Father? Not as a general rule. It is indeed true that between
the Father and the Son there was far more than the mutual
understanding or sharing of two hearts so closely united that
each anticipates and espouses the other's reactions: there was
direct vision, unfailing face-to-face presence. But, by a divine
mystery, this presence did not in any way affect our Lord's
human condition. He had sight of the Father at all times, but
he was not bound to read therein the decision he would have
to take. It was events, those 'masters given us by God' as Pascal
says; it was the normal flow of circumstances that called forth
responses from him, as from any other man. These responses
were those of the Son of God, they came to him from God the
Father, in whose presence he lived. But they were the responses

of a man, provoked by the impact of events on a human consciousness.

Clear as it is that our Lord knew where he was going and had a perfect insight into the consequences of his actions and the future awaiting him, it is equally evident that he allowed himself to be led by events. If, on the special occasion of his messianic entry into Jerusalem, for instance, our Lord's own initiative anticipated events, this was not to escape them, but to show that his usual submission was a free exercise of obedience. Whenever it happened that he upset the normal course of things by a miracle, it was not a mark of independence to lift the barriers surrounding human liberty, it was only that he suddenly found himself faced with a distress that moved him or faith that aroused his admiration. His reactions were those of God, of almighty power and boundless love, but they were always reactions or responses to human situations that this Incarnate God wished to experience, to live our human condition in real life. There was nothing contrived in his way of accepting events: they filled him with amazement or bitterness or joy, as they would any of us; he could be as defenceless to their blows as we are, or as deeply touched by their sweetness. But whether in joy or in distress, in all the experiences he underwent and all the emotions he felt, our Lord recognized the attentive look and the ever-active hand of his Father, he devoted himself to him and his work, he obeyed.

4. Obedience to the scriptures

Among the factors in his human condition in which our Lord could see the will of his Father, there was one that held a special place in his eyes, the holy scriptures. As all the children of Israel, he came to know them from his parents, from the elders of the village, from the readings in the synagogue. In them he venerated the sacred treasure of his race, the work of its geniuses and holy men, but first and foremost he saw in them the hand of the Father, the plan he had been following out ever since the first day of creation, to recapitulate the whole world in his Son.

In the light of this, our Lord did not seek the joy or satisfaction of understanding and grasping the whole of history,

but rather the means of interpreting the will of the Father as it
came to him in the events that occurred. Some did not depend
on him personally, but there was no reason for accepting them
blindly: these events had a message for him and he must give
them a meaning. Many others called for a decision: something
to be done or refused, an answer to be given. Where was
guidance to be found? In many cases his reaction was spontaneous and registered his way of thinking, his very nature, his
distress in the presence of suffering, his admiration at men's
faith, his anger at the distortions of God's word, his gratitude
to the Father, all welled up naturally from his soul. But often
we see him giving a reason for these responses, for instance his
fondness for sinners. 'It is mercy that wins favour with me, not
sacrifice.'[23] 'The poor have the gospel preached to them.'[24]
True, it was a case of defending and explaining a line of conduct that was considered surprising or scandalizing. But to be
able to apply the sacred text so happily, to be able to show
how his own actions fulfilled and threw light on centuries-old
prophecy, required more than incredibly apt presence of
mind; it meant that Jesus must have dwelt with the scriptures
and brought their light to bear on all he did.

To accomplish the scriptures Jesus did not have to reflect
or conform in any way; he just had to be what he was, the
Word of God. What had been uttered fragmentarily and expressed on the lips of others, had now become, in him, living
flesh with his own lips to speak with. He had no need to hear
any infidelity to it, since he actually was the Word. Nevertheless, he lived his identity with the scriptures, not by being
independent, but by being obedient. Fulfilling the scriptures
was natural to him, but as an obligation that it was impossible
for him to escape. Fulfilling the scriptures was for him, as for
all the children of Israel, a matter of attention and fidelity.
Born 'as a subject of the Law',[25] he was bound, like the rest of
his people, to observe it in its entirety, to the last iota and the
last dot.[26] In truth he alone saw the full implication of all these
demands. For his compatriots, for the scribes, as for our own
normal viewpoint, the Law only obliged in the case of explicit

[23] Matt. 9:13; cf. Hos. 6:6   [24] Matt. 11:5; cf. Is. 61:1
[25] Gal. 4:4   [26] Matt. 5:18

prescription with definite sanction attached. For our Lord all
scripture, from the slightest items of Law to the heartfelt
response arising from loyal understanding of what was written,
had the force of obligation. A word constantly on his lips to
recall the scriptures was 'must': God has laid it down, his will
must be done; God has promised, his commitments must be
kept; God has foretold, his word must be fulfilled. Laws and
promises go together; no one before Christ was the actual
instrument of the salvation promised by God, for no one could
so utterly surrender to God's will. Far from ever using his
familiarity with the scriptures to show his independence,
Christ held himself in constant readiness to obey them, with
the sole desire to fulfil the programme they laid down.

The passion, consummating our Lord's obedience to men
and events, was also the summit of his fidelity to scripture.
The 'must' binding our Lord as he sees his hour coming[27]
clearly came to him from the Father, from God's eternal
design. But this design presented itself to him in the meditation of the scriptures. When he yielded himself to the band of
men arresting him, our Lord brought out this meaning by
three things he said which, from three different angles, express
the same attitude of obedience. 'The time has come; behold,
the Son of man is to be betrayed into the hands of sinners'[28]
—obedience to men. 'Am I not to drink the cup which my
Father has appointed for me?'[29]—obedience to events. 'How
then should the scriptures be fulfilled, that it must be so?'[30]—
obedience to the scriptures. We have here three inseparable
aspects of the same obedience.

Corresponding to this 'must' at the onset of the passion
comes the final 'It is consummated'.[31] The same note of
obedience sounds, the same awareness of having carried the
fearful burden to the very end, of having accomplished to the
letter the programme laid down by the scriptures and having
clung unfailingly to the Father's will. All is consummated,
'the scriptures, the Father's will, Christ's sacrifice and the

---

[27] Mark 8:31; 10:38; John 3:14; 12:27
[28] Mark 14:41   [29] John 18:11
[30] Matt. 26:54   [31] John 19:30

salvation of the world'.[32] Just before putting the final touch
to his work and laying down his tools, our Lord, as if to make
sure his work is over, makes a last check with the scriptures.
Has he said and done all they asked of him, all that he was to
reveal in them? He seemed to find one last touch to include,
'I thirst!' he cried. This echo of the Psalms[33] recalled the most
disturbing feature of his death; God's silence over the crime
being committed had been willed and foreseen by him. It
showed also that, to his last breath, our Lord kept his gaze
fixed on scripture, reading therein what was to be his conduct
and his inspiration.

5. The obedience of the Son

In his obedience to men, to events and to the words of
Holy Writ, Jesus sought and found one thing only: the will
of his Father, the face of his Father. That was the secret of his
obedience, how to give his Father the proof of total love that
his heart thirsted for. His Father's will, excruciating as it
might be, was the only nourishment he needed.[34] Changing
stones into bread might appease his hunger, but it would also
mean cutting the very roots of his being, destroying all that life
meant. His sole source of strength was the absolute dependence of his life on God. Other men are of this world, they
have their 'friends and neighbours' in this world, they have
cut themselves off from God without losing the air they
breathe. For him, if he were to be cut off from his Father for
an instant, it would mean absolute isolation: 'He who has
sent me is with me; he has not left me all alone, since what I
do is always what pleases him.'[35] The will of the Father may
mean the most repugnant chalice, but the moment it is offered
by his hand, it becomes the living water without which he
would die of thirst: 'Am I not to drink the cup which my
Father has appointed for me?'[36] Hunger and thirst, food and
drink, what could be more vital: obeying the Father was for
our Lord a matter of life and death.

For him this obedience was not just a way of conforming to

[32] D. Mollat, *Bible de Jerusalem*, Paris, 1953, in loc.
[33] Ps. 21 (22):16; 68 (69):22   [34] John 4:34
[35] John 8:29   [36] John 18:11

and coinciding with the divine will; it was the expression of his very own personality, his unique inner relationship with the Father. It was only in obedience that he was what he was, the only-begotten and beloved Son. If he were capable of even a momentary trace of independent spirit, there would be something in him not coming from the Father, he could be partially something other than the Son, the Father could find in him something other than what he himself is and does. This is an unthinkable supposition: 'The Son cannot do anything at his own pleasure, he can only do what he sees his Father doing.'[37] He looks upon the Father, and sees himself in the Father's love, with no trace of veil or separation, doing the work of the Father: 'This my Father loves in me, that I am laying down my life.'[38] Whether it be his miracles, 'the actions my Father has enabled me to achieve';[39] or his words 'which I utter as the Father has bidden me';[40] or again his passion, 'the cup which my Father has appointed for me';[41] all the time it is his Father at work, and what can the Son do but be at work in the same way, with his gaze fixed upon his Father.[42]

Being the Son of God meant, for our Lord, doing the will of the Father, and the 'hour' when he finally revealed his true nature was also that in which he revealed, once and for all, how he had come to do the will of God. 'His hour' meant that of the passion. This secret he was in no hurry to reveal. The demons, in the lucidity of their hatred, had suspected it sooner than men, but he had imposed silence on them.[43] In a moment of inspiration, Peter had glimpsed the truth and made his profession in the name of the twelve, but they were 'strictly forbidden to tell any man'.[44] For the title, 'Son of God', remained ambivalent as long as Christ had not accomplished his final act of obedience. 'Son of God' meant protected by God, surrounded by his favour and predilection, defended against all threats and sheltered from all harm. These were glimpses of the truth, but they remained more general in meaning. Our Lord was now to remove all uncertainty.

[37] John 5:19
[38] John 10:17
[39] John 5:36
[40] John 12:50
[41] John 18:11
[42] John 5:17
[43] Mark 1:25; 3:11–12
[44] Matt. 16:16–20

Before declaring himself the Son of God, he waited to be handed over into the hands of men, becoming incapable (it would seem) of defending himself, suddenly deprived of his power. Then to the high priest's question: 'Art thou the Christ, the Son of the blessed God?' Jesus solemnly replied: 'I am.'[45] Now that his human situation had broken down and all human help was withdrawn, he could come out with his full title and speak of his glory, with no further concealment. 'Son of God', in this hour of his, could only mean a protection of a higher order, a close bond that no attack could ever reach. The unfolding of the passion did actually reveal, to eyes ready to see it, the secret of this protection and this bond: 'Truly, this man was the Son of God.'[46] To have come through this abyss of horror intact, to have kept his trust in God and yielded up to him his last breath with such assurance and simplicity, he must indeed be what he claimed to be, the only-begotten Son of God.

But it was not the power of the Son of God that was revealed in that hour; it was his obedience. His power was to show itself on the third day, at the resurrection; but it would owe nothing to men, it would be all God's work. It would be the seal of the Father on the obedience of his Son, testimony proving he had been right to base all his claims on his obedience alone, claiming the title of Son of God because he did God's work. Because our Lord proved to the world that he loved his Father and always acted only as the Father commanded him to,[47] in return the Father would show forth the glory of the Son and prove that he gave him all he asked. Because he proved himself the one who never failed the Father, the risen Christ is seen to be the one to whom the Father can refuse nothing. So Christ's obedience was not just a condition he must fulfil in order to enter his glory, it is built into the very heart of his glory; it expresses for ever what the Father is for the Son and what the Son is for the Father: 'When you have lifted up the Son of Man, then you will know that "I am" (God), and that I do nothing on my own authority.'[48]

[45] Mark 14:61   [46] Mark 15:39
[47] John 14:31   [48] John 8:28

6. *Obedience to God and obedience to creatures*

To obey belongs therefore to our Lord's very nature. Failure to appreciate this fully would mean failure to understand him rightly. But the recognition of this obedience would also seem to make it something we could not hope to imitate. If obedience is so 'built-in' to his nature, it is because it ties in with his situation as the Son, deriving all from the Father. But, precisely because he is the Son, Jesus has a direct awareness of this situation. He is in direct contact with the Father. He sees him act and, simultaneously, with his own human voice and hands he incarnates on earth the message relayed to him by the Father. But can we, without forcing the words, equate this direct contact to what we know as obedience? Obedience, for us, means leaving it to a superior to take decisions, for us to act accordingly. This kind of obedience normally requires faith, that is a condition in which, not having direct contact with the full issues involved, one trusts the word of another. So obedience inserts an intermediary between God and man. But there cannot be any intermediary between the Father and the Son. If our Lord stressed how far and how constantly he was subject to his Father, he equally clearly stressed the reason, namely, that he never lost direct awareness of being his Son. Would it not seem that to give this the name of obedience is straining the use of the word?

It is indeed true that our Lord was unique in this, and that his way of doing the will of his Father, as he is first to admit, belongs to him alone. How then could he impose upon his disciples the very attitude that he had to the Father: 'If you keep my commandments, you will abide in my love, just as I have kept my Father's commandments and abide in his love.'[49] If our Lord was not straining the meaning of words, it must be the same in both cases, for the disciples as for him; so there must have been, in his life on earth, as there is in ours, some real obscurity.

Only in the mystery of Christ's nature can we find an answer to this question. Our Lord declared that he lived in immediate union with his Father, receiving from him thereby direct

[49] John 15:10

guidance in all his actions—and, simultaneously, that he did so in the setting of a human life, subject to other wills than his own, depending on conditions laid down by others, accepting from others, from scripture, even from chance encounters, dictates to be acted upon. This is none other than the mystery of the incarnation, of God made man and able to obey because, like all men, he lives his life in dependence on other people and events. A mystery that deepens, and yet begins to light up, when it is seen to be the mystery of the Son. In Christ, human obedience with all its concomitant obscurity and submission to others is the medium revealing in its fullness the Son's direct and absolute dependence on the Father. Obedience to man, under the darkest and most inhuman conditions, was for Christ the predestined means of revealing his dearest secret: his filial love for his Father.

This mystery must find its counterpart in the Christian's obedience. If the Son of God became man, it was so that, in him, man should become a child of God. If his love for his Father expressed itself in obedience, it was so that man's obedience and every form of dependence he is subject to may serve to express man's filial love for the Father. If the direct contact of the Son with his Father culminated in the submission of Jesus to guards and executioners, it was so that the Christian, though victimized most cruelly, should never lose sight of the face of his Father.

This contact with the heavenly Father is accomplished in Christ Jesus. It is direct in so far as, in Christ, we can see the Father[50] and live with our gaze upon the Father, with the freedom and ease of a son. So it is true to say that our obedience should not stop at any man, however high in authority, but ever mount to God, who alone can make absolute demands on spiritual creatures. Still, this contact will always be obscure in so far as we can only adhere to Christ and to the Father by faith. Obedience and faith are not the same thing: Christ was obedient, but he did not need faith. But obedience for Christians, transforming natural submission into filial allegiance to the Father, is only possible with faith in Christ our Lord.

Faith in our Lord has to be lived in the Church and in

[50] Cf. John 14:9

obedience to the Church. Just as our Lord saw the scriptures imposing on him, in God's name, obedience to men and events, so the Christian finds in the same divine authority, the gospel transmitted to him by the Church, the meaning of his obedience in the world. In the scriptures our Lord could read infallibly the will of his Father; in the Church infallibly conveying to us the teaching of the gospel and the scriptures, we Christians can be sure of knowing just the kind of life that God gives us to live in the world and the kind of obedience that goes with it. So Christian obedience links up with Christ's obedience to the scriptures, both looking up to the Father. Our Lord teaches us that to obey the Church is to relive his own obedience: 'He who receives any one whom I send receives me; and he who receives me receives him who sent me.'[51]

Two forms of obedience are required in the Christian, different from each other, but indispensable to each other. There is the obedience Christ practised himself, to men and events, and there is the further obedience he required from his disciples, as he instructed or corrected them, as he sent them to proclaim his kingdom, as he led them in his footsteps. The first is practised by the Christian in his particular situation and action in the world, the second in his attitude within the Church. It is not always easy to reconcile them, and difficult problems may arise. But normally the two forms of obedience, each on its own level, go together and complement each other. The Christian sees God's will in the situations where he finds himself as a man, as a citizen, by reason of his work or position in the family, by obedience to the requirements of these various situations. Out of this natural obedience, his faith in Christ in the setting of obedience to the Church makes a specifically Christian obedience, a recognition of the hand of God and allegiance to his will. If he should fail in his duties as a man, his faith is vain and his fidelity to the Church is an illusion. But, for his fidelity to duty as a man to become the response of a child of God to his Father, it must be transformed into the obedience of Christ, in obedience to the gospel and the Church. Just as Christ made his obedience to men the perfect devotion to his Father, so the Church

51 John 13:20

makes the human lives of its children perfect devotion to God.

The transformation or transfiguration is achieved in obedience, in the feeling of distance and obscurity that always goes with obedience, by means of powers entrusted to men who have their limitations and shortcomings and whose authority can take on terribly harsh forms. The Christian is not shaken or scandalized at this. Since our Lord found no better way to show his intimate devotion to his Father than obedience to his creatures, it is normal that, to open to us the way to the same intimacy, he should put us on the path of obedience. If obedience is Christ's own instinctive reaction, how can we hope to know him unless we follow this profound instinct by the practice of his obedience? Such is the mission of the Church, such is the guarantee that the bridegroom gives her: the obedience she enjoins upon her children unites them to our Lord's obedience, makes them enter into his obedience as the Son.

Religious life in the Church springs from this need and the assurance of reliving and reproducing the obedience of our Lord. It is Christian obedience in its fullness; the religious does not lay claim to some more sublime form of obedience than his fellow-Christians; he is called to manifest in his whole life the meaning of Christian obedience, the meaning of our Lord's obedience.

This involves both aspects of obedience: dependence towards men and dedication to God. Religious life creates a whole world about the religious which, while not abolishing his duties towards natural societies and authorities, submits him also to a close network of relationships and dependences, concrete and spiritual. In itself, this life of dependence would not be more of more value than any other. But being wholly organized and lived in the Church, it benefits fully from the promises Christ made to the Church. The Spirit of God permeates its structure and its working; the obedience of Christ himself transforms the submission of his servants, dedicates it as an offering of love to the glory of the Father.

Religious life perpetuates in the Church the full witness of the gospel. There we see our Lord grouping his disciples around him, to enable them to lead the life of God's children, as announced in the gospel message, together, in real life, for the world to see. The disciples were not the only ones to live the gospel way of life, they were not necessarily the most faithful, but they had been chosen to live it together and publicly. So too the religious is not to compare or exalt his own way of life. Having answered the call of our Lord, out of obedience to him, he now keeps his gaze fixed upon his vocation in the Church—to bear witness to the obedience of Christ our Lord.

VIII

Prayer in the Gospel

Iᴛ ᴡᴀs ᴛʜᴇ ᴅᴀʏ our Lord had fed the five thousand. The crowd, carried away with enthusiasm over the miracle, surged round Jesus to carry him in triumph. But, realizing how misguided their enthusiasm was, he gave them the slip. Then 'he prevailed upon his disciples', shaking them out of any illusion, or the contagion of the crowd's enthusiasm, and he made them take to the boat again. With authority he dismissed the crowd and went into solitude to pray.[1] To see the full implication of an incident like this, we must try to grasp its exact meaning in the light of the gospel as a whole. The incident then shows up two opposite illusions. One would tend to reduce prayer for reasons of efficiency and generosity in action; the other would seek to find shelter from the harsh realities of life and the apostolate to escape in pursuit of so-called spiritual consolations. These are two opposite illusions containing complementary half-truths, but each of them fails to do justice to the prayer of the Christian and the prayer of Christ, as seen in the gospel setting.

1. Prayer for the kingdom of God

Prayer, in the gospel, is to do with the kingdom. It is quite clear that prayer, seen as a distinct occupation, held a large place in the life and activity of our Lord. He was seen to enter into prayer and to emerge from it. It was at the end of one

[1] Matt. 14:22-3

110

of such times, which certainly struck the apostles, that they asked him to teach them to pray and he taught them the 'Our Father'.[2] Though we have not a great deal of information on the frequency and duration of such times, we do know that they could last a great part of the night, even all night,[3] and that, at certain periods, praying could form a notable part of our Lord's activity.[4]

While the evangelists thus bring out an element that they consider of importance in the life of Jesus, it is evident from the context in which they put these hours of prolonged prayer that they saw them as inseparable from the activity taking up all our Lord's time, namely the proclamation of the gospel. Not one of the prayers so mentioned can be considered as an 'escape to God', a time of intimacy the Son had recourse to in order to forget his work and relish the presence of his Father. Every time our Lord put himself in prayer, it was because an important event was at hand or taking place, and for this event to bear fruit he had to accompany it and carry it along in prayer. St Luke is the most attentive in observing the importance of prayer in our Lord's conduct, and it is in his gospel that the close link between prayer and event is most manifest. 'Jesus stood there praying' at the time of his baptism, when the Father invested him with the Holy Spirit and sent him forth into the world as the servant charged with the task of taking away the sins of the world, as his Son for men to see and hear.[5] Jesus went out of Capharnaum, 'at very early dawn', to pray, and when overtaken by Peter and his companions trying to bring him home, his first word is to put them on the road forthwith: 'Let us go to the next country-towns, so that I can preach there too, for that is why I came out.'[6] Just before finally settling the choice of the twelve to be his apostles, the pillars of the Church, 'Jesus passed the whole night in prayer to God'.[7] While the apostles, alone on the lake amid the storm, puzzled by his strange reaction to the enthusiasm of the crowd over the multiplication of the loaves, feel tempted to desert him, our Lord was on the hillside that night and won for them

[2] Luke 11:1-2   [3] Mark 1:35; Luke 6:12
[4] Luke 5:15-16   [5] Luke 3:21-22
[6] Mark 1:38   [7] Luke 6:12

by prayer the faith that Peter would blurt out, as the desertions
went on: 'Lord, to whom should we go? Thou hast the words
of eternal life.'[8] Jesus was in prayer when the glory of God
transfigured him, at the same time designating him as destined
to meet death in Jerusalem.[9] It was in prayer that Jesus
obtained for Peter, in his temptation and fall, the gift of repentance and fidelity.[10] Our Lord prayed at the hour when he
entered upon his passion.[11] On every occasion prayer was
inseparable from his mission and the actions he had to accomplish.

All that our Lord told us about prayer he envisaged in
relation to the kingdom of God. This may sound surprising.
We have heard him say: 'Ask, and the gift will come, seek,
and you shall find. . . .'[12] Does this not mean that prayer may
normally be for anything at all, that an essential sign of faith
is to be able to express the first wish that comes into your head
with certainty of being heard: 'If you have faith, though it be
but like a grain of mustard seed, you have only to say to this
mountain, remove from this place to that, and it will remove.'[13]
'If you have faith, and do not hesitate, you will be able to do
more than I have done over the fig-tree; if you say to this
mountain, remove, and be cast into the sea, it will come
about.'[14] If one really has faith then one may ask for anything
at all, and the sign of having faith is to expect the impossible
from God.

This is certainly true, and we must not detract from the
word of the gospel. But the gospel itself tells us not to confuse
faith with more or less doubtful imitations. The words of
Christ we have just quoted come in a particular context. On
hearing his injunction to 'ask, and the gift will come', we do
have to imitate the man imploring in earnest, the determination and insistence of the man going round all his friends, the
persistent appeals of the widow demanding justice. But, to
find out what we have to ask for with such desperate persistence, we must hear the rest of our Lord's message: 'Why then,

[8] John 6:68
[10] Luke 22:32
[12] Luke 11:9
[14] Matt. 21:21

[9] Luke 9:28–31
[11] Luke 22:41; cf. John 17
[13] Matt. 17:19

if you, evil as you are, know well enough how to give your children what is good for them, is not your Father much more ready to give, from heaven, his gracious Spirit to those who ask him?'[15] The normal prayer of the Christian, as a child of God, is to ask the Father for his real treasure, the Holy Spirit. The two lessons on faith being able to move mountains both follow a miracle of our Lord's, namely the lunatic boy[16] and the withered fig-tree.[17] The first was worked to confirm a man in his faith, still frail; the second as a sign of warning to Jerusalem: the master is here to gather in the harvest, what sort of fruit is this? The inference is that, for those who take our Lord's power and his demands seriously, nothing is impossible.

Does this mean the Christian may not pray for personal needs? The petition in the Our Father, 'Give us this day our daily bread', shows that we can, but also on what conditions. One cannot reduce the petition to individual needs, isolating it from the petitions before and after it, from the priority given to God's kingdom and glory, and the community of sentiments and interests involved in the later petitions. While the need for bread is vital to man, for it to be wholly expressed in prayer it must invoke God's generosity on all who hunger. When you reckon up the intentions for prayer given in the gospel, you are surprised at their fewness and how they converge. Apart from the petitions in the Our Father, you find very little to add: 'What is good',[18] 'the Holy Spirit',[19] 'those who persecute you',[20] casting out evil spirits[21] 'labourers for the harvest',[22] 'that you may not enter into temptation'.[23] Every item here is within the framework of the Our Father and the kingdom of God. The Christian's prayer does not exclude any human needs, but puts them all in their right setting, in a community wherein all feel solidarity for the welfare of all others, wherein there reigns, if not a cloudless unity, a lasting concern to overcome all divisions in a spirit of forgiveness, wherein the overriding desire is for the accomplishment of the Father's will and the coming of his kingdom of holiness.

As we must take the gospel as a whole, so we must take the

[15] Luke 11:13   [16] Matt. 17:14–18   [17] Matt. 21:18–20
[18] Matt. 7:11   [19] Luke 11:12   [20] Matt. 5:44
[21] Cf. Mark 9:28   [22] Luke 10:2   [23] Matt. 26:41

Our Father as a whole. Then our Lord's promises are fulfilled to the letter. He who lives for God's will to be done can ask God for everything. If a man seeks the kingdom of God and his justice, 'all these things shall be yours without the asking'.[24] If a man does not really seek them, there is not faith, and what is taken for faith, the feeling of assurance people try desperately to achieve by dint of autosuggestion, is nothing but nervous energy whose intensity can sometimes produce apparent effects for a while, but whose spiritual efficacy is negligible. To imagine one can change the course of nature by supercharging one's battery of conviction is asking for disappointment. As Jesus said to Satan, who urged him to cast himself down from the temple, it is tempting God. Assuredly God could do anything to protect his Son, but only on the supposition he is acting as his Son, abandoning himself to the will of his Father, even unto death, when the Father willed it. Then he would raise him up to life again. All is possible to him who has faith: any miracle may arise from the hands of one who has espoused God's every wish. True prayer has for its object the kingdom of God, and all prayer is such only in so far as it is animated by this faith, that God is going to accomplish his work on earth.

2. *Persistence in prayer*

Seeking the will of God, seeking the coming of the kingdom—both take time. It is not enough to say a prayer once, no matter how much you mean it. Prayer according to the gospel involves waiting, because it is prayer with faith. Our Lord made this clear as he compared it to the persistent appeals of people in dire straits and in anguish. This is clear also from seeing him and seeing how his miracles came in reply to entreaties made to him. Our Lord did indeed work many miracles, but he did not display them as attractive articles for customers to come and get. He had not come to work miracles. He did so only in response to men's appeal, and this appeal had to be prolonged and intensified in order to be heard. Admittedly, when he found human misery present before him, he could not resist having pity on it: hunger,

[24] Matt. 6:33

disease, bereavement—he could not stand by unaffected. In the words of Martha, if he had been there, Lazarus would not have died. But apart from times when seized by emotion, Jesus often seemed to need to keep people waiting for his answer. The fact is that this answer depended on faith, and faith needed this test, this kind of challenge. Jairus came in search of him because his little girl was at death's door. Our Lord, as if not seeing the urgency and anguish of the father, allowed himself to be held up on the way and wasted precious minutes in conversation with a woman who was cured by now and no longer in need of him. It was as if he wanted to let death have time to act, as if, in order to be able to raise the child to life, he needed the father's faith to have gone through the extra test of being told that all was over and it was too late now. At this Jesus straightway reacted: 'No need to fear; thou hast only to believe.'[25] All depended on this faith, and this is what our Lord had to foster. Such was his concern also with the father of the lunatic boy, with the Canaanite woman, with the sisters of Lazarus, even with his own mother at Cana.

How are we to account for this time of waiting our Lord imposed on those whom he loved most? Was it to make their desire more intense? Rather it was to transform it into prayer and perseverance in faith. He wanted us to realize, not that he hesitates to hear our entreaty, but on the contrary that he is all generosity and fidelity and so will not grant our request till, obsessed with our own needs, we also realize his need to help us and to fill us with his riches. What is the point of his giving us things, if he does not make us capable of receiving his very self in his gifts? That is his motive in keeping us waiting. He has shown, by his spontaneous miracles in response to human suffering, that there are no limits to his power and goodness. Such signs should be enough to confirm us in the faith and conviction that, when he does delay, it is only a better way of hearing us by revealing himself to us such as he really is. If he granted all our desires just as we made them, they would never be more than whims, and he would never be able to make us know him. We should not bother with him once we got our gifts, we should be like babies

[25] Mark 5:36

towards him. We should never know his fidelity, for lack of
ever having given him our own, for fidelity can only be recognized mutually, and two persons who love each other can only
be sure of counting on each other when they have experienced
separation and absence. To pledge one's faith to someone
means one must not only accept, but of necessity be quite
willing, that the other be silent for a time at least. If we can
keep the certain conviction that God wishes to give us all
things, at times when we are left empty-handed, we are beginning to understand that he has better things to give us than
toys that catch our fancy: he wants to give us his word and
his fidelity, and for that he needs to see in what depths of
silence we are capable of still believing him.

This accounts for our Lord's reproach to those for whom he
had multiplied the loaves, that they were looking for him
'not because of the miracles you have seen, but because you
were fed with the loaves'.[26] In the miracle, the God-given sign
that Jesus could do all things and provide for their every need,
and so that they must trust themselves entirely to him, all they
saw was the immediate satisfaction of enjoying a good meal.
By making him king, they thought only to prolong this easy
source of benefits and make it their for good. They would
only have made Jesus a tool in the service of their needs,
making him an idol, and that is why he evaded their acclamations. Granted he was indeed king, as his miracle proved,
men must trust him and commit themselves to him, wherever
he may lead. Our Lord's silence towards the Canaanite woman,
as also towards our entreaties, transforms these cries of distress
into true prayer, linking them with a deep feeling of our need
for God. The more we plead, the more we become aware that
we know not what we ask, the more we discover how intently
and eagerly God follows the progress of our expectation.

Was our Lord's own prayer also subject to this? It is true he
did not live by faith, and that he had direct sight of the Father
and does just what he sees the Father doing,[27] that he is never
far from the Father, not doing anything on his own authority.[28]
Yet we see him praying for a long time,[29] pleading urgently, in

[26] John 6:26   [27] John 5:19
[28] John 8:28–29   [29] Luke 22:43

anguish and fear; he is not lingering in the delight of heavenly converse. We recognize in the prayer at Gethsemani the story of all prayer: the instinctive appeal to God of the creature in distress, founded and perfected in the prayer of the Son in his utter devotion to the will of the Father. Certainly the prayer of the agony, as also the fear arising in that hour, was exceptional, but our Lord's words had more than once shown that he lived in awareness of the hour he was waiting for,[30] when he would have his chalice to drink,[31] his baptism to undergo.[32] From his baptism by John, when mingling with the crowd of sinners he received in the Spirit the gift of his Father's love and mission to carry the sins of the world;[33] from the transfiguration recalling his glory and his death in Jerusalem,[34] right until the last sigh which in the apparent abandonment and silence of God[35] he yielded up to his Father[36] —our Lord's prayer followed the same pattern, the pattern of all prayer: thanksgiving and acceptance of his mission, for God's glory to be achieved.

3. Prayer in time of trial

Because it involves waiting patiently with faith in God, 'though the Lord hide his face from the men of Israel'[37] before granting them access to his glory, prayer is often—one may say normally—accompanied and threatened by trial, but it is also the believer's way of overcoming trial. Faith does not know itself till it has experienced trial, and it is only in trial that faith begins to realize in whom it is putting its trust. How can we believe for good and all in God's fidelity as long as no appearances have ever raised the slightest doubt about it? Until I am able to say to the tempter, in spite of all the facts he may allege in his support, that, even if they were ten times as disturbing, they would not shake my trust in God, I shall not know how much I do trust in him, how firmly he holds my trust. Nor shall I know how completely he deserves my trust for being so able to create it in me.

[30] John 12:27   [31] Mark 10:38
[32] Luke 12:50   [33] Matt. 3:15; John 1:29
[34] Luke 9:31   [35] Matt. 27:46
[36] Luke 23:46   [37] Is. 8:17

That prayer time and retreat time are times of trial is a fact
that St Ignatius taught from experience, when he warned his
retreatant that the bad sign is not that he should be tempted
but that he should remain inert, feeling no spiritual stirring,
being neither moved towards God nor tried by weariness and
desolation. If the devil is at work, in a person of good will, this
does not mean that God is far away; on the contrary it means
he is at hand and acting, since the adversary feels the threat
to him and seeks to counter it. This lesson is seen in the
gospels. After the manifestation of the Holy Spirit at his
baptism, the first thing that happened to our Lord was to be
driven by the Spirit into the desert[38] to experience loneliness
and temptation. When he entered into solitude and prayer at
Gethsemani, it was to encounter his adversary. At this time,
when he was to experience his greatest trial in prayer, our
Lord knew that in leaving his apostles he was leaving them
at the mercy of trial, as he had done the night after the miracle
of the loaves, when he made them sail back despite the storm.
It had to be, even he could not alter it: they had to be 'the
men who had kept to his side in his hours of trial';[39] it had to
be that 'Satan claimed power over them all, so that he can sift
them like wheat'.[40] Prayer is the sole defence: 'Watch and
pray, so that you may not succumb to temptation'[41]—not to
be sheltered from it, but to stand up to its violence.

Only our Lord's own prayer can preserve us from succumbing to temptation. The apostles fell asleep, being unable to
watch and pray, powerless to withstand the terrifying presence
of Satan. But, as they slept, their Master's prayer guarded
them. As it had won the grace of fidelity for them in the storm
on the lake, as it secured that Peter's faith should recover after
his fall, so now, with future centuries and eternity depending
on it, it still secures the faithfulness of his Church, of his saints
and martyrs, and the faithfulness of all our prayer.

4. *Prayer of thanksgiving*

Whether it be our Lord's own prayer or the prayer he seeks
in us, there is one permanent feature about it. Nowhere in

---

38 Mark 1:12   39 Luke 22:28
40 Luke 22:31   41 Matt. 26:41

the gospel does prayer appear as an escape from the world, a time spent on a higher plane of spiritual or other-worldly realities. It may indeed involve conditions, in particular solitude, or times set apart: 'When thou are praying. . . .'[42] It is not just the same as the spontaneous attitude of a soul that is faithful. The centre that gives it direction and force is something both divine and this-worldly: God's work, his ways, his will. Ultimately the essence of prayer in the gospel is the petition in the Our Father: 'Hallowed be thy name.' A strange formula at first sight, for could God ever do anything but have his holiness proclaimed? How could he expect from our prayer something that is bound to happen anyway? But there precisely is the essence of prayer, obtaining from God by our entreaties that he make manifest in his work his own handiwork, his power and his glory. For this work arises from his generosity, but how could God show his generosity if no one could recognize him in his gifts? To pray in this way is not just to bring one's will into line with him, but to await it with all one's hope and rejoice in God's work at the divine glory being revealed.

At this level our prayer, truly intent on the coming of God's kingdom and glory, naturally emerges as thanksgiving. This is undoubtedly the highest form of prayer in the gospel. It is far more than saying thank-you, an expression of gratitude that has to be made so that you are no longer beholden to a benefactor. It is joy and admiration at what God has done, an inspiration from on high seizing the creature at the showing forth of God's glory. It is far more than a human reaction: it is God's power that, after producing these wonders, stirs up in their wake a thrill of excitement, men's hearts being flooded with praise of God.

Thanksgiving in the gospel becomes deeper as we approach its centre, the mystery of Christ himself. This is especially noticeable in St Luke, who is the most alive to it, as also the most quick to point out the reactions going with prayer. There are the witnesses of miracles, who just happened to be there, but the sight of the miracle fills them with admiration as they go off praising God. There are people more closely involved,

[42] Matt. 6:6

E

the shepherds of Bethlehem, Simeon and Anna, making themselves heralds of the tidings of great joy, the first 'evangelists'.
There are the intimates, Elizabeth and John the Baptist,
sensitive to the very presence of the mystery and forthwith
flooded with the joy it brings. There is our Lady, all pure
service and thanksgiving, in whom absolute acceptance of the
divine will is at the same time perfect rejoicing in God's work.
Lastly, there is the unique exaltation of the Son, uniting
himself to the Father in the Holy Spirit.

All these go to show that thanksgiving, the purest sentiment
man can feel, truly detaching him for a time from his own
cares and pettiness to immerse him in the radiance of God's
glory, does not make him indifferent to God's world and work,
but makes him see the revelation of God's glory and God's
face in the very midst of this world. The highest examples are
the most significant. The 'Magnificat', the expression of pure
praise, looks with the same gaze of exultation on the marvels
wrought by the Lord for his handmaid and on the salvation
he brings to the hungry and little ones throughout the world.
So it is with our Lord himself. St Luke tells us his reaction to
the news of the results obtained by his disciples in their
mission: 'Jesus was filled with gladness by the Holy Spirit,
and said, "O Father who are Lord of heaven and earth, I give
thee praise that thou hast hidden all this from the wise and
prudent, and revealed it to little children. Be it so, Lord, since
this finds favour in thy sight. My Father has entrusted everything into my hands; none knows what the Son is, except the
Father, and none knows what the Father is, except the Son,
and those to whom it is the Son's good pleasure to reveal
him." '[43]

It is with the same joy that our Lord contemplates the divine
glory, seeing it at work in the midst of the world, on the least
privileged and in the ineffable exchanges linking the three
divine Persons in the Trinity. It all springs from the same
movement of love, the same response of thanksgiving, for the
same divine glory. Such too is the Christian's thanksgiving. He
is a child of God the Father, he shares with the beloved Son's
joy in the Spirit, he has the focus of his love in God—but it is

[43] Luke 10:21–22

on earth among men, in the midst of the Church with all its
troubles and hopes, that he must give expression to that love
and discover that joy in that same glory.

5. Our Lord's priestly prayer

The prayer in St John's gospel coming at the end of the
discourse after the last supper contains every aspect of Christian prayer and the full riches of our Lord's own prayer. There
we find the secret of so many silent prayers of his, of which the
gospels tell us nothing, except that our Lord did so prepare
and accompany his activity. In the light of this final prayer,
the few words that did escape his usual silence and were
recorded by his disciples fit together and take on new meaning,
yielding up their deepest secret.

This priestly prayer was indeed a prayer at a given time; it
came just after our Lord's last instructions, just before his
passion. However, the gospel does not enable us to say exactly
where or when it was pronounced.[44] The only indication John
gives is that this was the prayer of Jesus when 'his hour' had
come.[45] It is not so much, as in the case of other prayers
recorded by the evangelists, a prayer at a particular moment,
applicable at that moment, but rather a prayer spread out over
the whole passion. We may truly say this prayer formed the
very heart of the passion, it was the supreme act of Christ
giving his life, the act of a priest and victim, the sacrificial
form, without which the episodes of the tragedy up to the
crucifixion would be reduced to just a cruel execution: it
gave the passion and resurrection of our Lord their ultimate
explanation.

The deep significance of the passion is one of prayer, and
this prayer expressed the depth of it. What took place at this
'hour' was, beyond all the outrages and tortures of our Lord,
the encounter of the Father and the Son. It was an encounter
in the form of an entreaty, laden with all the sufferings of the
passion, but taking on the nature of a thanksgiving: 'I have
achieved the task thou gavest me to do . . . I have made thy

---

[44] Cf. A. George, S.M., 'L'heure de Jean XVII' in *Revue Biblique*,
1954, pp. 392–7
[45] John 17:1

name known to the men whom thou hast entrusted to me. . .
They have kept true to thy word. . . . They have found faith
to believe. . . . None of them has been lost. . . . This is my
desire that they may be with me where I am . . . so that the
love thou hast bestowed upon me may dwell in them, and I
too may dwell in them.'[46] An encounter in perfect intimacy
between Father and Son, but embracing the whole Church
and bringing it into the heart of this intimate union. Nowhere
does this union appear more strikingly, but nowhere also does
it show itself more completely open and ready to welcome all
the children of the Father into this infinite love.

The proof that God heard the prayer of the Son is that his
disciples can now make it their own. The Church, for which
Jesus prayed, has the Our Father for its own special prayer,
and in it the Church almost repeats the terms of our Lord's
priestly prayer. There is the same concern for the Father's
name and his glory, preoccupation with his kingdom and the
fulfilment of his will, the same desire for unity among brethren
and their preservation from evil. Our prayer is our Lord's
prayer, the one he taught us and coming from the bottom of
his heart. Just as the priestly prayer of our Lord expressed
not only his soul and his sentiments but also all he does and all
that he is, so the Our Father must be the expression of what
the Christian is, a child of God, living for his glory. Without
the priestly prayer to give meaning to the passion, it would be
a ghastly iniquity; without the passion fulfilling it, the priestly
prayer would have been a series of beautiful sentiments, but
devoid of real meaning. In the same way in the life of the
Christian there has to be both prayer and effective service as
inseparable aspects. If it does not lead to some efficacious
action, the Christian's prayer may be only an illusion; but
without prayer his action will be only a natural urge for
activity. In prayer the Christian puts before the Father all he
does from one end of the day to the other: his prayer is his life
itself, received from the hands of the Father, and lived out as
it comes in the joy of consecrating it wholly to him in return.

[46] John 17

IX

The Son's Thanksgiving

THE GOSPEL does not say a great deal about our Lord's thanksgiving, any more than it does about his prayer generally. It would seem that our Lord, naturally faithful to his instinct to seek privacy to be more united with his Father, shunned the crowd and popular gaze when he wanted to pray, and rarely let witnesses glimpse anything of his intimacy with the Father alone. Rare as such glimpses were, the ones recorded in the gospels tell us much of their meaning in depth. They fit in so well with everything about him, they reveal so convincingly the purpose of his whole life and the secret of his every action. In these few words of prayer, apparently slipping out of strictly guarded silence, we discover that we too, who are children of the Father, can be admitted into a sacred mystery, and we penetrate the depths of his heart, the very secret of the only-begotten Son.

Among the prayers that did slip out, the giving of thanks, though not the most frequently mentioned or prolonged, holds pride of place for the light it throws on our Lord's soul. When he needed to obtain from the Father a fruitful outcome, as in the choice of the apostles, or when he left them to bear the brunt of the storm and the disappointment after the feeding of the five thousand, or when he sought to secure Peter's faith in making his profession at Caesarea and recovering from the denials—on all these occasions Jesus spent hours, sometimes nights, in prayer to his Father, and this persistence in supplication is the most striking thing about him. By contrast, his giving of thanks seemed to well up in sudden spurts, like waves of emotion, provoked by some event or at the prospect of some decision. But these waves were only the crests of a more continuous flood surging through the life of Christ and flowing into everything he did.

1. 'Revealed to little ones'

The seventy-two disciples came back full of rejoicing; Lord, they said, even the devils are made subject to us through thy name. He said to them, I watched while Satan was cast down like a lightning flash from heaven. . . . But you, instead of rejoicing that the devils are made subject to you, should be rejoicing that your names are enrolled in heaven.

At this time, Jesus was filled with gladness by the Holy Spirit, and said, O Father, who are Lord of heaven and earth, I give thee praise that thou hast hidden all this from the wise and the prudent, and revealed it to little children. Be it so, Lord, since this finds favour in thy sight. My Father has trusted everything into my hands; none knows what the Son is, except the Father, and none knows what the Father is, except the Son, and those to whom it is the Son's good pleasure to reveal him.[1]

Come to me, all you that labour and are burdened; I will give you rest. Take my yoke upon yourselves, and learn from me; I am gentle and humble of heart; and you shall find rest for your souls. For my yoke is easy, and my burden light.[2]

In this thanksgiving, our Lord's divine sonship appears in its unique grandeur, but at the same time he shows us how deeply he is rooted in our human nature, subject to the same reactions and responding to the same sentiments. It began with the joy of the disciples, amazed to see the power they were endowed with by the very fact of belonging to Jesus and acting in his name. 'Even the devils are made subject to us through thy name': they saw the powers of evil forced to

[1] Luke 10:17–22   [2] Matt. 11:28–30

acknowledge defeat. Our Lord was immediately stirred by this radiant joy, naïve as it was, like the first discoveries of childhood, and it gave rise to profound repercussions within his soul. He too saw the devils put to flight, but beyond this manifestation in time he could contemplate the ultimate victory, Satan dispossessed of his power. His joy was far more wonderful, but also more complete and solid, for it was free from all possible illusion and fixed on the essential truth. There is a finer joy than seeing devils put to flight, a joy not feeding on what it sees but on what it believes—God's promises: 'Your names are enrolled in heaven.' So our Lord's joy, touched off by the joy of his disciples and amplified in his own soul, in its turn affects the disciples and enables them to join and share it with him: 'Rejoice!'

There and then a much more powerful wave of emotion seemed to carry our Lord away altogether. The emotion shared with his disciples, amplified as it was in him, had been of the order of ordinary human sentiments, when suddenly it seemed to undergo a transformation. A kind of joy came upon him, prompted by what had passed—St Luke notes the connection: 'In that same hour'—but with its origin elsewhere and of far greater impact. A deep stirring of soul came over him, lifted him up, giving his speech an unprecedented note of power and far-reaching plenitude of meaning. It was the Holy Spirit releasing his power, putting the Son face to face with the Father. Then there burst forth the thanksgiving in the truest sense, our Lord no longer addressing those about him, but turning to his Father he confesses his glory and his greatness: 'I give thee praise, O Father!', 'I thank thee, Father.'

This praise and thanksgiving is two-fold, and in this it conveys a precious lesson. Our Lord thanked the Father that he himself was his only-begotten Son, that he belonged to him alone, that he could be really known by him alone, that he himself alone could share his Father's intimate union wholly and exclusively; and yet at the same time that in him the Father throws open to little ones the unfathomable riches of this incommunicable sonship. It was this sight of the Father opening his divine treasures to those who have none, that released this outburst of praise and thanksgiving. Such is our

Lord's human nature: at all times, of course, he was aware
of being the Son; but being a man his consciousness reacts to
impulses coming to him. Seeing the generosity of the Father to
his children was for our Lord one more experience bringing
home his sonship. Just because he is the only-begotten Son,
for ever living at the source of all sonship, every manifestation
of divine liberality reminds him of the unique relation of love
to which he owes his being. Because he is the Son owing his
whole being to the Father, because he also embodies perfectly
the absolute dependence and radical helplessness of the
creature, his joy in being the object of the Father's love surges
up anew in contact with the poor, those who, possessing
nothing, can only receive all things. Thus his thanksgiving is
inseparably that of creature and Creator, that of the poor and
of the Son, that of one having nothing of his own and one who
can truly return to the Father all that he receives from him.

We have here, though without any exceptional outward
manifestation, the same thing as we saw revealed at our
Lord's baptism and transfiguration. Being in possession of the
Holy Spirit, our Lord is in direct contact with the Father and
the heavens were opened to him. At the baptism and transfiguration, the Spirit was manifested bringing the Son the love
wherewith the Father enfolds him: 'Thou art my beloved
Son'. Here the Spirit enables our Lord to return his love to
the Father in vivid awareness of his sonship. In the case of
the Father, this love is all initiative and giving. In the case of
the Son, it is all welcoming and grateful acceptance: 'I bless
and thank thee, Father!' Mutually there is radiant content-
ment, unfailing attachment, absolute understanding and perfect unity in the Holy Spirit.

Because inseparable from the Father, the Son's thanksgiving must needs cling to his infinite generosity. It springs
from it and goes with it, emerging in its turn as more
generosity. This thanksgiving is an overspill of generous love
and leads to giving: 'Come to me, all you that labour and are
burdened.' The Son has accepted everything, but it is so as to
give it all, to share with those who have nothing the mystery
of love that constitutes Father and Son. It was at the sight of
the poor that the wave of thanksgiving came over Jesus, and

it brought him back to the poor. The Father has entrusted
everything to him, and 'he can only do what he sees his
Father doing',[3] so he shares all the Father gives him with
others. Alone in knowing the Father and in being able to love
him as the only-begotten Son, far from counting this gift as a
privilege to cling on to for himself,[4] he saw in it only a chance
to share it. His way of thanking God for being the Son is to
reveal the Father 'to little ones', to make them children of
God, able to turn to know the Father's generosity and give
thanks with the very same response as the divine Son: 'Abba,
Father!'[5]

2. The raising of Lazarus

Jesus once more sighing to himself, came to the tomb;
it was a cave, and a stone had been put over the mouth of it.
Take away the stone, Jesus told them. And Martha, the dead
man's sister, said to him, Lord, the air is foul by now; he has
been four days dead. Why, Jesus said to her, have I not told
thee that if thou hast faith, thou wilt see God glorified? So
they took the stone away.

And Jesus lifted his eyes to heaven, Father, he said, I
thank thee for hearing my prayer. For myself I know that
thou hearest me at all times, but I say this for the sake of
the multitude standing around, that they may learn to
believe it is thou who hast sent me.[6]

In a different scene, in a setting and presentation peculiar
to John's gospel, our Lord's thanksgiving at the tomb of
Lazarus is very like the preceding scene. There is the same
consciousness of being in the presence of the Father and being
the only one to have full knowledge of him, conscious of holding and expecting all from him, with no shadow of uncertainty.
There is also the same striking reaction, the impression produced on the soul of Jesus by the encounter between human
distress and divine generosity. He too was distressed to see the
tears of Martha and Mary and the people with them, he sighed
deeply before the tomb of his friend, for he knew what suffer-

---

[3] John 5:19   [4] Cf. Phil. 2:6
[5] Gal. 4:6   [6] John 11:38–42

ing and death meant, as he knew the part played by Satan. He
rejoiced that the Father had enabled him to triumph over the
powers of darkness, to be 'the resurrection and the life' and to
help both those who die and those who are bereaved. Above
all he gave thanks that he could bring to those who believed
in him the revelation of him that sent him: 'That they may
learn to believe it is thou who hast sent me.' To make the
Father known to men, to manifest to them his sacred name,[7]
the object of his own love and veneration, this was all our
Lord's joy and the unfailing source of thanksgiving in him.

His thanksgiving also means his sacrificing himself to the
Father, and his attitude in raising Lazarus shows this clearly.
Previously his thanksgiving had ended in an invitation to
those who are suffering: 'Come to me . . . I will refresh
you.' It would almost imply that at his mere presence, in the
radiance of his gentleness and humility, distress would turn
to joy. But here we have our Lord's friends in grief going to
him and at first obtaining no relief, far from it. Our Lord is
the first to be filled with grief, though he could have pre-
vented his friend's death if he had been present;[8] he was
overcome with grief over this bereavement to the point of
being overwhelmed. But it had to be that God should be
glorified in that way, 'to bring honour to the Son of God'.[9] It
meant that Jesus had to bear the anguish of his friends for four
days, had to pass for being thoughtless and heartless;[10] he had
to let Lazarus die so as to go along afterwards to raise him up,
realizing the risks he ran in Jerusalem,[11] knowing that this
outstanding miracle on so prominent a person would seem a
challenge to his enemies[12] and hasten his undoing. Jesus knew
all that, but since it was to give glory to the Father and
strengthen the faith of his disciples, it gave him joy and gladness;[13] they would see the glory of God,[14] they would see what
the Son could do for the Father and what the Father was doing
for the Son. In this way thanksgiving in our Lord was not only
close to human suffering, it identified itself with it and bore

[7] John 17:6
[8] John 11:32
[9] John 11:4
[10] John 11:37
[11] John 11:8
[12] John 11:48
[13] John 11:15, 26
[14] John 11:40

the burden of it without shirking, up to the most acute form
of distress. It is stronger than death even and it rejoices, not in
preventing death doing its work, but in triumphing over
death after undergoing it, no matter what powers it may
display.

3. *The eucharist*

'And he took bread, and when he had given thanks he
broke it and gave it to them saying, This is my body, which
is to be given for you. Do this in remembrance of me.'[15]

Our Lord's thanksgiving here would seem reduced to a
minimum: just a word or so and a familiar gesture, customary
among the Jews before a meal, in particular for a religious
meal such as the Passover. Yet Christian tradition has rightly
fastened on this expression, eucharist, meaning thanksgiving,
and made it the name of the action our Lord performed at the
last supper and renews daily in his Church. This is truly the
Lord's thanksgiving.

Unlike the previous occasion, this one did not arise from
any onset of emotion. One might almost think it was said
without any emotion, if one did not recall the keynote of the
whole of the last supper and the atmosphere of self-sacrifice,
affection and solemnity surrounding it. It was not an onset of
emotion, but a deep and heart-felt emotion that had been
saved up for years: 'I have longed and longed to share this
paschal meal with you before my passion.'[16] This was the hour
for which he had come into the world, which he had been
thinking about as he listened to the scriptures, which had
guided every fibre of his being ever since he came into this
world: 'See, my God, I am coming to do thy will', 'as it is
written of me in the roll of the book.'[17] His life is coming to
an end, he knows it, and he knows why. It is not ending in
solitude. He is with those whom the Father has given him and
whom he has kept for this hour. They have to be there, for
without them he cannot do what he is about to do. He is doing
it for them, and they must know, so they can tell all men
about it and go on doing it till the end of time. The emotion
filling our Lord at this hour is related to every aspect of the

[15] Luke 22:19   [16] Luke 22:15   [17] Heb. 10:7; cf. Ps. 39 (40): 7–8

situation he is in: the awareness of a man whose end is near
and knows he is accomplishing the decisive act of his life, the
affection of a friend for the companions he has involved in his
own destiny and whom he will never see again with the eyes
of mortal flesh, lastly the love of the Son at last able to offer
the Father the sacrifice worthy of him.

The secret of this emotion, making it one of thanksgiving,
the deepest our Lord has ever experienced so far, is that it
embraces the mystery of God in all his glory. This is the hour
when the Son is to reveal to the world what the Father is. 'Lord,
let us see the Father',[18] said Philip, and our Lord was surprised. How was it that Philip, after living so long with him,
had not realized that it was enough to watch him in order to
know the Father? Seeing him dealing with people, like children united in God's care for them with all the warmth of a
home; hearing him speak of the Father, his greatness, his
justice and his choice of them; seeing him in prayer before the
Father, carried away with admiration, veneration and absolute
trust—how could Philip not see that the Father was there,
before him, within reach of his prayer which he both inspired
and responded to? It was true of course that Philip and the
others could not yet know it all. They had not yet grasped
how much the Father deserved their love and trust; they could
not know how devoted the Father is to his children and how
much he is a Father to them. They had not yet entered into our
Lord's secret, they had not heard all the Father said to the
Son and all that the Son said in return. For them to enter into
this mystery, our Lord needed to die.

He was to die in the most cruel circumstances, letting sin
release all its powers. For our Lord to render the Father
supreme witness, he had to be delivered into the hands of
sinners, he had to experience the horror of the innocent falling
defenceless into the hands of criminals bent on destruction,
it had to be that God himself should abandon him to us and
let us exhaust on him all the injustice and cruelty, all the
hatred and cowardice that sin in us can invent. Now that the
loyalty of his own followers has collapsed; now that all his
powers—the note of authority in his speech, the imposing

[18] John 14:8

marvel of miracle-working, even the mastery over his own sentiments—seem about to lose their effect; now that he is not to be the master leading, but the sufferer undergoing trials, Jesus can now indeed give thanks to his Father. It is 'his hour', the hour when he is no longer the miracle-worker that men follow 'because of the loaves', or the prophet speaking as no man ever spoke, or the Messiah men want to raise to power, but nothing more nor less than the Son, he whose whole life is to render glory to the Father, to do his will and show forth his love, as the beloved Son: 'This my Father loves in me, that I am laying down my life.'[19] This he does as he consecrates the bread and wine, he yields his body to be broken and his blood to be shed. By one and the same act, with one and the same resolution, by the total surrender of his life, he responds to the Father's love and makes us the final gift of his love. By thus enabling our helplessness to draw inexhaustible strength, and providing a way for the Father to go on for ever giving us his Son, Jesus entered upon a giving of thanks that endured throughout every moment of the passion.

From the supper onwards every thought was of his death. He had made his body our soul's food, so it must be sacrificed. He had made his blood the drink for our souls, so it must be shed. He had said the words, they must take effect, they must be kept. It only remained for him now to go to the bitter end of these words, letting Judas do his worst; now the passion was 'on': it had been started by our Lord's eucharistic thanksgiving; it embodied his gratitude, glorification of God and generosity to men, spilling out of his heart and taking the form of an outward and final thanksgiving action.

4. The priestly prayer

'Father, the time has come; give glory now to thy Son, that thy Son may give glory to thee.'[20]

What the synoptics portray in the eucharist thanksgiving, St John conveys in the priestly prayer. Though in the form of asking, this prayer was couched in terms of thanksgiving; but asking and giving thanks are inseparable for our Lord, as we saw at the grave of Lazarus. Never more than at this moment

[19] John 10:17   [20] John 17:1

when he prayed for the fruitfulness of his life and death and
for the future of all his work, never did Jesus show such
enthusiasm and spontaneity, such unshakable assurance of his
union with the Father, of coming up to his expectations and
of sharing his joy in its fullness—but also of holding in his
hands the life and happiness of his followers, and of being able
to fill them with his own happiness. The things that were to
disappear during the passion, the Father's presence close and
reassuring, joy in being his and carrying out his instructions,
the feeling of veneration in contact with his greatness and
holiness, all these are concentrated in this priestly prayer and
go to make it the ideal example of our Lord's thanksgiving
prayer.

Whether the prayer was said at the cenacle or on the road
to Gethsemani, it cannot be detached either from the supper
or from the passion. The tone belongs to the discourse after
the last supper, but the matter now is to do with the passion.
Having done all that he had to do, and only able to let events
take their course, Jesus goes forth. All that remains for him
to do is to 'consecrate' himself,[21] to transform into a willing
and holy sacrifice the cruel injustice of which he is to be the
victim. Judas has accepted his thirty pieces of silver, but he
has not yet handed him over, and he can only do so when
Jesus hands himself over. He has already given himself up by
means of the eucharistic consecration, but his followers must
realize that interior decisions of his own are determining
the impending events. When our Lord finally makes the decision, Judas can come—in St John's gospel[22] the betrayal
follows forthwith—the series of tortures can start, sin can
embark on its task; but it is too late, they have already lost,
they can only execute the work of God and glorify both the
Father, who has the whole tragic action under control, and the
Son who accepts and undergoes it with the whole of his willing
thanksgiving.

5. The passion

How can we speak of thanksgiving at the time our Lord is
being crushed by his passion? We feel crushed by it ourselves,

[21] John 17:19   [22] John 18:3

when we try to follow it, which we can only do from afar,
begging God to help us to enter into this mystery. Two facts
emerge from a bare reading of the gospel accounts: on the
one hand, our Lord was really submerged by the passion, pain
sank into every part of him, body and soul; on the other, our
Lord remained unshaken in his giving of thanks to God. It
was no longer the joyful thanksgiving seen hitherto, nor the
calm assurance in the face of the Father as he raised Lazarus
from the dead. As soon as he is caught up in the diabolic
machinery, as soon as the anguish of the agony descends upon
him, Jesus is flooded with suffering, and all his powers of soul
and body are only just enough for him not to founder. He
masters his fear and sorrow, but how much it takes out of
him! To the very end he keeps his strength of judgment and
decision: not for a moment does he even appear to give way
or lose control; he dies in full possession of his faculties,
knowing where he is going, and at the moment he wills it. But
there is not a word from him that suggests a moment of relaxation, nor any intermission for him to breathe freely or shake
off his suffering somewhat. The burden is on him all the time,
always just as overwhelming. The few words he utters are
dictated to him, almost forced out of him, by his situation. He
has to tell Judas, and the guards arresting him, those who
judged him and the women who weep for him, why it is he is
going to his death. Men must know that he forgives them and
that he is saving them. Once the essential is said, he is silent.
It is not a silence of contempt; primarily it is because he is
overwhelmed; he has no strength to waste, he has not the
requisite degree of freedom of mind to express what he feels,
even to speak about his Father. The passion of Christ was
human suffering like ours and it took possession of him wholly
and entirely.

So it is that, throughout the long hours when he was showing 'the greatest love a man can show'[23] and that for us, we
hear hardly a single intimate thought for us or a word to tell
us of the love overflowing in his heart. So too, though this is
the hour when 'the world must be convinced that I love the
Father',[24] the time to achieve his desire to glorify the Father,[25]

[23] John 15:13   [24] John 14:31   [25] John 17:1

and to receive from him the only glory that means anything
to him, the Father's own;[26] yet our Lord now appears in no
condition to attempt even that tone of joyful abandon to the
Father which he alone can express. Normally, when he addressed the Father, he seemed already to enjoy the answer to
his prayer, but here we catch none of this, and nothing in our
Lord's tone now reveals such confident assurance. Can we still
say that, in this condition so like our own wretchedness and
the powerlessness it reduces us to, Jesus still lives in thanksgiving and in the direct and beatific possession of God?

We can and we must also say we know the reason—that even
in the passion we can still recognize the attitude of thankful-
ness to the Father, unchanged though veiled for us, the same
that we have detected in our Lord throughout his life. Indeed,
the thanksgiving is not just the moment of calm and assurance
wherewith our Lord gathered his forces in preparation for the
struggle; and it is far more than a firm resolve of allegiance
once determined upon and not withdrawn. In actual fact,
thanksgiving permeates the whole passion and floods it with
meaning. Moreover, it is the passion that really manifests the
most characteristic features of thanksgiving.

We heard our Lord burst into thanksgiving on seeing Satan
fall like lightning from heaven, and in the passion the time
had come for the encounter with the adversary.[27] The powers
of darkness now not only can lead him and take him along, as
in the desert,[28] but also lay hands upon him and do their
worst upon him. By the mouth of Herod they repeat the
temptation: 'If thou art the Son of God, work a miracle.'[29]
They could hurl the same challenge: 'If thou art the Son of
God, cast thyself down, come down from the cross.'[30] The
reply is the same: 'There is life for man in all that proceeds
from the mouth of God',[31] 'Am I not to drink that cup which
my Father himself has appointed for me?'[32] What our Lord
rejoiced to see in anticipation is now realized in the passion,
'the prince of this world cast out'.[33]

[26] John 17:5
[27] Luke 22:53
[28] Luke 4:5, 9
[29] Luke 4:3; 23:8
[30] Matt. 4:6; 27:40
[31] Matt. 4:4:
[32] John 18:11
[33] John 12:31

The core of our Lord's thanksgiving was his consciousness of being the Son and knowing his Father so intimately, knowing exactly all that he wished and accomplishing it in every detail. In the passion it is this all the time: 'Father, only as thy will is, not as mine is',[34] 'All is consummated.'[35] The essence of the passion is not, for the gospels or for our Lord himself, the overwhelming amount of his sufferings: it is that they enable him to reveal what he is—the Messiah, the Saviour of the world, the Son of Good—and by the same token to reveal the Father, for having sent such a Saviour and given birth to such a Son. Before Caiaphas, before Pilate, before the crowd milling round Calvary, and before the 'prince of this world', Jesus solemnly professed to be who he is: 'As you say, I am a king.'[36] 'And moreover, I tell you this; you will see the Son of man again, when he is seated at the right hand of God's power and comes on the clouds of heaven.'[37] 'Thou art, then, the Son of God? You say rightly, I am.'[38] His profession of faith hitherto had come out with an explosion of joy and gratitude; now he reaffirms it amid mortal agony and knowing that it is condemning him to frightful torments, but it is no less firm and spontaneous, and it takes on a far greater significance. What he had meant before, only he and the father could fathom, and it was only to the Father he was speaking; in the passion he can convey this revelation to men.

At this hour he really is the Son, he is on his own, he is cut off from all his disciples and friends; he has disappointed all the hopes set on him; he had multiplied miracles, and now he is powerless; he had won over crowds, and now is incapable of putting two sentences together; all his defences are down, he is disarmed against fear and anguish, disarmed against every form of treachery and cruelty, he is lost. In this state, if he says he is God's Son, it must be that between him and God there exists an imperishable and invulnerable bond that no disappointment can ever break, an intimacy that none can violate, an indestructible bond of loyalty. To be God's Son does not mean, as Satan supposed or as men imagine, to be able to count on miracles, to be sheltered from harm, to force

34 Mark 14:36   35 John 19:30   36 John 18:37
37 Matt. 26:64   38 Luke 22:70

men's hearts; it means to expect strength from the Father's
will alone; it means, when everything seems to show that God
is abandoning him, to be able to entrust his soul into the
Father's hands like a child. Such was our Lord's supreme witness, with the same basis and inspiration as his thanksgiving.
It was wholly and entirely thanksgiving, not so much in words
and outpouring of the heart, as in action carried out to the
very end, till all was consummated.

A proof that the passion of Christ was the ideal moment
of thanksgiving is that therein he accomplished what he had
promised in previous moments of joyful exultation: 'Come to
me, all you that labour . . . and I will refresh you', 'I am
the resurrection and the life'. While his sufferings are yet on
him and the crowd around him can still see only failure and
desolation, already the good thief on the cross beside him
turns to him: 'Remember me when thou comest into thy
kingdom';[39] and Jesus, knowing now that God has entrusted
all to him, without a moment's hesitation to turn to the ever-
present Father, can promise him: 'This day thou shalt be
with me in Paradise.'[40] What was hidden to the wise and
prudent God had just revealed to one of his little ones. A man
who had carried a heavy burden of sin and the weight of the
justice of men was the first to be admitted to see just how
gentle and humble of heart the Son of God could be.

6. *The resurrection*

It might be taken for granted that we should next contemplate the Son's thanksgiving when raised up by his Father,
the outpouring of mutual admiration, gratitude and love
between him who decided the whole plan and his Son who
had executed it all so perfectly. This would be a legitimate
and inspiring subject of contemplation, helping us to enter
into the mystery of the Blessed Trinity, giving us a true and
concrete example of the loving encounter between the three
Persons. But no scripture text actually portrays things for us
in this way, so we must be discreet, for to clothe the mystery in
features of our own imagining could lead us astray.

Still we are not entirely left outside the threshold, we who

[39] Luke 23:42   [40] Ibid. 43

have received the Spirit of God enabling us to join with the Son in his cry of love for the Father.[41] We know by faith that the essence of the resurrection, of which the gospel apparitions are only samples, is the entry of Jesus into his glory. God raised him up from the dead;[42] God has exalted him and made him sit at his right hand;[43] God has made him Lord and Christ,[44] prince and Saviour,[45] sovereign judge of the living and the dead;[46] he has given him 'that name which is greater than any other name'.[47] The early Church never lost sight of the resurrection as the decisive turning-point that was at the origin of its existence as of all its action in this world. Stephen, at the point of death, saw Jesus at the right hand of the Father, showing precisely that the early Christians were not afraid to contemplate this ineffable union in a concrete form. This they were entitled to do, as we also can do after them, since they had seen him with their own eyes, eaten and drunk with him, and so knew that the risen Christ was no less human than the Master they had followed from the lake of Galilee. The Christ whom the Father welcomed into his glory was the Son of man who had lived among them and made them his friends and who, even after his resurrection, was as simple and friendly, as human by nature as they had always known him.

So to contemplate the thanksgiving of the Son when glorified by his Father, there is only one way, that taken by the first witnesses—to return to the episodes of the mortal life of Jesus, giving them their full dimensions as we unfold them now in the light of his resurrection. The thanksgiving of the risen Jesus is still the same as when he heard the disciples tell him of their successful mission: 'I saw Satan fall from heaven. . . . None knoweth the Son. . . . Come to me. . . .' No word need be changed; it remains just as true—even more true, now that what was only a happy flash of light in the lifetime of Jesus has now become his everlasting joy. The joy of being able to reveal the Father: the joy of being the resurrection and the life for those that mourn; the joy of seeing

[41] Gal. 4:6
[42] Acts 2:24, 32; 3:15, 26; 4.10; 5:30; 10:40; 13:33; 17:31
[43] Acts 2:33; 5:31   [44] Acts 2:36   [45] Acts 5:31
[46] Acts 10:42; 17:31   [47] Phil. 2:9; Eph. 1:21

men's eyes opening to his light; the joy of being their daily bread, the ever-enduring source of strength for them; the joy, finally, of being the head of his Church, of having received from the Father this body as his completion,[48] of being united to this spotless bride.[49] This mysterious truth plunged St Paul into permanent thanksgiving and sustained him in all his apostolic endeavours. The thanksgiving of all the apostles, the thanksgiving of the Church in its spreading through the world, has as its source and origin, unique and perfect, eternal and for ever finding expression in joyful human sentiments, the thanksgiving of the Son of God, our Lord Jesus Christ.

[48] Eph. 1 : 22–23   [49] Eph. 5 : 27

X

The Gospel and Bread

BREAD IS ALMOST as prominent in the gospel as in the thoughts of a housewife or the breadwinner in a family. Apart from the number of meals we see our Lord share in, from Cana to his farewell gathering on ascension day, the thought of bread, man's staple food, is often present and our Lord often seizes the opportunity to speak about it. 'Man cannot live by bread alone', he answered the tempter.[1] 'Do not be anxious about your life, what you shall eat',[2] he said in the sermon on the Mount. But he would have us pray: 'Give us this day our daily bread.'[3] He reproached the crowds for following him 'because you were fed with the loaves',[4] but he took the initiative in multiplying the loaves. To give us his flesh to eat he would take bread into his hands; and it was by his way of breaking the bread that the disciples at Emmaus were to recognize the risen Jesus.

What are we to learn from these different ways of acting and speaking about bread? At first sight they seem concerned with such varied matters that it is hard to link them up. What value are we to attach to bread or food? Are we to concern ourselves with it or not? Is it something desirable or to be tolerated just as a necessary adjunct in life? One finds so many paradoxes and apparent contradictions on the point that one tends to apply them alternately according to circumstances,

[1] Matt. 4:4
[2] Matt. 6:25
[3] Matt. 6:10
[4] John 6:26

even when we do not trade on them and make out we are following the gospel when we are only quoting the texts that suit us. But fidelity to the gospel requires that we accept all these sayings, with undiminished force, and loyally try to integrate them and carry them out in our lives. We need not be surprised at these paradoxes; we should see in them the great paradox at the heart of Christianity, the sign of contradiction and of salvation, without which Christ's teaching would be a vain construction containing no nourishment for the soul.

No need to examine every mention of food in the gospel: three main episodes will do—the multiplication of the loaves, the last supper, and the meals of the risen Jesus. In these three quite different sets of circumstances, a significant degree of continuity can be found.

1. The multiplication of the loaves

On the evening of the day our Lord multiplied the loaves, five thousand men, carried away with enthusiasm at such an unprecedented miracle, far more significant for them than the usual healings of unknown people, swarmed around to acclaim Jesus. This was the man, the one sent by God to take in hand the destiny of his people, to deliver them from their enemies, to set up on earth a kingdom of peace and justice: here was the king of Israel. But Jesus slipped away from this demonstration. He prevailed upon his disciples to embark again and obliged them to sail across the lake. He made the crowds return to their homes too, and he went away to pray in solitude.

We cannot help feeling that our Lord's conduct was disconcerting, and we can understand the apostles trying to oppose it. He had led these people into the wilderness, undertaken to feed them all, calmly set them down in groups, in an atmosphere of solemnity and peace; he had made the apostles distribute the loaves and fishes as he blessed them, uniting all these people of all different religious and social levels and interests at the same meal, and he had aroused in them the same pitch of enthusiasm and the same high hopes. Was this not really a way of presenting himself as a new liberator, more powerful than Moses, equally able to gather and lead the people, but able moreover to produce this miracle from his own hands without waiting for manna to come down from heaven? He himself, the next day in the synagogue at Capharnum, would bring out this difference: 'It was not Moses who gave you the bread from heaven.'[5] If he would not let himself be proclaimed king of Israel, why work miracles that were bound to convey the impression that he was?

In all our Lord's miracles, the multiplication of loaves along with all the rest, there remains an element of ambiguity— something puzzling in the nature of Christian life and our Lord's presence in this world of men. Two surprising aspects can be detected in our Lord's attitude with regard to miracles. On the one hand he exercised considerable reserve; he imposed silence often on those he cured,[6] taking them on one side and sending them straight home,[7] so as to keep them away from the crowds. These precautions seem to us naïve. Did our Lord think that, when a blind man recovered his sight or a deaf-and-dumb man was healed, people would not get to know about it straight away? Could he really be surprised to find people talking all the more about such things when he asked them to keep them quiet? What use would there be in asking Jairus to keep it quiet about his little girl being restored to life, when all Capharnum was outside talking about it? Did he hope to reduce the number of sick coming to him? Why then, on the other hand, did he heal them all, even at the touch of his garments? How are we to reconcile this reserve and this easy access? How could our Lord work so many miracles and expect people not to talk about them? It could not be lack of understanding, nor could it be play-acting. Are we to say the texts contain contradictions?

No, they only need closer looking at, and then we shall see that, while certainly working a great many miracles, Jesus never presented himself as a professional performer of miracles. He had not come to work miracles, to invite the general public to benefit from his powers and see if he could do as he promised: he never organized performances of miracle-working. When he did work miracles, it was because they were really and truly forced out of him. Miracles did not

---

[5] John 6:32   [6] Mark 1:44; 5:43   [7] Mark 7:36; 8:26

come from him 'at any old time'; they were conditioned by
two definite stimuli, human misery and faith. 'Moved with
pity' or 'seeing his faith'—these two indications constantly
occur as a prelude to a miracle, and they are the only motives
the gospels assign. Jesus could not bear to stand by and see
suffering. If he had been present at Bethany, Martha said,
he would not have let Lazarus die. For his friend to fall a
victim to death, Jesus had to postpone his own arrival. The
sick, the lame, the lepers, who came to him were sure of being
cured; all they had to do was to show him their wretched condition. These were commonest cases. But there were others,
equally significant, especially when the distress was not
directly present to our Lord, when someone else came to
represent it to him, such as our Lady at the marriage feast at
Cana, the centurion for his servant, the Canaanite woman for
her daughter. Then our Lord required more urgent intercession; sometimes he even seemed to take little interest at the
first mention of the need. In reality he only wanted to arouse
more lively faith, and he tells us himself that it was their faith
he was won by. Thus he was showing the truth of what he
taught his followers: 'If you have faith, though it be but like
a grain of mustard seed, you have only to say to this mountain,
Remove from this place to that, and it will remove.'[8]

Apart from these two considerations, faith and human
misery, our Lord had not come to upset the course of nature.
He had no intention of changing the course of existence, either
for himself or for his apostles, or for the crowds about him. He
preached absolute trust in God who 'takes every hair of your
head into his reckoning', but he added that the time for such
trust is when one is at the mercy of those who can kill the
body.[9] This is the explanation of his attitude over multiplying
the loaves: when he saw the hunger of the crowd, deprived of
normal means of sustenance, he obeyed his instinct of pity for
them; but once this emergency help was given, he referred
people to their ordinary way of life, their bread-winning and
their shopping at the bakers. But the five thousand misunderstood: in this extraordinary measure they thought they saw
the signal that the kingdom they expected was at hand, they

[8] Matt. 17:19   [9] Matt. 10:28-33

imagined they had found someone to be responsible for feeding them always. As the Samaritan woman thought she could see herself freed from the daily task of fetching water, so they thought they were entering a 'welfare world', a world with no hunger or thirst, as such needs would be met for the asking, a world without tears or hardship, because some 'good fairy' would come between them and all harm—an ever-recurring dream that our Lord summed up sternly: 'You seek me, not because you saw signs, but because you ate your fill of the loaves.'[10] In their blindness they had not seen it as the work of God, but only as food to eat: they had not risen to faith, they had failed to recognize that if, in Jesus, the most human pity was at the service of divine power, then it was up to them to follow his guidance and inspiration, not just bring his pity into line with their own wishful thinking.

The lesson of the multiplication of the loaves is that of our Lord's whole life, and of his passion: 'I am a king', but 'my kingdom does not belong to this world'.[11] But it would be a mistaken view of this answer to see in it a repudiation of the kingdoms that do belong to this world. They are not the kingdom of God, right enough, but they are indispensable, and the kingdom of God cannot do without them. By referring men to their own devices and normal means of subsistence, by refusing to be their king on the lines of their wishful thinking, our Lord assigned the right basis to economic and political life, as necessities founded on human nature and problems that man has to tackle with his own powers of body and mind. Bread is won at the sweat of man's brow,[12] so 'if anyone will not work, let him not eat'.[13] Peace and security are the affairs of public authorities. Though not infallible, doctors and hygiene and natural remedies are the normal means of preserving or recovering health. It is certainly true that health and peace and food always come from divine providence. If they should fail, it is often due to the sins of men, and we must pray day by day for God to grant these things, causing his sun to shine and his rain to fall on the fields of the just and of the sinner. There is no question of counting on miracles or favouritism

<hr />

[10] John 6:26
[11] John 18:36
[12] Gen. 3:19
[13] 2 Thess. 3:10

on our behalf. The principles of agriculture, as of social and
economic life, are things that men just have to discover and
apply for their benefit.

Our Lord made quite clear the validity of such things in
their own right, but he did more. By sending the five thousand
back to their homes, as also the sick people he had cured, not
only did he show that these were exceptional favours called for
by some crying emergency, and that he was not intending to
put doctors or bakers out of business; but also he was giving
doctors and bakers, along with all other men's trades or pro-
fessions, a new significance and a new dimension: that of
charity. By distributing to the five thousand as much bread as
they wanted,[14] Jesus had not thought of giving any bakers who
happened to be there the idea that their work would not be
needed any more; but on the contrary that they should always
try to serve loaves as good as those they had just tasted and see
that even the poor around them should have their fair share.
This did not mean under-rating the trade, far from it, and at
the same time it indicated the terms on which a Christian
should follow his trade, with concern to satisfy any human
needs and 'give every satisfaction' in more than name.

To provide men with food, or clothing, or medical care, to
secure for them the benefits of justice and peace—these are
great things for a man seeking to find a meaning in his work;
they form a human task on which the subsistence and development of humanity on earth does really depend. Our
Lord's miracles do not relieve men of such tasks in any degree,
they only throw a new light on them, so as to see them in his
light. For a Christian alive to the gospel, feeding and clothing
and caring for men or defending them in any way, are all ways
of seeing them and serving them as our Lord does. It means
being on the alert against all that may harm them, every kind
of deprivation or injustice, on the alert to help those without
adequate clothing or lodging. It means being like our Lord in
making oneself accessible to every form of distress. Whether
he is a farmer, a doctor or a statesman, the Christian cannot
thereby claim any superiority of competence or conscientious-
ness over anyone else, nor does he enjoy any such privilege

[14] John 6:11

simply and solely because of the work he does. What superiority he may have should show in his attentiveness to men's needs, in being quick to respond to wrongs and injustices as often as they occur; with boldness and confidence in God's support, so never tiring in finding opportunities; with a realization of the beatitudes, so instinctively seeking out 'the least of my brethren', the most neglected; with a Christ-like fellow feeling that attracts and wins the hearts of men.

2. *The last supper*

The bread that Jesus took into his hands to change into his body was the bread that was on the table, made with the same flour and kneaded with the same hands as hundreds of other similar loaves of bread. Nowadays, when people are more consciously aware of the meaning of human work, we like to think of the eucharist as consecrating both the gifts of nature and the fruit of man's work. If this idea is to be fully worked out and if it is to be a real inspiration to action, as distinct from inspiring oratory and enthusiasm on great occasions, we must try to see more clearly the connection between bread and the eucharist, and between man's work and the action of Christ.

In choosing bread to give to his disciples, saying 'This is my body', Jesus was acting in virtue of his omnipotent power, which could have transformed into his body any other elements. As he chose bread in preference to all others, we need only accept his gift in all simplicity and gratitude. However, in view of his constant reference to bread, and his multiplication of the loaves, as well as in view of the particular setting he devised for the celebration of the eucharist, we are quite entitled, in the measure of enlightenment he affords us, to see if we can understand the motives for his choice.

The way our Lord stresses that the bread he is giving the apostles is the same body that he is to give up for them is significant. If the bread is becoming his body, it is because his body is already nourishment: 'My flesh is food indeed',[15] he had already said in the synagogue at Capharnum. Nourishment means something substantial and rich in life-giving

[15] John 6:55

energy, and something that can be assimilated, received and absorbed. Jesus is indeed so completely given to men that they can receive him whole and entire. His time, his strength, his honour, his life itself, he has kept nothing for himself. The very hour in which he is consecrating this bread is just the time when he is going to show publicly that he has given himself in earnest: like bread, he belongs to men who can do as they wish with him. But, even as they think they are destroying him, they are only releasing energies stored within him since the incarnation. Every word of his, every movement, every heart-beat, every thought or feeling, had always been so utterly devoid of self-seeking, so filled with God's generosity and charged with his power, that they were for every man and for all humanity an everlasting source of strength and light, 'living bread'. However, though manifested in the course of his life on earth by the power of his words and works, this divine energy had remained subject to the limitations of human activity, acting in contact with immediate surroundings, within a limited radius, by the normal ways and means of human influence. For it to reach and feed all men, death had to come and break down these barriers, the grain of seed had to be buried in the earth and have its protecting and insulating coverings removed. Then, when he had exhausted his capability and given all he had, Jesus really and truly became the food of those believing in him, the ever-available food and life of his Church.

These powers that he gives us, to sustain our life, have passed through this earth. The power of his love is divine, but it saves us only by virtue of becoming human, passing through his human heart, through his 'blood and sweat and tears'. All his human substance, unfailingly transformed by the power of love, he derived from this earth and the nourishment it affords. The bread he took from the supper-table to change into his body, at his word, for thirty years he had made his daily food to build up his body. Any man eating food can say, this is becoming my body, as that is in fact what happens to the foreign body. Jesus indeed did something very different, but not something unrelated to the food he had taken hitherto. At the moment he gave his body and his whole self as our food for all time, he made the bread he had eaten for thirty years, the bread human beings would eat for the rest of time, capable of becoming his body, in the Church. At this moment when his mortal body was about to perish to become the seed of 'his body which is the Church', need we be surprised that the bread he had lived on should be made capable of becoming, wherever the words of our Lord are duly pronounced over it, his own body transformed in glory?

By this action our Lord finally gave full meaning to the bread that men make and that all men eat. By multiplying the loaves, when bread was lacking, our Lord had clearly marked its value as men's ordinary food. By now changing it into his body, he revealed the ultimate purpose bread should serve. That one piece should be set aside to become a consecrated host is not only something that ennobles all bread throughout the world, it is infinitely more. Just as the bread at the last supper represented for our Lord all the bread he had previously taken and eaten to build this body of his which he was giving up for us, so the living bread we receive from his hands in the eucharist lends new meaning to 'our daily bread'. If our Lord, in his love for us, in some way used all the bread he ever took on earth to form his body to become our food, it was so that we, receiving his body and his love, should be made capable of transforming into an offering to God and food for our brethren all the human energy we derive from earthly food.

The eucharist gives bread its true value—this is not only true in the case of consecrated particles, but also for all the bread the earth produces. It is not enough to have bread in sufficient supply to make hosts: all men must have enough to keep up their strength, and that requires the efforts of farm-hands and bakers, the brain-work of economists and politicians. To meet inevitable shortages in some places, to resist the injustices bound to occur in a world where sin is at work, men must ever be on the alert. The Christian has no monopoly in this task, but our Lord's pity in feeding the multitude binds him too and assures him that, if he seeks justice in the kingdom of God, his faith and charity can count on getting anything from God, even the multiplication of loaves. But where will he find this faith and charity, and the courage to face human distress and despair day by day, if not in him who has sacrificed himself for all men's sins and made himself the nourishment for all men's needs? To help all mankind to be able to eat their bread in peace, we need the holy eucharist.

As long as men do not eat the eucharistic bread, they will not eat their bread in peace, they will always know hunger. Only the bread our Lord gives is able to satisfy the most imperious hunger of men, the hunger for the meal where God gathers his children about his table and fills them with his joy. Christians most preoccupied with providing everyone with their daily bread must not forget that, for our Lord, the multiplication of loaves was only a preliminary. Christians must indeed try to see that they act efficiently and cannot be content with vague pity or good will out of touch with real life. But they know that, even in their action, the most valuable and the main thing is not the bread it secures for men but the joy and hope it brings to the poor to find themselves loved with something of our Lord's love.

3. The meals taken by the risen Jesus

Meals, of such frequent occurrence in the gospels, loom quite large in the brief resurrection episodes. On rejoining his disciples, Jesus wanted to show them he was not a ghost,[16] but he also wanted to relive with them some of the most friendly times in human life, when intimacy can be, if not always most profound, at least the most spontaneous and whole-hearted, thereby fostering friendship at every level. By going on with this, now in his new glorified state, Jesus was giving them the proof they most needed just then of a most incredible fact. In his new glorified state, though no longer subject to our limitations and sufferings, though no part of him now is subject to death or decline, so that the tomb could never claim any trace of his body; yet nothing had changed in his reactions, in his heart, in his person. He is exactly the same man they knew, they find him again undiminished in any way.

They found him again in the same setting in which he had taken his leave of them, that of a meal. Every meal with the

[16] Luke 24:39

risen Jesus could not fail to recall his last meal before his passion. Then he had warned them that this was the last time he would be drinking of the fruit of the vine with them till the day they would all drink it together in the kingdom of his Father.[17] And here he was again seated among them 'breaking the bread' and sharing it between them, just as he had done for the five thousand and for the apostles at the last supper.[18] These points recorded by the evangelists have a real significance: in each of the meals in the risen life, the last supper is present and not just as a memory, however touching. No doubt there is little point in seeking to show whether our Lord's 'breaking of bread' for the disciples at Emmaus was the eucharist or not, but as we read the gospel resurrection narratives it is clear that the master who came to sit and eat with his disciples was indeed he who had given himself to them as their food.

He showed them his body and the traces of suffering left on it, he made them feel this body which now belonged to them since he had given it to them. It was still the same, though not tied down by space and weight, it could make itself visible at will, and so could be present unknown to them; it was radiant with life and invulnerable to age and death. This body restored to them the familiar presence, his features and gestures, his way of speaking and looking at them, his whole person. Jesus had become the centre of their life: when he was not there they felt lost; his strength carried them along; his words, stern and disturbing as they were at times, always set them on the road to truth; his ever-available devotion to their needs, his unreserved and unselfish affection for them—in all those things he had been the sheet-anchor of their life. The risen Jesus became all this for them anew, and more than before. All those things that he had given them day after day as he lived his life with them, he had now given them once and for all by sacrificing himself to death for them. Moreover he was giving it all to them, now that he rejoined them, in a form that he would take henceforward for his Church, the form of food, of the bread that Christians would share among them and make the source of their life.

[17] Matt. 26:29   [18] Luke 9:16; 22:19; 24:30

The life this eucharistic bread brings us is involved in the
world and its struggles, all the more for having passed through
death. Each of the four gospels, in somewhat different con-
texts, closes with an episode amounting to the same thing:
Jesus sending his apostles to bring the good news to the
world. The presentation of this in St Matthew is the most
striking. The scene is impressive and yet simple, vaster than
the divine intervention on Sinai and yet as simple as the
humblest passage in the gospel story. Jesus suddenly appeared
to them, and the apostles, 'when they saw him there, fell down
to worship him'[19] in adoration, for divine omnipotence belongs
to him and he is the Lord of the world and of all time. But he
is exactly the same as he had always been, with no outward
apparatus of glory about him; his Sinai is only a modest hill,
and his apostles a small group of ordinary men. There is the
same contrast in the mission he entrusts to them: it is for all
the peoples of the world for all time, but it consists in setting
out on foot, as before, resuming the itinerant way of life they
had shared with our Lord, not long since, along dusty and
thirsty roads around the villages of Galilee where he had pur-
posely made this rendezvous with them. Their Galilee was
henceforward to be the whole world, but the way of life awaiting them would be the same as they had experienced with our
Lord, arriving as strangers wherever they went, at the mercy
of the attitude or humour of whomsoever they might encounter, at the disposal of the poor and sick and distressed,
constantly eyed by jealous rivals or the ill-will of adversaries.

When Jesus disappeared from their sight and they found
themselves on their own again, did they remember the night
after his most ambitious miracle, when he launched them on
their own, in darkness and storm over the neighbouring lake,
while he stole away from them? Their present situation
seemed much the same. Here they were left to their own
devices, obliged to have recourse to natural resources to keep
body and soul together, to reckon and deal with ordinary men
and their customs and laws. All this was to be the framework
and the stuff of the new life they were to live. From her birth
the Church has been subject to the laws of economics and the

[19] Matt. 28:17

social and political facts of life of the civilizations where her
mission has been. She has been subject to them, not as unfortunate necessities to put up with, but as the basic setting
in which to live the divine charity beating in her heart. One of
the Church's first actions was to appoint deacons to see to the
provision of food for the Christian communities. Soon after
that St Paul would be organizing collections in the communities he had founded, to help out the Church in Jerusalem,
reminding them of the importance of work and its Christian
significance, as a means of serving those more in need. From
one end of the gospel to the other, the need for bread recalls
the same lesson to Christians. If they overlook the duties
involved in helping men to earn their living, in the name of
the charity of Christ, Christians are failing in obedience to
the gospel. But to respond to these demands with the freedom
and detachment, with the tact and warmth of welcome and
friendliness that people expect in those trying to keep them—
and without these the service of men can easily degenerate into
the urge to lord it over people—if our charity is to be from
God, if it is to reveal God, we Christians need the eucharistic
bread, the body of Christ who so empties himself and identified
himself with every man on earth that he is their food and
their life.

F

XI

The Priesthood of the New Covenant

WHETHER AS A PRIEST seeking to grasp the full meaning of his vocation, of the sacrament that consecrated him and the pastoral responsibilities that are his, or whether as a lay person trying to discover his true position and task with regard to the priesthood of the Church, the Christian must naturally fall back on the last supper and the words of Christ: 'I have chosen you. . . . I will not call you servants; I call you friends. . . . Do this in memory of me. . . . They do not belong to this world.' Our Lord's words, confided to his followers as a last testament as he enters on the passion, seem to define the essence of the Christian priesthood and describe what the priest of Christ should be. The Church has constantly rehearsed these words down the centuries ever finding new inspiration. Nowadays, when the Christian priesthood raises burning questions, we may be quite certain that meditation on the last supper will help us to see things more clearly.

1. The covenant on Mount Sinai

'This is my blood of the New Covenant . . . do this for a commemoration of me': as they received their mission to go on doing as the master said 'until he comes', the apostles were also given to understand that what the master did was itself a reaffirmation of one of God's greatest interventions in human history—his covenant with the people of Israel on Mount

Sinai. As we read in our missal this mention of '*novi et aeterni testamanti*', we also are given to understand something of what was the significance, in human history, of God's entry into alliance with his people and their life, which is involved in the covenant.

The covenant on Sinai was not itself the new covenant and we are no longer governed by it. But it is of direct interest to us, because it helps by comparison towards a better grasp of the new covenant. Reduced to its essentials, the covenant at Sinai was made up of three elements: history, Law and sacrifice.

First of all, the intermingled history of Yahweh and the people of Israel; the history of God revealing himself, from the call of Abraham to the marvels of the Exodus, by signs of divine power and by a continuity of interest showing conscious design; the history of God now assuming responsibility to pursue this design for the future and destiny of his people.

This undertaking involved a counterpart: God undertook to secure for ever the destiny of Israel on one condition, that Israel should really live as God's people, adopting his way of thinking and feeling about things, accepting the dictates of his Law. Knowing what Yahweh had already done for them and what he could do for them in the future, was Israel ready to live as God's people, with all the demands and guarantees this commitment involved? By free choice the Israelites took this decision and accepted the Law.

Then, when all was ready to be sealed, signed and delivered, there only remained to translate it into a sacred rite, so making it an inviolable covenant. This was the object of the solemn sacrifice celebrated by Moses according to the exact instructions given by God. The blood of the victims, sprinkled partly upon the altar of God, partly on the assembled people, set up between them an indestructible community of life. From then on there could be no question of Israel having the option of renewing or withdrawing. Its decision was now incorporated in a sacrifice; it was, so to say, clasped between God's hands, and it had become a sacred deed that no human power could annul. The twelve stone pillars erected about the altar were to remain permanent witnesses for the centuries to come.

By sacrifice, in any religion, man has found access to the numinous realm of the sacred, but it was mostly by rites constantly repeated and only involving part of his life. The covenant of God with Israel meant incomparably more. The sacrifice on Sinai conveyed to the chosen people that, by accepting the law, governing as it did every aspect of their lives, the whole life of the people would take on a new and consecrated value. Entering into fellowship with God once and for all, they are now his guests and sit at his table. For good or ill they could not escape God's passionate concern for them, and they now had no choice but mutual fidelity or incurring God's anger. The history of Israel was to unfold and prove the earnestness of this covenant throughout more than a thousand years.

2. *The new covenant*

If he had not been performing a rite connected in some way with that of Sinai, Jesus would not have said: 'This is my blood of the new covenant, shed for many.'[1] This mention of the new, as opposed to the old, was far more than a pious association of ideas. It provides a far deeper understanding of the mystery being performed in the hands of our Lord.

The covenant on Sinai was the climax of a long series of special interventions by God: arousing faith in Abraham and his descendants, sustaining the courage of Moses, claiming his people from the power of Egypt, tirelessly upholding their fidelity so often on the point of breaking down, Yahweh had 'carried his people as if on eagle's wings',[2] with many marvels to help, till they reached his chosen spot on Sinai, and thereby revealed his power and fidelity. Under appearances quite unassuming and unspectacular, Jesus did the same with his twelve apostles. He too had chosen the men he wanted, prepared them gradually and set them on the road to faith through ups and downs of trust and misgiving, showing himself to be in possession of almighty miraculous powers, though not immune from the attacks of the powers of evil. On this evening his task was nearing its end: he had loved and preserved those whom he had chosen to be his and 'none of

[1] Mark 14:24   [2] Ex. 19:4

them had been lost . . .'.[3] He still had the decisive step to take, making these men, united by a year or two spent in common following him, into his Church to be throughout the centuries his body in action and his gospel proclaimed and lived in this world. Moreover, just as Yahweh had gathered in his law all the rules governing the life he had made his people lead to bring them to Sinai, so our Lord gathered in one single commandment the guiding principle of the life he led and taught his disciples to follow: 'Love one another, even as I have loved you.'[4] A new commandment, the charter of the new covenant, the Christian law is not an assemblage of rules, but it remains an obligation with binding force: one cannot be a Christian without loving one's neighbour, one cannot love one's neighbour as a Christian except as taught in the gospel by the concrete example of our Lord.

As the old covenant on Sinai, so also the new is concluded in the form of a sacrifice, and, because the Christian priesthood has this same sacrifice as its *raison d'être*, we must study it at some length. This sacrifice is mysterious in many respects, and there is something puzzling even about its manner of performance. It has little if anything in common with the traditional rites performed in the temple of Jerusalem on the beasts offered as victims. It seems to take place at two levels of time, with little or no sign of continuity discernible between the two. On the one hand, at the last supper Jesus did seem to proceed according to a veritable ritual, setting himself before God, taking into his hands an offering of bread and wine, performing actions whose meaning was assigned by the words: 'This is my body, this is my blood, this is the new covenant', and ending by their all receiving in common the sacred elements offered to God. On the other hand, the rite seemed to remain unfinished and unfulfilled, in that Jesus spoke of his body being given up and his blood being shed, which seemed then to be only words. It would seem that they could only take on meaning by awaiting the crucifixion the following day. But on Calvary all sign of ritual was absent: all that could be seen was the ordinary apparatus of human justice, and the presence of the two thieves on either side brought out the fact that

[3] John 17:12   [4] John 13:34

Jesus' death was a common execution. A supreme act of boundless love on his part, but how see in it a sacrificial act? And how could Jesus incorporate it in advance with the rite he had performed at the last supper?

These points can be explained if one remembers that what is involved is a new covenant and therefore a new kind of sacrifice. Our Lord's breaking away from the old ritual was a sign that he was consciously inaugurating a new dispensation and quite freely settling the new terms and conditions. The apparent distance separating the rite of the last supper from our Lord's death on the cross brings out an essential aspect of this new sacrifice. It was the sacrifice of Jesus Christ but it is also the sacrifice he left to his disciples and which his Church has the task of offering 'until he comes'. In the truest sense, this sacrifice was unique and was offered only once and for all, when Jesus breathed his last on Calvary. Only the shedding of our Lord's blood could duly seal the new covenant, matching God's adoption of all humanity with a fitting response, the Son's act of thanksgiving expressed in total obedience. Upon the cross alone this new covenant was perfectly consummated and God's own expectation truly fulfilled. There, the blood shed was no longer a symbol but an actual proof of devotion. There was rendered to the Father love for love. For man there is now no possible communion with God save through the cross of Christ. But the cross takes on its value as a ritual sacrifice by its attachment to the last supper and the rite performed then. Because our Lord, while still a free man, gave his disciples his body and blood, he revealed to them that his death was something quite different from a mere execution carried out by Roman and Jewish police. Because, while still completely at liberty to come and go, he publicly assigned himself to death, he made it clear in advance that from the moment men came to arrest and take him bound, every one of his movements, though apparently forced on him by the powers of darkness plotting against him, would in reality be the unfolding of a ceremonial minutely provided for by the will of the Father. Between the ritual at the supper and this unfolding of the passion, there is far more than type-symbolism, there is inseparable connection: the last supper enabled the passion to be wholly and entirely a sacred action, the victim's being led to the final immolation.

Conversely, the passion enables the last supper to be, for the first time in the history of divine worship in the world, something other than a symbolic rite. It was the free decision of Christ, distributing his body and blood to his disciples, that set in motion the ruthless machinery of the passion. Jesus handed himself over to sinful humanity, and they would treat him as only sin knew how, heaping on him all the inventions of which cruelty is capable. But it was our Lord who had taken the initiative, otherwise there would never have been 'an hour for Satan and the powers of darkness'. The gospel narratives, especially St John's, bring out this wonderful contrast between the two phases of the single action forming the sacrifice of Jesus: his freedom and ease in making the plans, his spontaneity and friendliness, his command over the future, up to the evening of the supper; then, from the agony onwards, the blind and crushing release of all the forces of evil, driving Christ on to his death, though never depriving him in any way of his sovereign mastery. When he gave up the ghost, in full self-possession, he bore witness that he had, 'on the day before he suffered', freely used the power of giving his disciples his body and blood as their food and drink.

The agony in the garden of Gethsemani formed the transition between these two phases and linked them together. It revealed the mysterious connection between the supper and the passion. It brought out the deep earnestness of the ritual performed at the supper, by showing that it was not just the announcement of something in words but an irrevocable commitment to something being done. It uncovered the depth of this commitment by showing what was meant by this body and blood being given and shed for many. It manifested by its outcome the sacrificial character of the whole passion. Up to his last sigh, up to the great cry he uttered to God before expiring, in the depths of powerlessness and horror, our Lord's decision and prayer in the agony went on unfailingly transforming every moment of torture and every detail of the ignoble execution of justice into a sacred elevation and a perfect sacrifice.

3. *The implications of the last supper*

In the light of the cross every word and deed of our Lord at the supper takes on its full meaning. The supper was a meal, and it was from the ingredients of this meal, bread and wine, that Jesus formed the food and drink he gave his disciples. We are quite accustomed nowadays to see in this choice the sign that our Lord came to consecrate and transform the work of man. It is a commonplace among commentators and the hymns sung at the offertory. This is all quite true and confirmed in biblical tradition. As he took the bread and wine into his hands, Jesus was also taking in hand the working of nature, the part played by the seasons and the gradual growth of seeds, together with the efforts of men, the skill of the vine-grower and the toil of farm or house work.

But of course the bread and wine were not on the table at the supper just to restore man's strength, they were ingredients of a festive repast between friends, and this is what our Lord made the basis of his sacrificial ritual. Any meal together is a gesture of some significance for human beings. Eating and drinking—not merely satisfying brute hunger—in company with friends and neighbours, sharing their pleasure, adding to the satisfaction of instinct the joy of meeting and talking to people, all this represents something of civilized value. Quite naturally in many religions, and notably that of Israel, sacrifice to God ended in a meal. The higher the religious sense, the more spiritual was the meaning of these sacrificial meals. In pagan cults they were the outward sign that the forces of abundance and peace, regenerated in the domain of nature by the sacred rites, are restored in the fullness of their fruitfulness. In the religion of Israel sacrifice had become covenant and its significance was very different. Nature was no longer the domain of blind and capricious forces, it was the domain of God. God had installed his people in his holy land, not as strangers but as his guests for ever, to live in fruitful collaboration between 'the work of their hands'[5] and the God-given fertility of the soil under his rain and sun. The sacrificial repast was one of covenant, the sign that his people were

[5] Deut. 16:15

faithful to him and Yahweh had rewarded their labours with divine generosity.

All this was there at the last supper too. By gathering the apostles about his table, recalling how he had longed for this brotherly gathering, Jesus, as on so many occasions, showed the value he set upon a meal together, a time when men enjoy the fruits of body and mind, giving free rein to their thoughts and sentiments. However this value may not be without alloy, and our Lord needed to purify it. Before taking up the bread and wine, the elements of a natural communion, Jesus was to show clearly what kind of human gathering he had come to consecrate, what sort of meal he was to make into his holy eucharist. It was then he took off his cloak, took a towel and a basin to wash the feet of the apostles. This washing of feet he made the necessary preparation for participation in the supper.

In this our Lord reveals the weakness in a common illusion. We imagine too easily that Christ's consecration immediately gives a sacred value to all human activity, but this would be assigning to it a quasi-magic efficacy. To hear certain accounts of the offertory of the Mass, you might think it only needed a few words of prayer and a verse or two of a hymn for all human endeavour and achievement to be gathered straight-away on the altar, fit to be offered to God and become the body of his Son. All this may be perfectly true, but only on the understanding that the only human achievement and en-deavour, the only human values that can duly be offered on the altar of Christ and included in his consecrating action are those which, in one way or another, spring from his charity and bear its hall-mark. Just as the covenant on Sinai required the life of the chosen people to be lived according to the law of Yahweh, for it to be given a sacred value, so the new covenant consecrates the whole life and work of Christians on con-dition they spring from charity, the charter of this covenant.

We must therefore recognize that at the last supper our Lord did consecrate all the joys and hardships of our human condition, as expressed in a meal with brotherly love. He himself took the trouble to make this clear. He began this meal, that he was to share with them after so much longing, by indicating how to enter into the spirit of it. In kneeling to wash the feet of his apostles, implying that unless they were ready to accept the disconcerting experience of seeing their master in the guise of a slave he could not have them at his table, Jesus taught them that the meal he was making his holy eucharist was one in which those at table and those serving are equally guests. He was discarding nothing of the warmth and intimacy of human fellowship about the table, provided they went with the least spectacular and most anonymous service and devotion, that of the slave at his task.

That done, Jesus could take into his hands bread from the fields of his country and wine from the grapes of Judea. He could gather up his whole life, nourished on such bread and wine, affording him the energies he then transformed into self-sacrificing effort and finally into pure charity, until the last drop of his blood. In a surge of thanksgiving to the Father, he consecrated to him this bread and wine which he changed into his body and blood, and so consecrated this body and blood which he made the victim of the sacrifice he was instituting; and he consecrated likewise 'those whom the Father had given him'[6] and who would do this in remembrance of him till he came again. So the table laid by Peter and John became the altar of the new covenant; the brotherly gathering of the twelve at the close of the day became the sacred repast at which God gave himself in communion to his apostles; and the guests at this table became the priests of the new covenant.

As revealed at the last supper, this new covenant bears the same three aspects that featured in the old. It is a history, a law and a sacrifice, all in one. If one neglects either of these three components one can claim no part in this covenant. One cannot be a Christian if one does not accept the gospel record, the law of charity and the eucharistic sacrifice. A charity that thought to dispense with the gospel story, the living familiarity with the Christ of the gospels, to be guided by human needs as they occur, by the highest ideals of right conduct, may lead to heroic service, but it is not Christian charity. Nor would it be so, if it thought to live the gospel and bring men the witness of Christ without seeking it at the ever-living spring

[6] John 17:11

of the sacraments of his Church, where Christ is not only in men's remembrance or affection, but also really and truly present and active, in particular in the holy eucharist. Some Christian men with the best of intentions may tend to overlook the indispensable role of the sacramental order. But the vast majority live in the opposite illusion and imagine that 'the practice of their religious duties' and 'frequenting the sacraments' dispense them from getting to know the gospel and the teaching of our Lord and from service to their fellow men. They think they belong to the gospel and they do not hear Christ telling them to go and learn the lesson of the Old Testament prophets: 'Go home and find out what the words mean. It is mercy that wins favour with me, not sacrifice.'[7] To approach the holy eucharist, we must have accepted the spirit of our Lord washing their feet. To receive the eucharist as did the Christians at Corinth, blamed by St Paul for letting barriers of class and money intervene in the place where the meal was held, is to make oneself 'guilty of profaning the body and blood of the Lord'.[8] Not that the body of the Lord, risen and invulnerable, could be itself affected by such profanation; but because to receive the eucharist without charity was violating the new covenant in its most fundamental law at the very moment of outwardly adhering to it by sharing in the sacrifice that established it. To receive the body our Lord sacrificed even unto death, and to refuse to think of one's brethren, is an insult to his redemptive love and makes a mockery of his supreme self-sacrifice.

Gospel, charity, eucharist: the close linking of these three factors in the last supper is no coincidence, still less caprice on the part of God. Christian life, of its nature, involves the life of man being transformed by the understanding of the story of Christ. True, the human heart has remarkable resources of unselfish devotion and abnegation; it is capable of heroic allegiances and of a deep and painful awareness of misery and sin. But all these aspirations remain uncertain and precarious, till given their true inspiration and purpose: God in Christ, reconciling the world. The Christian cannot ignore in himself or others, the consciousness of disgust for evil and the aspira-

[7] Matt. 9:13; cf. 12:7   [8] 1 Cor. 11:27

tion to keep his conscience loyal and clear; but he also knows that the only refusal of sin that was wholly perfect was that of Christ, that the only rejection of wickedness with no trace of condescension or pride was that of Jesus in the presence of his 'chalice' at Gethsemani. If the sacrament of penance gives us the assurance that our sins are washed away by it, it is because it consecrates and transforms our poor creaturely sorrow in contact with the sorrow and horror of sin our Lord had in dying for our sins. The contrition of the penitent sinner takes its rise from the sorrow of our Lord's broken heart. The fidelity of Christian husbands and wives is won for them by the fidelity of our Lord to his Church. So it is with all the sacraments: they consecrate our lives by making them the prolongation of the life of Christ in the lives of other men. So the divine purpose in the covenant is achieved: God making men share his life and his family. More than the rest, the eucharist, the sacrament of the new covenant, embodies this basic plan. In the eucharist the Christian finds the guarantee that his charity is genuine because it arises, not from his own poor heart, but from our Lord; he finds the incentive urging him to imitate our Lord whose charity he bears within him; and he finds the assurance that this charity in him is capable of overcoming his weaknesses and making him live for the service of God and the brethren. There can be no true Christian charity unless it feeds on the gospel and the eucharist, and unless it reaches out to the Mass to consecrate it in the hands of Christ to the salvation of men and the glory of God.

4. The priest of the new covenant

The above account of the new covenant will help us to understand the priesthood going with it. Some ways of describing the Christian priesthood, directly applying to it features of the levitical priesthood straight from the Old Testament, for instance stressing its separateness from the people, tend to forget that Christ's sacrifice is not a levitical sacrifice. As the priest of the new covenant, Christ has affinity, not to Aaron, but to Moses, offering the sacrifice of the covenant as head of the whole people. To describe the Christian priesthood the

Old Testament can certainly help, provided it is not literally superimposed but transposed into the new covenant.

Here there is only one priest, Jesus Christ. Not only do the priests of the Church derive their priesthood from him, but the meaning of their priesthood is to show forth the unique and exclusive role of Jesus Christ. The priest is the permanent sign that the Christian receives absolutely everything from the Lord. Of the three elements composing the Christian life, the gospel, the law of charity and the eucharist, there is one, namely charity, which does directly depend on individual men: it is up to them to make the effort it calls for and to see the priorities it involves. But this charity itself is a gift of God, and the presence of the priest is there to remind men of it. God has entrusted to the priest the ministry of the word and of the eucharist. No doubt every Christian has his share in heralding and furthering the gospel in the world, as the gospel is proclaimed by the Church as a whole. St Paul thanked all the members of his community at Philippi 'for taking so full a part in the work of Christ's gospel'.[9] But the priest is specially commissioned to ensure the full transmission of the word of God in the scriptures and in the gospel which is their fulfilment. He is, in a sense, directly responsible for the text of the scriptures and their official interpretation in the Church. He thereby shows that Christianity must always be the imitation of the life led two thousand years ago by Jesus of Nazareth, not necessarily in detail, but in the Spirit inspiring all his actions and given generously still to those who contemplate them.

Every Christian, in his way, has a share likewise in the Mass celebrated by the whole Church, but only the priest's hands are consecrated to take and distribute the body of the Lord. By receiving the eucharist from the hands of the priest, the Christian is reminded that the charity within him does not come from his own resources, but is the overspill of the boundless charity that led Christ to Calvary and made him our servant. At the offertory, as he entrusts the bread and wine to the hands of the priest, as the fruit of his own efforts, the Christian recognizes that his whole life, with its success and

[9] Phil. 1:5

failure, and the love of God in him crowning it all, must—if it is to escape its own limitations and share in God's own boundless love—be gathered up in turn by the hands of Christ and incorporated in his eucharist, his sacrificial act of thanksgiving to the Father.

The presence of the priest, then, shows forth in the Church the divine authority of the word of Christ and the divine efficacy of his sacraments. He is not an exclusive agent of the word of God, which all Christians must convey to the world, nor of all the sacraments: any person can confer baptism, and the spouses mutually confer the sacrament of marriage, while the priest is only the witness representing the person of Christ. But in the sacramental order, as in that of the word, he is a reminder of divine initiative and transcendance. Teaching in the name of the Church, he enables Christians to receive his word with an attitude of faith, not for any value or quality of its own, but because it comes from our Lord. He is an indispensable channel of the full sacramental life and he prevents us forgetting that all our riches come from the hands of Christ and must pass through these same hands back to the Father. Not all the gifts from the Father to his children need pass through the hands of the priest, but his presence reminds us that all that we are and all the good we do comes from above, 'sent down by the Father of all'.

In view of all this, a spirituality of the priesthood must needs be marked with the character investing the priest with authority and power and designating him to take care of the full transmission of the word of God and the tradition of the Church. These are tasks that call for faithfulness at all times, and they may involve dangers of over-literalism. To play an important part can lead, if one is not careful, to just acting a part. To guard against this danger, the priest must have a profound sense of the absolute sovereignty of God, whose representative he is, and a heart burning with something of God's own passion for the salvation of men.

If he does not keep his mind on the sovereign greatness of God, if he does not constantly recall with conviction that it is only from the Father and through the Son that all light, all truth and all strength come to us, that the slightest stirring of grace is a gift of divine generosity, the priest soon tends to take himself for an indispensable intermediary. All the disciples of the Lord are 'unprofitable servants', but those who are commissioned to show the world the gratuitous and sovereign nature of God's approach to men's souls must realize more than all others that they are unprofitable to God. Before God, all men are empty-handed; but the hands of the priest, through whom divine riches pass, have less right than any others ever to clutch these treasures in any way. All that they receive from God belongs to the Church of his Son Jesus Christ.

The priest in the Mass gives men the riches of God all present in the host, now become the body of Christ. In preparation for this he receives from men, to change into the body of Christ, the fruit of God's gifts to them forming the substance of their lives, as well as the charity that is in them. Between these two phases of the Mass, between the communion whereby he gives God to men and the offertory whereby he should give men to God, the life of the priest finds fulfilment. If he really has given Christ in the gospel and the sacraments, he cannot fail to take an interest in the effect produced by Christ in those who have received him. Being a witness with inside knowledge of the divine generosity at work, the priest must realize the passionate expectation of God, who gave up his Son so that men should love God as their Father. Enthusiasm and zeal in the apostolate are an integral part of the priestly vocation.

Of course they are not the monopoly of the priest. Every Christian living in the charity of Christ feels constrained to take seriously the words he prays: 'Hallowed be thy name, thy kingdom come!' The priest has no monopoly of the apostolic spirit and missionary zeal for the kingdom, any more than he can claim any superior type of holiness. That zeal is the common concern of the whole Church, priests and lay folk alike. In the case of the priest this concern normally takes on the form of his actual vocation and task in the Church: his job is to strive for the sacred and sacramental order, he naturally tries to convert the goodwill and generous efforts of people about him into action on the sacramental and ecclesiastical plane.

The ministry of the word and the sacramental ministry, these two functions are of the essence of the priesthood. But it does not follow that a priest can always exercise the two together or to the same extent. He can only distribute the sacraments to an established Christian community, and he may have to start by creating one. Before achieving this he will have to proclaim the gospel and it may be a long business. It may take many years, and a priest who seems to devote himself wholly to this approachwork cannot be accused of neglecting his mission. Proclaiming the gospel is not less priestly than baptizing or giving holy communion, and a priest doing that only would not be falling short of his task as a priest, unless he proclaimed the gospel with no consideration of baptism or sacraments, unless he preached a repentance that never led to Christ's forgiveness in the confessional, unless he preached a charity with no desire to feed on the eucharist and be gathered by the Church and transformed on the altar into the charity of Christ.

5. *Priest and layman*

The implications of the new covenant will help us also to form a right relationship between priest and layman. The priest is distinct from the layman, essentially and radically. To try to remove this distinction would distort his whole nature as a priest, as well as the gratuitousness of grace and the authority of Christ in what he ordained. But this difference does not necessarily mean the priest is 'out on his own'. It imposes on him a certain way of life affecting his behaviour, and it would be a strange thing if a priest seemed anxious to disguise his character, when it is his mission to appear and present himself in the name of Christ, as his spokesman and deputy. But it is clear also that this mission, far from inducing the priest to keep away from and ignore the layman, makes it his duty for him to keep in the closest contact with the layman.

The vocation of the priest is not to live in a 'sacred' world with only rare openings on to the 'profane' world where the layman moves and has his being, but to help the profane world itself to become consecrated. Though the profane and the sacred are different, they do not constitute two different worlds. The land of Israel was a holy land, because it was where the people lived the covenant of Yahweh in real life and where its deeds were transformed: sin became a profanation, fidelity to the law made life a consecrated thing. So too the Christian in the new covenant does not make two parts to his life, one sacred in which he comes to hear the gospel and receive the sacraments, the other profane where he has to adjust all he hears and does on the sacred plane down to the ordinary everyday level. If there are places and ceremonies, churches and sacraments, where God's sacred presence is intensified, it is to radiate this presence over the lives of Christians and make them holy. Everything a Christian does, every one of his decisions, should aim at being directly inspired by the gospel and animated by Christ's love at work in the sacraments. Thus his whole life will be a true sacrifice; consecrated by the hands of Christ and united to his sacrifice, his life is lived 'unto God', in unfailing thanksgiving rendered to the Father.

In the case of Israel, strictly speaking it was enough for them to observe the law of Yahweh to the letter, for their sacrifice to confer a sacred value on the life of the chosen people. But in the new covenant there is a much closer and more necessary connection between sacrifice, the law of charity and the Christian way of life. The law of charity as proclaimed in the gospel does not consist in a code of rules, but in a spirit constantly finding new modes of expression. There is no quick answer in the matter of charity, no rule of thumb can guarantee we are fulfilling its requirements; we must always be returning to the gospel and enquiring what it demands of us. This constant confrontation between the words of scripture and our fulfilment of it in charity supposes also a constant dialogue between priest and layman. It supposes that the priest is closely enough in touch with the layman to supply him, amid the complexity of everyday matters, with just the right note or interpretation he needs of the words of scripture. It supposes that the layman has the happy combination of responsibility and submission to enable him to be attentive to the word and law of God transmitted by the priest in the name of the Church, and then acting accordingly, to make his own responsible decisions.

This special relationship of priest and layman may take various forms. The priest may be a 'secular' priest, to use an expression that seems somewhat out of date and liable to be misunderstood. Such a priest embodies this relationship 'in the world', as we say. Living as a rule in a parish, he lives the same kind of life as his parishioners: in the country, it is affected by the seasons and the usual concerns of farming people; in the town it is the usual busy urban or suburban life of streets and households. Or the priest may be a 'religious' and live apart from the common life of men. Even in this case, cut off from the world and dedicated to a way of life that is impracticable for lay folk with family and social commitments, he is only cut off from them in outward appearance. As a religious he affirms, by his poverty, charity and obedience, the message of the kingdom of God that the layman has to observe amid preoccupations of money, family and social relations. By his vocation he lives the letter of the beatitudes, he is there to help his layman brother to live their spirit, the spirit of the gospel which is the only true spirit of Christianity. Whether secular or religious, whether closer to the normal life of lay people or more cut off from it, the priest is ever their companion on the way.

How this relationship should work out in practice, and how the priest is to make the layman aware of his presence, representing the authority of Christ in the gospel and his efficacious presence in the sacraments, belongs to the Church, the unerring confidant of Christ, to judge according to circumstances. But to judge from history, the forms this presence can take may be extremely varied and hardly any legitimate human activity is, by its nature, incompatible with the priesthood. In this domain, the golden rule of St Ignatius in the *Spiritual Exercises* seems to have its application: '*tantum quantum . . .*' 'Man has to use things as far as they help and abstain from them where they hinder his purpose' (God's glory). The more any form of life enables the priest to be with the layman in depth as regards developments that are really needed, the more this life enables him to feed the layman on the gospel and the sacraments, the more priestly his life is.

In truth, the more the priest and the layman live in Church

united in depth, the less their respective roles are likely to get mixed up. The phrase 'the priesthood of the laity' could be only a misleading slogan if it claimed for lay people powers that God, in his concern to show that they are beyond any ordinary human powers, has entrusted to priests alone. But it expresses a profound truth that is part of our faith, if it is understood in its right sense: all members of the Church are consecrated and all their actions should tend to become daily more consciously and wholly the actions of Christ in them, the unique action of Christ giving himself to men and dedicating himself to his Father. The more lay people live by this 'priestly' spirit, the more they deepen their need to live after the model of Christ in the presence of God, by his grace and his will and referring all glory to him; then the more they will be anxious to seek from priests the riches they can bring down from God, his gifts to feed and consecrate their souls. On his side, the more the priest grows in realization of his priestly mission, the more he deepens in himself the urge to transmit to the laity the purest spirit of the gospel, so as to feed and consecrate their charity, the more also will he realize that his mission as a priest requires him to live in the same spirit and to bear witness by his whole life to the charity of Christ our Lord, whom he holds each day in his hands. In this way he will be meeting the layman on his right ground; and in this way he will constantly find example and inspiration on seeing how lay people welcome the gospel and dedicate themselves to the charity of Christ.

XII

The Gospel and the Mass

SOME PEOPLE imagine that they have to make a choice between the living riches of the gospels and 'the frequentation of the sacraments'. In the gospel, hearing our Lord's demands and appeals to men, they feel 'this means them' and they recognize their shortcomings, but not without hope. They know they do not measure up to his words, but they find strength in his example. By contrast, sometimes, the sacraments of confession and communion, even Mass itself, seem devoid of meaning and leave them cold. They keep them up, to be faithful to the Church, but just the necessary minimum and as expeditiously as possible. Such people nowadays who claim, not without courage, to be followers of Christ, seeking loyally to live by the gospel and spread its light around them, would seem to share the same indifference for the sacraments and the same apathy as the most nominal 'practising' Catholics.

This lack of genuine interest in the sacraments no doubt betrays a weakness in the faith. But it can also result from too hasty and human a look at the gospel, too concerned to measure the practical or subjective impact of the text. The gospel does of course contain the sacraments too, in briefly indicated forms that may not strike us very much, but they are concentrated and rich in meaning. In the case of the eucharist, it apparently takes up little space in the gospels, just as even daily communion takes up little space in our day's work and may pass almost unnoticed. But the whole of the gospel is

170

really there in the eucharist, as also the whole of the life of Christians should find its source in the eucharist. We see this in the accounts of the last supper.

1. The longed-for paschal meal

The supper was not only the last meal our Lord had with his apostles, and the tone of gravity the gospel narratives take on here does not only come from the solemnity of the time at the imminent approach of the passion. The gospels stress the close connection between our Lord's last acts and decisions while still at liberty, and all his previous deeds, all his life so far. 'I have longed and longed to share this paschal meal with you before my passion.'[1] St John even more solemnly indicates the significance of this farewell meal: 'Before the paschal feast began, Jesus already knew that the time had come for his passage from this world to the Father. He still loved those who were his own, whom he was leaving in the world, and he would give them the uttermost proof of his love.'[2] Our Lord's words and St John's comment throw into relief the unique significance of this meal, both in relation to the passion that was to follow and the whole previous life of Christ. The meal was a fulfilment and also a commitment: long in advance our Lord's heart was filled with desire for it, as he had been impatient for the accomplishment of his 'baptism'.[3]

The gospels do not usually tell us much of the intimate thoughts of Jesus, and they are mostly respectfully silent on the secret communing of the Son with the Father in the Holy Spirit, but they do record a few confidences of this kind whose converging value is precious. Knowing what is in store for him (though he had no need, for his knowledge to match his task, to see the events of his life and death unfolded for him as in a preview of a film), Jesus knew he was approaching a fearful crisis: a charge, laid upon him by God, a 'must' that he had to go through at all costs, would make him fall into the hands of his enemies and lead to a most cruel death. The gospels are full of allusions to this, more frequent as the passion approaches, and renewed even after it when the resurrection

[1] Luke 22:15   [2] John 13:1   [3] Luke 12:50

had come to explain everything: 'It was necessary that Christ should suffer.'[4] Clearly such expressions as 'everything . . . must be fulfilled', were our Lord's way of expressing a thought that was constantly in his mind and on his lips. But this kind of expression, though concerned with our Lord's own person, is part of his teaching and retains an accent of objectivity. These imperatives are spoken of in the third person, as concerning the Christ and the Son of man, meaning of course himself; but in taking on that character he was to play a part and play it in a particular way, carrying out someone else's wishes and intentions that simply must be executed, being those of God. In view of this, the gospel imperatives are always for our Lord categorical, providing a final explanation of his actions and accounting for the extraordinary life he led. Still, they do not express all that goes on in his heart, they are in a sense intended mainly for the benefit of others; they do not reveal our Lord's personal reaction, the echo in his heart of this divine imperative. Some of our Lord's more intimate sayings allow us to catch a glimpse of more secret depths in him.

Sometimes we hear our Lord no longer speaking of himself in the third person, stating his mission as the Son of man, but more freely, in the first person, simply opening his heart and expressing his own response to the divine law governing his life. Then precious words come from his lips, recorded by the evangelists: 'The fire I have come to cast . . . the chalice I have to drink . . . the baptism wherewith I am to be baptised. . . .' There is still the same imperative note, the plan God has drawn for the life of his Son, but here the Son expresses what the plan means to him and how he lives it interiorly. It is a fire consuming him, a baptism surging over him, a chalice he must drink. These are also the words St Luke puts on our Lord's lips at the opening of the supper, loaded with the same obligation, now even more imminent; they express his desire for this farewell meal as a prelude to his passion. Fire, baptism, chalice, meal—it is significant that these words, expressing our Lord's most intimate feelings, his most heartfelt sentiments about the mission planned for him,

[4] Luke 24:27; cf. v. 7 and v. 44.

are precisely the words describing his sacraments, baptism, confirmation, eucharist. This is no coincidence, still less a literary device to match the terminology of the sacraments with that of our Lord. It is the natural outcome of the fact that the sacraments have their origin in the most intimate depths of our Lord's heart: not just in the actions of Christ, last supper, agony and passion, but in the personal value these actions had for him, both in suffering and in fulfilment of his hopes. In the moments where we do have an insight into his mind, it seems absorbed by the phases of his action which are to give rise to this sacrament.

2. *The gift of the Lord*

In the light of these brief but illuminating flashes in the gospel record it is easier to grasp just what happened at the last supper. Our Lord had awaited it long and eagerly, and in it he enshrined his whole life and death. The bread he picked up from the table and shared with the apostles, he made into his body that was to be given up and done to death. In choosing bread for this it was not just a demonstration of power or a matter of convenience, it had to be thus. Ever since he came into this world his body had been our food; the body he now gave them to eat, he had put it at their disposal every day he spent with them. His work, his suffering, his strength and all the resources of his mind and heart, he had wholly put at men's disposal. Not only did he dedicate his whole life to them, but he expressed this dedication in his way of life: nowhere to lay his head, no shelter, no means of avoiding harassing and tiresome people, a willing prey to all forms of distress, the first to suffer from all the forms of suffering that found their way to him.

Out of this dedicated life our Lord has made a way of nourishing us, a gift that we can really and truly take into ourselves. There are people, generous in their way and anxious to dedicate themselves to the service of others, who accept their services and even take them for granted, but no one is notably better for having known them. Such people remain, you might say, enclosed in their own zeal and they leave other people enclosed in their troubles. There is no real contact or communing with them. But in the case of our Lord, he does communicate himself and his treasures are life to his followers: a spring of living water welling up to eternal life.[5] His example is winning and his presence makes an immediate impact, his words strike deep, his truth carries conviction, his pardon imparts new heart; what he gives is himself, and he enables us to receive him. That our bread and wine should become his body and blood, might conceivably have just meant the natural marvel of all food, the living assimilation of all in nature, miraculously gathered in an expressive symbol. But because our Lord, out of the bread and wine he made into himself, always made the material of a life wholly lived for us, the body he gave us at the supper is really our living bread and the blood he gave us to drink in the chalice is the spring of everlasting life for us.

Thus the eucharist is not only the crowning of the Lord's work and the uttermost proof of his love; it is the very substance of his being and his life and death. The reason why he had 'longed and longed for this meal' was because he was able thereby to accomplish in its entirety and in one single act all that he had come on earth to do: to give himself to us as the food of our souls, to make himself our life.

3. The sacramental gift

This great act fulfilling our Lord's desire and containing within it the whole of his life was in itself something so simple as to be almost insignificant. What our Lord had been doing ever since he came among us, but only in a succession of partial actions incomplete in themselves as all our human actions are, on the evening of the last supper he did in an absolute and irrevocable way. He was no longer giving himself in speech, in looks, in deeds of power and kindness; he was no longer giving his daily solicitude, his ever-alert attentiveness to people, his unwearying patience. In one single definitive act he released all his treasures, made himself wholly present and spent the whole of his being. To achieve this giving,

[5] John 4:14

involving all his love, our Lord just said a few words: 'This is my body; this is my blood, shed for you. . . .' We have here not just simplicity of expression, which alone can serve in moments of great emotion: we have a radical exclusion of all emotion or explanation. There was no question of making himself understood, or appealing to the hearts of his hearers; it only needed an act to be performed, words to be pronounced, a rite to be executed, and all was complete. At the moment our Lord pronounced the words that he had been looking forward to all his life, there is no allusion to his compassion for the crowds, his tender solicitude for the suffering and for children, his passionate concern for the honour of the Father, his delicacy and respect in dealing with sinners, his ardent appeals to all men—all these features so characteristic of our Lord seem now to escape notice.

This is partly because it is of the very nature of a rite to be unemotional. In all religion, more or less purely as it is more genuine, ritual action tends to be stripped of all that emotion or intelligence might add to the essential religious ceremony. As man penetrates in ritual into the sacred sphere, he feels he must leave behind him on the threshold his ordinary reactions, and that he cannot hope to reach God by arousing his own powers of mind and heart. A rite owes its efficacy not to being invented by man, but to its relation to some divine intervention. This divine intervention or revelation, which so many religions have sought in vain in so many forms, the religion of Israel could rightly claim, basing it on un-doubted experience of unique effectiveness. The rites of the Jewish people were valid in that they perpetuated the memory of the covenant with the true God and rendered present to the people God's word and his promises. At the supper Jesus adopted the most solemn of these rites, those of the Pasch and of Sinai. His last meal was a paschal meal,[6] and the blood he gave his apostles was the blood of the new covenant.[7] So it is not surprising that, being the celebrant, Jesus kept to the essential form and limited himself strictly to stating the divine fact produced by his words, his body and blood given in sacrifice and made food and drink. In two sentences our Lord

[6] Luke 22:15   [7] Luke 22:20

gave us, living and substantial, the final fulfilment of all he
ever said, the power behind all his miracles, all the unfathomable riches of the incarnate Word.

The rite of the last supper had features of its own of even
greater simplicity. Its way of recalling the rites of the Pasch
and the covenant bring out its originality. The paschal meal
celebrated by Jewish families involved some solemnity intended to impress on their minds the memory of the great
events by which God had liberated his people. Readings,
chants and ritual customs, all contributed to put the partici-
pants into an atmosphere of expectation, and to arouse the
sacred memories handed down by their fathers. As for the
rites recalling the covenant, the inspiring scenes recorded
in Exodus, Deuteronomy and Josue bear witness that Israel
did not separate, in its memory or in its rites, the conclusion of the covenant from the sacred setting of Sinai or of
Shechem.[8]

The institution of the eucharist was in simpler form; the
words were effective in themselves, they were enough to
constitute the new covenant and make it valid in all parts of
the world for all time. True, they would not have had this
effect apart from the sacrifice that followed them: Jesus really
and truly gave his body, so he would have to give himself up
to the hands of Judas and shed every drop of his blood: his
words could not fail to take effect. The supper is inseparable
from the cross, the moment the one proclaimed the other; the
supper stated what happened on the cross, stated it in advance,
with the sovereign efficacy of divine words; if he had not
intended the cross, Jesus would not have pronounced the
words at the supper. When the Church, continuing to offer to
God the one true sacrifice the world has produced, the
sacrifice on the cross, celebrates Mass day by day, she does not
portray the scene of the crucifixion in her ritual, but the
scene of the last supper, and this has a message for us. If one
were to think in terms of the Jewish rites of the Pasch and the
covenant, one could imagine the Mass so constructed as to
recall the sacrifice it is intended to render present, and one
would expect to see the accounts of the passion featured

[8] Cf. Jos. 24

prominently in every Mass. But the ordinary of the Mass contains only brief allusions to the passion, and the heart of the Mass consists of the account of the supper and the pronouncing of the words of consecration. It could almost seem that the passion is set aside in the prayers of the Mass to leave pride of place to the supper. Are we to say there is not much left of the passion if it is not definitely recalled and remembered in detail? With the passion seemingly emptied of its contents, how can the Mass claim to represent it in any way?

The answer is not difficult: the secret is in the real presence of Christ in the Mass, this presence being the presence of the crucified who consummated his sacrifice by undergoing death and triumphing over it by his resurrection. No gospel narrative, no expression of remembrance or emotion can add any significance to the sheer fact of this presence. The whole passion is in that presence, no longer in the past events that went to form it, but in their substance as experienced by our Lord, in the love they called for, in what they made him for all eternity, a man having lived and suffered and experienced death as the Son of God, worthily in sight of his Father.

For the first time in human history, ritual fully achieves its purpose: to render present the event it symbolizes. But it only does so by stripping itself of the forms it had hitherto assumed and needed to recall the past event and create a religious setting. The words of consecration at Mass have their effect, not for any power of appealing to the imagination or by virtue of any ritualistic setting, but by the decision of our Lord consummated by his death and ratified by his resurrection. Apart from any outward ceremony, the Church can, in exceptional circumstances such as a concentration camp, authorize a priest just to pronounce the words of the last supper over bread and wine and so offer the sacrifice of the Mass. True, it still remains a rite, the only way for human beings to render present a divine intervention. Of this human thing, called rite, Christ has made his sacrament. The simplifying effect we observed in human rites reaches its maximum simplification in the Christian sacrament.

4. The mystery of faith

This helps us to understand how, on the one hand, our Lord's life and passion are made present in the Mass, with all the richness of the gospel, and yet, on the other hand, all these wonderful details seem to disappear in the Mass. They do disappear, in one sense, it is true. They disappear from memory and imagination, they disappear under the aspect of visible events that could be described in their temporal and passing context, they disappear to make way for the everlasting, invisible and spiritual reality of Christ risen from the dead offering to the Father the sacrifice he consummated in the days of his mortal flesh. The gospel remains indispensable, of course, revealing God to us, and we cannot realize what Christ is, what he does and wants us to do, without being ever attentive to his words and his life. So it is that Mass begins with readings culminating in the gospel. But once our memory is thus refreshed, the understanding of the mystery of Christ set before us once again, then memory, emotion and understanding must yield pride of place to faith. In the same way, after our Lord had lived with the disciples long enough for their faith to be duly formed, he left them because 'it was better for them',[9] so that being filled with the Holy Spirit, they should learn to recognize in their Master the fullness of the Spirit, the communication of the Father to the Son. It was not to make them forget anything of what they had learned from him during his mortal life, far from it, but so that they should find him where he is, at the right hand of the Father, the head of redeemed humanity.

In like manner the Mass forces us to go right to the heart of our faith. In it we have Christ our Lord living, the fullness of the godhead, for us to receive, and to make us capable of receiving this gift the Mass demands the total and absolute allegiance, that of faith. There is faith already in our allegiance to the gospel message, but in this basic acceptance of Christ there are bound to be all sorts of personal factors, our own experience, our 'personal equation'. This is perfectly normal: given that the gospel presents the life of a human

[9] John 16:7

being, the words and scenes are bound to have overtones that appeal to mind and heart. This is the very meaning of the incarnation, to present God to us in a form we can appreciate by our senses, so as to make us love the invisible reality dwelling in him, as the Christmas Preface says: *'ut dum visibiliter Deum cognoscimus, per hunc in invisibilium amorem rapiamur'*.

But the visible really must lead us on to the invisible reality; we always tend to pick on the points in the gospel that favour our ideas and wishes, twisting our Lord's miracles and sayings to suit us (as we saw in the multiplication of the loaves), confusing the beatitudes with preconceived notions, and identifying our adversaries with the pharisees. There is a permanent temptation for people to distort the gospel to favour their own politics, or their way of thinking or feeling about things. Like the disciples at Capharnum, many who follow Jesus willingly to hear him speak of the kingdom and manifest his power, part company with him when he shows up the uncertain nature of their allegiance: 'You are looking for me . . . because you were fed with the loaves and had your fill.'[10] It is a stern reproach and may seem hard on people who had been so anxious to hear him that they forgot to eat, but their illusion is too dangerous to let off lightly and our Lord clearly condemned this wrong idea of his gospel message.

Clearing up this point after the multiplication of the loaves, to put his disciples right and restore them to genuine faith, our Lord confronted them with the mystery in its most direct form, that of the eucharist. In order to enter into the gospel and 'work in God's service', what was needed was 'to believe in the man whom he has sent',[11] the acid test of faith. Taking this to the limit, the time when faith is crystallized in the purest form, with no human admixture, is when faith is prepared to eat the Lord's flesh and drink his blood,[12] acknowledging all the living riches of the Word incarnate under the inert appearances of bread and wine. The gospel reaches fulfilment in the Mass, and that is what our Lord was leading the disciples to, knowing that many would fall by the wayside, but also know-

[10] John 6:26   [11] John 6:28–29   [12] John 6:54

ing that in the Mass their faith would find all the food it needed for its perfection: 'You can have no life in yourselves, unless you eat the flesh of the Son of man, and drink his blood';[13] for otherwise you will not know what it means to believe in me. To receive our Lord in the eucharist, accepting the reality of the Mass in its bare essentials as a simple statement of what is happening, that is really to accept the full implications of the gospel and to receive in its fullness what it brings with it, faith. In the Mass our Lord asks exactly the same faith as he was asking for on every page of the gospel: if he asks for it here in the most complete form, it is because he also is giving himself wholly and entirely.

As the life of Christ led up to the last supper, as his gospel led up to the eucharist, as the allegiance he demanded led up to the faith of the Church at Mass, so in its turn the eucharist imparts his vital strength and becomes the Christian's daily food, the means of living by the gospel. In the eucharist Christ gives us all his gospel message, living and fulfilled in him, so that the gospel message may fill our lives. It would be falling short of the gospel to leave it where it leads to the holy eucharist; but it is underestimating the eucharist to make it an end in itself just a privileged communing of the soul with the Lord, or even a massive gathering of Christians in unity of purpose. The Mass is all these things for each and every one of God's children gathered about his table. Because it is a communing, a meal, a unity of Christians, the Mass is already initiating us into life everlasting; it does indeed put us in communion also 'with those who have gone before us, sealed with the sign of faith' and all the saints in heaven. But this communing is achieved in faith and it remains beyond our present sight and grasp. Until the day when the Lord shall come to make all who are his sit down at his table, the Mass will go on making us live in the service of his kingdom. Neither Mass nor communion are strictly speaking the final purpose of the Christian life: this can be nothing less than the coming of God's kingdom, the perfect accomplishment of his will, on earth as in heaven. On earth, it means fidelity to the whole of the gospel message; in heaven it means the vision of God face

[13] John 6:54

to face that is to absorb and unfold the communing hitherto experienced in faith alone.

Our Lord, in one single action, at the last supper, gathered up the whole of his gospel and gave himself up for our salvation and the honour of his Father; we Christians must so feed on his strength and love in the eucharist that all our actions, day by day, may become the expression of the gospel in our lives.

XIII

'Mary kept all these words'

THE PASSION of our Lord was the time for the fulfilment of God's designs, for the mystery on which he had been working since the dawn of this world to yield up its secret. The last moments of a man's life, the last few agonizing words, often throw a flood of light on all he has done and reveal the secret of his soul. In our Lord's last words and death the Church is all attention to gather the final secret God reveals in his Son, a secret governing all he did and explaining so much that is puzzling to us.

1. The Church in the person of Mary

At this last hour the Church is there, first and foremost, in the person of our Lady. St John's gospel clearly stresses that the hour when all was consummated for Jesus revealed as it were a new dimension and a new figure in his mother. The words Jesus addressed to her: 'Behold thy son', cannot be considered merely as concerned to settle his mother's future now she was left on her own. It does include this concern, for Mary's future was involved, but Mary's future now is the fate of the whole Church. Our Lord's desire to provide for his mother has the wider implication of all the other aspects of his death: the royal inscription above his head on the cross, the sharing of his garments, the cry 'I thirst', the piercing of his side. In all these details in fulfilment of prophecies, it is made manifest that Jesus is the long-awaited Messiah and his death is the salvation of the world. The words concerning our Lady cannot be an exception to this. They have the brevity and power of creative words, achieving what they express. What they achieve is to create a new bond between our Lady and St John. It is conceivable that Jesus might confide his mother to his most faithful friend, though one would expect Mary, when she lost her son, to turn to her own relations to take care of her. But John still had his own mother and so, in taking Mary to be his mother, it must mean that the death of Jesus set up a new relationship between him and Mary, more deep than flesh and blood. John was the first to be aware of this, because he alone of the apostles was there at Calvary. But his whole version of the incident shows that he was conscious of being a witness of events in which we are all involved. The whole Church was there present.

The Church was there primarily in the person of Mary: in her alone the Church grasped what was happening and gave it the allegiance of absolute faith. The other people there, Nicodemus, the Roman officer, Mary Magdalen, even John himself, though certainly struck by the extraordinary atmosphere of this scene, were far from grasping its full meaning. Swept along by events and carried away by forces they could do nothing about, passive witnesses of a conflict going on that did not make sense for them, they had to wait for the resurrection and Pentecost for it all to come clear. Mary alone was in full possession of the Holy Spirit and attuned to the stirrings of his grace. Long since she had become accustomed to keep in her heart and humbly ponder over all the words of Jesus, to be the food of her soul and to guide her way, thus anticipating and indicating the attitude of the Church down the centuries, living and going forward with eyes fixed on our Lord and his message. So, at the hour when God was revealing to the world the last word on his work of salvation, the ultimate meaning of Christ's coming and his person, his deepest secret, Mary was there to hear this secret, to gather it from his lips and impart it to the whole Church.

For us in our turn to be faithful to the instinct of our Lady, and docile to the Spirit guiding her, the best means is not to force one's heart and try to imagine the reflections and

G

prayers of our Lady. Such attempts are bound to be disappointed. The way to join in our Lady's meditation is to join
her as she embodies the Church, listen to the words within us
as she did, and let ourselves be penetrated by their meaning
as she was. Her whole instinct was to open her heart without
reserve to these words, making them the very law of her being.
Never taken up with concerns of her own, she sought only to
listen to God. We must listen to God with her, and treasure
the few words Jesus spoke with difficulty in the course of his
death agony. What light they throw, on the evening of Good
Friday, upon the words that our Lady had been keeping in
her heart and pondering, all those years, never exhausting
their full riches!

2. 'All is consummated'

'Jesus of Nazareth, King of the Jews', said the proclamation
over the cross of Jesus to all that passed by. It was put up by
Pilate, but Pilate did not invent it. It was dictated to him in
spite of themselves by the chief priests, and solemnly confirmed
by Jesus, saying, 'I am a king.' Jesus has not accepted this title
for long, less than a week, since his triumphal entry into
Jerusalem; to be exact it is since the leaders of his people
rejected him and decided he must die. This title which he had
formerly shunned, amid the enthusiasm of the multiplication
of the loaves, this title that he had never before wanted to
assume, he does accept and claim it now that all ambiguity
is gone, when no one can expect to see him set up his kingdom
in this world. And it is true that he is a king from this hour
onwards, reigning over the repentant thief and the Roman
centurion, over the onlookers beating their breasts. So it was
true, as the angel announced to Mary: 'He shall be great, and
men shall know him for the Son of the most high; the Lord
God will give him the throne of his father David, and he shall
reign over the house of Jacob eternally.'[1] Here is the son of
David ruling his people, and here is the throne God has set up
for him: in truth God's words are fulfilled, but in what a
strange way!

'Did you not know I must be about my Father's business?'[2]

[1] Luke 1:32   [2] Luke 2:49

At the age of twelve Jesus had reminded his mother of this
lesson. Assuredly she knew that her Son must be about his
heavenly Father's business, but why did it need saying so
firmly? She had long wondered, turning over in her mind this
answer she had never quite understood or felt happy about. At
the foot of the cross Mary understood it all: this is what was
meant by his Father's business, this fearful business wherein
she could take no part! No doubt she now relived the suffering
of former years, but at a depth she had never before realized:
the anguish of feeling an inexorable decree weighing down
upon the head of Jesus and of being able to do nothing to
relieve it, the feeling of being defenceless against this awful
horror. But there is a difference now; it does not lighten her
grief, but it enables her to bear it unbowed, not letting any of
it escape. In the past, so as to devote himself to his Father's
business, Jesus had withdrawn from her, keeping his secret for
himself. Now that he is wholly immersed in this business, he
allows her to join him in it. She keeps her gaze upon him,
contemplating him for three long hours, entering with him
into this fearful mystery of horror and love, wherein he still
finds his Father.

'What have you to do with me? My hour has not yet come.'[3]
This is another of the mysterious sayings of Jesus that Mary
kept pondering on, knowing that they would reveal the will
of God to her one day, when she understood. This day had
come: his hour had come now, the hour when she finds him
again, but as in the past, seemingly separated from her. There
is only a foot or so between them, but it seems to form a
chasm. He is nailed to his death on the cross, and she can do
nothing for him. Like every other man, like children dying
before their mother's eyes, he has to die alone.

But Mary has now reached the heart of the mystery of the
cross, because she follows exactly the plan of the redemption,
the sharpest sword of suffering is also the source of her joy.
This is the hour when, for her as for Jesus, all the words of
God, all the 'great things' she sang of in the 'Magnificat', find
their fulfilment. The hour when the sword prophesied by
Simeon strikes is also the hour when the angel's message is

[3] John 2:3

fully accomplished: 'Rejoice, thou who are full of grace!' Joy, which we always imagine as an escape from sorrow, as a compensation for grief, becomes in Mary the suffering itself transformed by God, and this new aspect of her sorrow takes its rise at the foot of the cross.

What was there between herself and him? Now only the most holy and sweet will of the Father came between them. What separated Mary from her Son was not the guards nor any decree of fate : beyond the cruelty of man and the savagery of sin venting its fury on Jesus, Mary clung to the will of the Father that kept her separated from suffering as he did. Between herself and him, she saw only this divine will: may it alone be done and not hers! In this she was now like her Son. He was not really dying alone, he was never alone, as he was at all times 'about his Father's business' and present to him. So also Mary, though separated from him by the will of the Father, found herself in this hour enfolded in the same embrace wherewith the Father welcomed and gathered to himself his beloved Son.

'Woman, behold thy son.' This meant the same combination of boundless suffering and purest joy, at one and the same moment the most terrible blow to a mother's love and the blossoming in her heart of a new motherhood as vast as the world. It was the farewell of death, an end to the deepest bonds of human love, the feeling of absolute loneliness. What could John and all the others do for her now? Would it not be better to leave her alone? At this hour when everything should conspire to leave Mary alone with her sorrow, the unimaginable happens: she is conscious of really becoming the mother of John and the infant Church. This is the Father's doing, it is the hour he has chosen. God, from whom all fatherhood comes, who would not suffer Abraham to lay a hand on his son, God had chosen this hour to deliver up his only Son into the hands of sinners, to abandon his beloved Son to all the inventions of their hate and to all the cruelty and baseness of sin. So much did he love the world. Mary, with her gaze fixed upon Jesus, who is dying in order to show what the love of the Father means, is conscious of being introduced into this mystery of fatherly love at a level she had never experienced before. In union now with the Father, she offers her Son and delivers him up for the world: 'God so loved the world', and we can now add: 'Mary so loved the world.'

'Woman, behold thy son.' This word that any mother might hate to hear, finds Mary more than willing to accept with all her heart and readiness to respond. Since she is in a position to sacrifice Jesus to save John, John must no longer be a stranger; no one must ever be a stranger to her, as she has sacrificed all she loved most for them. John is hers now, and so are all men. This is the hour when the Father opens his glory for Jesus to enter and gives him the right to spread it over all humanity, now redeemed. He establishes him as Lord of all creation, with a wonderful sovereignty of love surpassing all other human influence, putting him in direct contact with the personal mystery of every man, and enabling him to unite all his fellow men in his love, making them one body with himself. This is the hour when Mary receives her unique place in this Mystical Body, now coming into the world. At this hour the word spoken by Jesus has its effect: Mary discovers that she clings to John as her own son, now she must love Jesus in the hearts of his brethren.

A whole series of memories faithfully kept and pondered in her heart arise afresh and take on new meaning. His birth at Bethlehem, as it were on the wayside far from home, in the midst of strangers. From then on her home had been open to all in need, strangers and poor. God had kept her intimate union with Jesus free from all exclusiveness or human barriers. He was preparing her for this hour, making her ready to share this wonderful intimate union with all men, welcoming them all as brothers of her Son, as her own children. From Good Friday onwards she has no home; she will live with others. But the Father's arms, as they gather up his dying Son, enfold her as well and bring her into the home where all humanity finds rest, the Church. From that day onwards, Mary's home is the Church of Christ.

3. The mother present in the Church

From then onwards our Lady's presence was felt throughout the Church, enabling the Church to possess, from the very

beginning, the fullness of faith and love. Our Lady is so closely
identified with the Church that her presence on Calvary and
her action in the Church can only be fully understood in
relation to the Church's central mystery, the eucharistic sacrifice. Our Lady led the way for the Church in understanding
and joining in the action involving the whole life of the
Church, offering her son for the salvation of the world. In her,
the sacrifice of Christ, once accomplished, becomes the sacrifice
of the Church. In her the Church, as it offers to the Father the
sacrifice of the Son, can offer it as the Church's sacrifice, the
gift to God of all she possesses. What our Lady offered was not
her own body and blood, but the body and blood that meant so
much more to her, and this meant offering her whole self.
This absolute self-sacrificing love of hers spreads to the whole
Church. Plunged in the depth of suffering, like her Son, she
was sensitive to the response aroused by him: the prayer of the
repentant thief, the fidelity of John, the devotion of Mary
Magdalen, the contrition of the onlookers. She gathers up these
responses of repentant or faithful love and links them with her
own oblation. With her, the Church now takes part in the
mystery of the cross, entering into the suffering of her Lord,
linking to it the tears of her sinful children and the blood of her
martyrs.

Offertory leads to communion. God only calls for our blood
or our tears to transform them into joy with him. Of the
mystery accomplished on Calvary, in her as in the Church, our
Lady, who had borne such a crushing burden of grief, must
certainly have experienced the divine weight of joy and glory
at the resurrection. But the gospels tell us nothing of her
experience of Jesus in his glory, perhaps as being too intimate
and wonderful to be related. Where imagination fails us, the
answer is to contemplate the sole glimpse of our Lady after
the resurrection recorded in scripture, the last mention of her
on earth: at prayer in the midst of the disciples reunited in the
joy of seeing the risen Lord and in the expectation of the
coming of the Holy Spirit.

What can our Lady's prayer have been? We need not rely
on imagination; faith is enough to guide us. As on Calvary, her
prayer is none other than that of the Church: joining in the

sacrifice of Christ, offering it to the Father in thanksgiving and finding in it the food of her soul. In the past, before the Church came into being, Mary treasured the words of Jesus as the guide and nourishment of her life. Then the hour came when she had to sacrifice all she had, with the death of her only Son, and when she received back from God this same Son transfigured in glory. Since that day all had become clear for her, all was light. Once she had seen the fulfilment of all those words, she no longer needed to puzzle out their meaning. Waiting for the second coming of her Son, to take her up into his glory, as the Church will go on doing 'until he comes', our Lady found her nourishment in the eucharist where she also found, ever living and present and invulnerable to the passing years, that same mystery that she shared on Good Friday and on Easter Day and all the days of her life.

About her, the Church, for whose benefit she lived on, also possessed, in the eucharist, the fullness of the mysteries of Christ and the message of all his words, but the Church had not yet been able to grasp these riches. The apostles and disciples gathered around our Lady had heard Jesus speak, but they had been far from understanding all he had to each them. They still had a long way to go. It would now be necessary for them, in the light of the Holy Spirit and the apostolic strengthening he would bring them, to grow in realization of all they had seen and heard. It would also be necessary for the Church, down the centuries, to pursue the example of attentiveness and submission to God's word that Mary had lived from the annunciation to the resurrection. Our Lady was there present at the earliest beginnings of the Church's effort to learn. Scarcely had the Church heard the parting words of Jesus, when Mary was in prayer in their midst teaching the Church to 'keep all these words in her heart'.

XIV

The Gift of the Spirit

THE SUPREME GIFT the Father makes to his children is the gift of the Holy Spirit: *'Altissimi donum Dei'*. True, God begins by giving us the Son, and in him giving us his beloved and only-begotten Son he has given us 'all things with him'.[1] But God only entirely gives us his Son by giving us the Holy Spirit in whom Father and Son meet and express their union. Christ is for us, but above all it is true that 'we are for Christ'[2] and 'we belong to Christ',[3] and also that to belong to Christ we must have received his Spirit: 'A man cannot belong to Christ unless he has the Spirit of Christ.'[4] 'The gift which was promised by my Father',[5] 'the fulfilment of the Father's promise',[6] the assurance of being his children and his heirs,[7] all that is none other than the Holy Spirit.

This gift of the Holy Spirit was made to us on the cross. Until Christ had been publicly 'lifted up' for the world to see, until he had finally revealed the secret of his life and death showing how he loved the Father, 'the Spirit had not yet been given to me'.[8] When the soldier had pierced the side of Jesus with the lance, and when, from his body that had shed all its blood for us, the last drops of blood and water flowed out,[9] then the Church was born 'of water and the Holy Spirit', of the water of baptism and of the Spirit of God.

[1] Rom. 8:32
[2] 1 Cor. 3:23
[3] 2 Cor. 10:7
[4] Rom. 8:9
[5] Luke 24:49
[6] Acts 1:4
[7] Rom. 8:16
[8] John 7:39
[9] John 19:34

1. The baptism of the cross

Though Christian baptism has its prototype in the baptism of Jesus by John the Baptist, and though it puts us in a similar position in the sight of God and the world to that of Jesus at the Jordan and in the wilderness, yet it does not exactly derive from this episode, but rather from the mystery of our redemption, from the death and resurrection of our Lord. 'By baptism, we have been taken up into his death . . . we have been buried with him, died like him, that so, just as Christ was raised up by his Father's power from the dead, we too might live and move in a new kind of existence.'[10] Our Lord himself, when he spoke of his baptism, did not refer to the initial episode at the Jordan, but to the final episode at Calvary: 'Have you strength to drink of the cup I am to drink of, to be baptized with the baptism I am to be baptized with?'[11] was his question to the sons of Zebedee soliciting places of honour in his kingdom. 'I came to cast fire upon the earth; and would that it were already kindled! I have a baptism to be baptized with; and how I am constrained until it is accomplished!'[12] These are precious clues to our Lord's feelings: it is almost as though he could bear this heavy secret no longer and lets it slip out. It is a little disturbing to hear this: in our Lord's anxiety, what has become of the luminous vision at the Jordan, and the calm assurance with which he then reduced the tempter to silence? Has the voice from heaven become silent, and is the Spirit no longer with him, bringing the Son the evidence of the Father's joy and affection?

In these glimpses we see the sombre glow of the agony and Calvary, but it is the glow of divine glory. The baptism towards which our Lord was advancing, and which carried with it this charge laid upon him, is not the baptism given him by John. It is the baptism of Jesus, that John could only foretell, the baptism Jesus would give because only he could take it. The scene at the Jordan remains prophetic: John baptizes Jesus in the water and forthwith God reveals himself over the head of Jesus; but it is not what John does that calls forth the divine manifestation, and this manifestation is not strictly a

[10] Rom. 6:3-4   [11] Mark 10:38   [12] Luke 12:49-50

baptism. It is a divine briefing, revealing what Jesus is and
what he is to do: he is the beloved Son of God, and he is to
offer the Father the sacrifice he calls for, which will be his
joy; the Son possesses the Spirit in all his fullness and he is
setting out to accomplish the task given him by his Father.

This divine briefing is executed in the passion. This time it
really is a baptism, a baptism from God. Jesus is now not just
mingling with the crowd of sinners; he is publicly and
solemnly declared a blasphemer and he dies as a criminal—
because of men's sin, of course, but basically by the premedi-
tated plan of God determining to give up his own Son, to
abandon him to the mercy of sinners, to let sin unleash all its
resources upon him, to make him bear the sins of the world.
Indeed a horrible and merciless baptism, but ultimately from
God: God himself plunges his Son into these terrible depths,
and the agony beginning at Gethsemani is truly an encounter
between Jesus and the Father.

Like the baptism in the Jordan, the baptism in the passion
is a revelation of the Trinity, in a way the supreme revelation
of it. Because the trial is carried to its uttermost extent, because
the prince of darkness is allowed to display all his power, the
interplay of the three divine Persons can be seen at work in
the fullest sense. At this hour Jesus drains the cup his Father
holds out to him, and in this terrible draught he finds the
strength to undergo his torture to the bitter end and to die in
full possession of his freedom. At this hour, as on the pinnacle
of the temple, Satan offers him a way of putting an end to his
tortures and turning the people in his favour: 'Come down
from that cross, if thou art the Son of God!'[13] At this hour,
'knowing well that the Father had left everything in his
hands',[14] Jesus breathes his last; and over his head a title
mocks his royal power, for having refused to hold it from
anyone but the Father. The force that holds Christ fastened to
his cross is not just the nails, it is the voice of the Father in his
heart. This voice that seems so fearful and cruel, and now so
distant, our Lord could still hear repeating to him: 'Thou art
my beloved Son.' If the Father could call for this martyrdom
from his Son, if he could expect human flesh to undergo such

[13] Matt. 27:40   [14] John 13:3

torture and a human heart to experience such agony, it was
because the Spirit was upon him. The Spirit that drove Jesus
to his encounter with the tempter led him to this hour. The
Spirit that enabled Jesus to speak with divine authority and
gave him power over all forms of evil; the Spirit that was
always leading him along his way and unfolding his destiny,
now rested upon the motionless, crucified, silent Christ, wholly
defenceless, in order to consecrate his sacrifice, transforming
his suffering into obedience, his helplessness into allegiance,
his horror for sin into pardon and love, so that he was in deed
and in truth 'the joy of His Father'.

When 'all is consummated' and the great waters of suffering
and anguish finally close over the head of Christ, his baptism
also is complete and God's revelation likewise: with a great
cry, Jesus yields up his soul into the hands of the Father.
Having loved him to the uttermost, he shows us what it is to
be the Son, and of such a Father, to involve such sacrifice; and
as he gives all down to his last breath to his Father, he shows
us what the Spirit of God can achieve in human flesh. By the
same token, the baptism of Jesus becomes ours. Having loved
his own to the uttermost, having borne the shame and horror
of all sin, giving his life for his enemies, he carries all humanity
with him in his death and presents it to his Father. Out of the
grain of wheat buried in the ground a new world comes forth;
the Church is born. Out of the wounded side the soldier's lance
brings forth, with the last drops of his blood, the water wherein
John, as the first witness of Christian baptism, recognizes the
gift of the Spirit.

2. *Pentecost*

'Exalted at God's right hand, he has claimed from his Father
his promise to bestow the Holy Spirit, and he has poured out
that Spirit. . . .'[15]

Pentecost is the time when the risen Christ, 'who has become
a life-giving spirit',[16] bestowed upon the Church the gift of
the Spirit to be its very life. We are tempted to concentrate on
the outward manifestations of the outpouring of the Holy
Spirit on Whitsunday, the mighty wind, the tongues of flame,

[15] Acts 2:33   [16] 1 Cor. 15:45

the gift of tongues and miraculous healing. But in all the
sermons in the early chapters of the Acts, St Peter constantly
strives to lead his hearers beyond these things, which were still
only signs. What they saw seemed very wonderful, but it was
only the outer casing of the reality. The decisive event was an
interior one, the Holy Spirit had taken possession of the
disciples' hearts, purifying, regenerating and transforming
them. Nowadays we are less struck by the spectacular signs
and wonders than the people of Jerusalem were, but we may
not be more spiritual. We are always inclined to imagine the
gift of the Holy Spirit either as some secret outpouring, with
some element of magic, or else as merely a matter of psychological influences. But to have a truly spiritual view of the
Holy Spirit and his action in the Church, we must always
closely associate the gift of the Spirit with Christ our Lord to
whom we owe this gift.

For our Lord, giving the Holy Spirit is not a case of sharing
some secret and unprecedented power, not even a divine
power such as being able to raise the dead. The Spirit our Lord
gives us is just what he receives himself from the Father, the
Holy Spirit by whom he was conceived as man, and who
enabled him throughout his life on earth to speak and act as
the only-begotten well-loved Son. So, to give us his Spirit
means for our Lord not just giving something infinitely
precious, but giving the very secret of his personality. The
basic experience of the Church, bringing it into existence and
investing it for all time with its unique identity in this world,
is its certainty, in receiving the Holy Spirit, of having received
from its Master, not just an infinitely precious gift, but of quite
simply possessing *him*. If the risen Christ is not now visible to
us, it is not that he is playing a game of hide-and-seek. It is
because he is hidden in the invisible mystery of God, in the
depths of the Spirit, and he is now able to supersede all the
barriers and limitations of the flesh. He can now be wholly
present and living in every part of his Church.

His disciples no longer have their Master before their eyes,
they no longer have his voice to guide them, or the fear of his
reproaches to restrain them, or the magnetism of his personality to pull them together and lead them on. Jesus is no longer

there with his own courage and assurance to stop any tendency to disunion or slackness. As in all other human institutions, everything should conspire towards a gradual but inevitable frittering away of his work, with the survival of his unique, superhuman prestige, but liable to the usual interplay of mingled motives and forces that affect all human endeavours—and yet the unprecedented happens: though he has died, Jesus goes on living in his disciples, uniting them as he had never succeeded in doing during his lifetime. He now enables them to confront, with an enthusiasm that he himself had not always manifested, the same adversaries and the same trials as himself. He enables them to proclaim, with invincible assurance, a gospel message that previously they found hard to take for themselves and had accepted only because they could not say no to their Master. This incredible transformation, this indisputable survival of the Master's presence with his disciples, this irresistible influence perpetuated amid all vicissitudes and guided at all times by an active head, spells the Church of Christ, his body living in this world.

The Church, yes, and the Holy Spirit. If the power of Christ is still such, if it can give rock-like strength to Peter, hitherto scared of a servant maid; if he can change pharisees into disciples of his gospel and touch the heart of Saul the persecutor, this does not mean God gives him some magic power, some psychological sleight-of-hand capable of conjuring up new personalities from nowhere. It is the power of the Spirit that can transform Paul in an instant, but only because it reaches down to his heart, touching him at the very centre of his personality, that mainspring of his being that Paul himself was to call 'a man's own spirit that is within him'.[17] Otherwise it would not be the same man converted, it would be a mere substitution of some other creature, without father or mother, with no roots in this world, almost a mythical personage. Only the Creator can speak to his creature and call him by the name he has given him; he alone can find the secret of speaking to the heart he has made; only the Spirit of God is capable of arousing the spirit that is within us. If Jesus could convert Saul by telling him: 'I am Jesus whom you are persecuting,'[18] it

[17] 1 Cor. 2:11   [18] Acts 9:5

proves that the risen Lord identified himself with his disciples and made their life his own, and it also proves that no heart can escape the irresistible power of Christ and 'the Lord's Spirit'.[19]

In all Christians, as in Christ our Lord, spiritual life and apostolic life converge into one; attentiveness to the Spirit of God and devoted service to all human needs go hand in hand. Christ in his mortal flesh lived purely by the Spirit, and the presence of his Father, the voice and love of his Father, impregnated every fibre of his flesh and inspired everything he did. So now, risen in the flesh by the power of the Spirit, Christ can thereby reach all human flesh and redeem it all. His whole life, everything in the gospel story, every word he spoke and every moment he lived through, everything he experienced in his own body and blood, now perpetuated for us in the eucharist with the sacrifice of his whole life—all that, by the power of the Spirit, is recapitulated in the risen Christ. By the eucharist and by the power of the Holy Spirit, all that can take shape in our flesh and blood, our sweat and tears, can consecrate our lives in the service of God's kingdom and enrich them with God's joy and plentiful redemption.

[19] 2 Cor. 3:17

XV

Christis the Life of the New-Born Church

F OR ME, life means Christ!'¹ St Paul's exclamation arouses
an echo in every Christian with any real faith. Christian
life reminds him of Jesus Christ on all sides. The crucifix
in his room reminds him that his own joys and griefs have as
their witness the Christ who died on Calvary and rose again
on Easter day. From Christmas to Advent, the series of Christian
feasts constantly brings him into contact with Jesus. Whether
it be the face of the child in the crib or the boy Jesus, or the
face of the Master teaching and training his followers, or the
face of Christ disfigured by suffering or radiant in glory, he
can never hide from the divine face wherein he knows he will
see, at our Lord's coming, his own everlasting destiny. Baptized into the death of Christ, marked by each sign of the cross
he makes, fed with his flesh and blood—all these things cannot
be just so many touching souvenirs and remembrances: Jesus
Christ must really mean everything in the life of a Christian.

How can this be? Apart from fine phrases and comparisons,
how is it possible, in the day-to-day round of concrete situations, to achieve this transformation of life that makes a
Christian really conscious that, for him, 'life means Christ?'
It belongs to the Holy Spirit to bring souls to this conscious
awareness, and the Spirit has his own interior way of speaking
to each individual spirit of man. But the experience is
primarily the experience of the whole Church. The Holy

¹ Phil. 1 : 21

197

Spirit, in the writings he has inspired in the new covenant, has left us a faithful record of this experience, as lived by the new-born Church. To learn to live the life of Christ, we can read the Acts of the Apostles and their epistles, and there we can watch the Church in action, we can see what Christ means to her, how she maintains contact with him and finds life in him alone.

1. The temptation to live in the past

As we read these New Testament records we notice two misapprehensions tending to lead the disciples astray as to the real mind of Christ. One was to try to keep him to a way of life that was over and done with. The other was to try to get him involved in plans for a future here below. The second is the more obvious. Right up to the moment of the ascension, the disciples expected Christ 'to restore the dominion to Israel here and now'.[2] Devoted as they were to his person, they could not refrain from making the most of it in the interests of the new era they hoped for, with him as the liberator of Israel.[3] Jesus would have none of these ambitions. To set him up as a liberator of Israel meant being more interested in Israel or in liberation than in himself, and this meant not understanding him at all. Jesus wanted men to follow him with faith in him. Just as some of the disciples of Christ failed to see this, so some Christians tend to fail today. Anxious to be with 'this day and age' and concerned for the future that lies ahead, they follow humanistic and fascinating schemes, seeing in Christ only a prophet of a grandiose future on earth and the liberator of humanity. The danger is that they are more concerned with this would-be liberated humanity than with the person of Christ himself.

The other temptation was mentioned less often, and the occasions for it were rare and short-lived. It can be seen after the resurrection, when Jesus appeared to many of his followers but did not let them enjoy his presence to any great extent. When Mary Magdalen tried to cling to his feet, as she had done before, Jesus made her realize that such signs of devotion were all right as long as he still lived subject to death,[4] but now she

[2] Acts 1:6   [3] Cf. Luke 24:21   [4] Cf. John 12:8

must grow out of them: 'Do not cling to me thus; I have not yet gone up to my Father's side . . .'[5] She must not try to keep our Lord now that he is risen; she must return to the brethren and tell them Jesus is alive.

This is the clearest case, but it helps us to understand other episodes not so clearly worked out. It helps us to see why the risen Jesus, when he appeared to his disciples, never stayed long with them. As soon as he had made himself known and settled all their doubts and hesitations he left them, with instructions what to do: to proclaim his resurrection,[6] to forgive sins,[7] to preach the gospel.[8]

The lesson of the apparitions seems clear to us now. For the apostles it only became clear with Pentecost. If the Holy Spirit had not come to enlighten them, they might have gone on a long time living on memories, piously fostering a cult for a Lord who was alive but not with them now. The little group lying low behind closed doors when the Master had left them could not forget all they had been through. The disciples of Emmaus, even before finding faith and while they still thought their hopes and memories had failed, were full of it all and only too anxious to relate it to the chance passer-by. But when they had walked with the risen Christ, and when the disciples had all been made witnesses of the triumphal outcome of our Lord's story, these memories had taken on far greater fascination for them. How could they ever weary of rehearsing this wonderful story? So theoretically one might imagine these hundred-and-odd faithful souls perpetuating the cult of Jesus with religious enthusiasm. One might imagine their assurance and sincerity winning them recruits and forming a sect, 'the sect of Jesus'. His memory might thus have been preserved for years, even centuries, and history might have been the richer for it, though not notably altered. One more sect, some wonderful sayings, a figure with an attraction surpassing other men but fading with the passage of time, with an appeal winning many hearts, but with no power to release the world from its burden.

This temptation to live in the past, which might conceivably

---

[5] John 20:17   [6] Matt. 28:10; John 20:17
[7] John 20:23   [8] Matt. 28:19

have involved the disciples of Jesus, had they not been guided through it, is something to be reckoned with still today. For some Christians Jesus is only a memory, a figure as in a dream. Some seek him only to find consolation or express sympathy and concern at the sight of his life. Some imagine they know him, while they are only feeding their imagination. Some think to find union with him, while only satisfying frustrated sensibility. Some think they have put him in the centre of their life, when they have only found a suitable place for him in their own intellectual system. There are so many ways of travestying the gospels with no more substance than a fairy tale, and of mistaking prayer for a refuge or escape from real life.

2. *The impact of the Holy Spirit*

It takes the Holy Spirit to guide us through such temptations, as it did for the apostles after the resurrection. Pentecost made the whole world new because that day the Church was brought into the world. Peter and his companions no longer merely sought to recall the master to mind, they suddenly felt impelled by the Holy Spirit and wholly committed to the God's work there and then. The Acts of the Apostles described the transformation in their attitude: 'Peter, with the eleven apostles at his side, stood there . . .'[9] confronting the gathering crowds. For the first time the Church confronted the world at large. She had only one message for them: the work of God saving the world by the death of his Son Jesus Christ. To proclaim this message did involve recalling memories of the mortal life of Jesus of Nazareth and the events of his life, death and resurrection. But these memories which, only yesterday, would have been just a personal heritage of a group of friends clinging together for protection, had now become a message to be broadcast to all men. 'Men of Judea, and all you who are dwelling in Jerusalem'[10]—men from all different countries. The life of Jesus now took on new dimensions: God was bringing about his great design, reconciling the world to himself, in his Son.

[9] Acts 2 : 14   [10] Acts 2 : 14

Thus, as soon as the Church is alive to her mission, she finds just the right attitude to her Lord and Master. Of all he did in life, his miracles, his sayings, his actions and all his response to human experience, the Church carefully gathered all she could. It was clearly our Lord's intention, in grouping witnesses around him, from first to last, to ensure the recording of those memories for future generations. Realizing this intention the Church would gather them up and put them on record in the gospels. But the Church's fidelity was not merely to produce a correct record. Now that the risen Christ was enthroned at God's right hand, all that he said must be fulfilled in men's hearts. Now that the beatitudes had become a reality, the time had come for the poor to have the gospel preached to them. Now that the seed of the parables was beginning to germinate, it was time to see it was sown throughout the world. Now that the blood shed on the cross had been gathered to heaven by God, it was time to proclaim to all men that their sins were forgiven and invite them to the new covenant. Such was the message of Peter on Pentecost day, and such was the message repeated constantly in the early chapters of the Acts of the Apostles.

3. The Spirit, the presence of Christ

As we follow the steps of the early Church, we see a two-fold development constantly and faithfully adhered to. On the one hand there is the impulse of the Spirit, the signs of his power being multiplied and his action pursued in men's hearts, so that the Church takes great strides forward, over land and sea, from Jerusalem to Samaria, from Antioch to Ephesus, from Corinth to Rome. Each stride brought new conquests, but also new adversaries and more fearful threats, harsher persecutions and graver problems to solve. The Spirit was always with them, enlightening, sustaining, enabling them to win hearts and inspire devotion. But at the same time as the Spirit launched the Church towards new conquests, he also brought their minds back to the actual memories of Jesus, and made them dwell on his features and way of acting, so as to find therein the light they needed in their problems and the strength to overcome obstacles and threats. Each time Peter found himself up against a difficult situation, he turned to the life of Jesus to seek the response the Spirit of Jesus would dictate to him. When confronted by the lame man at the Beautiful Gate, when summoned by the Sanhedrin and ordered to keep silence, when he was involved in the incidents at Joppa and Caesarea concerning the Roman officer Cornelius—while conscious of the guidance of the Spirit, Peter also recalled what he had seen and heard at the side of Jesus, and there he learns that what the Spirit moves him to do is just the natural expression of what our Lord would do, and he finds God continuing in his apostles the work of Christ. For the early Christian community, the manifestations of the Spirit and their memories of our Lord's own life go hand in hand.

Of course, both are equally from the Holy Spirit. Both go together by their very nature, being the fulfilment of promises made by our Lord before leaving his disciples. It was the Holy Spirit who would 'recall to their minds everything that Jesus had said to them';[11] and the same Spirit would enable them to stand up to all interrogation and judgment on their apostolate, however harsh and formidable their adversaries might be.[12]

Thus the Church, though for ever on pilgrimage away from Christ, keeps her gaze fixed on him to find out which way to go forward in each day and age, and finds his guidance at every step. Far from this gaze paralysing the Church by concern for a past that is over and done with, on the contrary it is an inspiration to the Church's forward-looking progress and sustains its apostolic endeavour. So it is that the person of our Lord, far from growing more remote or faint with the passage of time, remains for ever living and inspiring for his followers. This is the fulfilment of his promise: 'I am with you all through the days that are coming, until the consummation of the world.'[13] This might have been taken to mean constant and faithful assistance, with powerful protection when needed. But it meant, really and truly, an actual presence, the presence of the man who had walked with them on hot and dusty roads, the presence of the friend who had sat down to meals with

[11] John 14:26   [12] Cf. Matt. 10:8–20; John 16:8–11
[13] Matt. 28:20

them, the presence of the teacher whose words immediately brought them light. All this, which they had enjoyed for many months together, living with Jesus, the apostles found again as they made their way about the world 'teaching and preaching Jesus as the Christ'.[14] All this also the Christian of today can experience in the same living way in the measure in which he too embarks on the service of the kingdom of God and devotes his life to the gospel.

4. *The Spirit, the action of Christ*

The more completely the Christian is committed to the service of the kingdom, the closer he finds Christ's presence and the more personal and intimate his relations with the Master. Here again the Acts are revealing. The first Christians especially those dedicated to the apostolate, soon realized that their life was a prolonged reproduction of our Lord's. In their journeyings, their conversations and speeches, their controversies and worries and anxieties, they grasped that the work was going on which had filled the life of Jesus, as they carried about the world the word of God. The setting was now different. Mediterranean ports had replaced the roads of Palestine: the wise men of Athens replaced the scribes of Jerusalem; slaves in Corinth replaced the poor in Galilee. Details mattered little, given the work was the same as our Lord's daily round, sowing the seed of the word of God. Though they no longer heard his lips explain the parables of the kingdom, these parables came to life before their eyes. The seed that is the word of God was being sown throughout the world;[15] men's hearts were receiving the word of God;[16] 'the word of the Lord spread and prevailed'.[17] In calling all this by the name of the 'word', the early Christians were not just using a convenient comparison. They were showing their conviction that they could see the harvest our Lord had come to sow on earth, and their joy in having a share in it and in finding him with them in their daily task. For them 'the ministry of the word'[18] is none other than 'serving the Lord Jesus'.[19] Proclaim-

---

[14] Acts 5:42
[15] Acts 13:49
[16] Ibid. 8:14; 11:1
[17] Acts 19:20; cf. 6:7; 12:24
[18] Acts 6:4; cf. 20:24
[19] Ibid. 20:19

ing the word is proclaiming Jesus.[20] The mission of the
apostles, as they understand it, is an exact counterpart of the
ministry of our Lord. When in danger from the Sanhedrin,
their prayer was to ask God that the ministry of Jesus should
go on by their hands: 'Look down upon their threats, Lord,
now as of old; enable thy servants to preach thy word confidently, by stretching out thy hand to heal; and let signs and
miracles be performed in the name of Jesus, thy holy Son.'[21] As
bearers of the word of God entrusted to them by Jesus, they
do more than imitate him: their action reproduces his, even
in the details of the signs going with it.

If there were times when the living presence of Christ was
closer, and when the first Christians felt they were going
through just what he had gone through, they were the times
of persecution. Then we see, even in the sober account given,
a privileged experience at work, the joy of living and sharing
the most precious moments of the life of Christ. The first time
the apostles were scourged 'they left the presence of the Coun-
cil rejoicing that they had been found worthy to suffer
indignity for the name of Jesus'.[22] They were happy to have
known something of the passion of Christ, happy to fulfil his
words in their own person, happy to have tasted the joy he
promised and to be following so closely in his footsteps. When
St Paul was arrested at Jerusalem and summoned in turn
before the Sanhedrin, the Roman governor Felix and King
Agrippa, one can feel St Luke's emotion as he relates it with
our Lord's words in his ears: 'Men will be laying hands upon
you and persecuting you; they will give you up to the syna-
gogues, and to prison, and drag you into the presence of kings
and governors on my account.'[23]

It would seem that in these episodes of persecution on his
account, the witnesses were quick to observe details that might
otherwise have been neglected, mere coincidences, you might
say, between their situation and our Lord's. The trial of
Stephen before the Sanhedrin struck his fellow Christians as
a kind of repeat performance of the trial of Jesus. There were
the same accusations of wanting to destroy the temple.[24]

[20] Acts 5:42; 8:35   [21] Acts 4:29–30   [22] Acts 5:41
[23] Luke 21:12   [24] Acts 6:13; Matt. 26:59

There was the vision of the Son of man in his glory at the right hand of the Father[25] as our Lord had described.[26] Then there were his last words: 'Lord Jesus, receive my spirit', his prayer for forgiveness for his executioners and the loud cry before dying.[27] These points of similarity with the last moments of our Lord were treasured as precious signs by the early Church. They showed that between Jesus and Stephen God had set up a close kinship, visible in outward likeness. Jesus himself, linking the prediction of his death with warnings to his followers, had told them they had to 'take up their cross'[28] and 'drink the cup he was to drink'[29] so sharing in his own sufferings. Without going out of their way to find coincidences, the early Christians were not long in recognizing, when the time came, how their persecutions gave them a share and an insight into the mystery of the passion of their Master.

5. 'Life means Christ'

Surprisingly enough, the apostle most attentive to this insight and sharing with Christ was St Paul. Content not to have 'known Christ in merely human fashion',[30] when it becomes a question of the mystery of the cross he was anxious to follow it in detail. The circumstances of his arrest in Jerusalem were a case in point, as we have seen. He had gone up to Jerusalem 'bound in the Spirit',[31] and realizing that imprisonment and afflictions awaited him there: like our Lord, he would be 'delivered into the hands of Gentiles'.[32] Clearly St Luke, as he related this episode, was thinking of Jesus towards the end of his life, going up to Jerusalem where he too was 'delivered into the hands of Gentiles'. There was also the same atmosphere of Gethsemani in St Paul's words: 'The Lord's will be done.'[33] It may be that other witnesses did not immediately grasp these likenesses, but St Luke did—not just for literary effect, but because he knew the early Christians would be alive to their significance.

In this St Luke knew he was expressing what St Paul wanted him to. There is no doubt how St Paul felt about it: he had

---

[25] Acts 7:66 [26] Matt. 26:64 [27] Acts 7:59
[28] Mark 8:34 [29] Mark 10:38 [30] 2 Cor. 5:16
[31] Acts 20:22 [32] Luke 18:32 [33] Acts 21:14

constantly before him the definite and vivid picture of Christ crucified. True, he did not linger on descriptions of other episodes in the passion, but Christ's having suffered this death, 'death on a cross'[34] was not just an episode, it was the heart and soul of St Paul's message, 'preaching Christ crucified'.[35] Wherever he went St Paul portrayed 'Christ as crucified', and did so 'publicly before their eyes'.[36] His greatest boast and the credentials he quoted for his defence were that 'he bore the scars of the Lord Jesus printed on his body'.[37] Some have thought this might mean the 'stigmata', but no such sign was necessary for St Paul to realize that 'in his sufferings . . . and in his flesh he completed what was lacking in Christ's afflictions'.[38]

St Paul is well aware of what he is saying, and he is too dedicated to his mission, too devoted to his master, to be carried away by sentiment. He wants 'to know . . . what it is to share his sufferings',[39] and he does not find the answer in emotion, but in his task as an apostle. He is rejected by the Jews, 'asking for signs and wonders', and scorned by the Greeks, 'intent on their philosophy';[40] he is concerned to stand 'crucified to the world',[41] and this is no rhetoric, it is sober fact. In preaching Christ crucified, he finds himself in the same situation as our Lord on the cross, rejected by his fellow Jews and condemned by the Gentiles. He does know what it is to share his sufferings and in just the same cause. The burden is so overwhelming at times that he cannot refrain from reminding his Christians, so inclined to forget, what his life has been. He has:

> so often looked death in the face. Five times the Jews scourged me, and spared me but one lash in the forty; three times I was beaten with rods, once I was stoned; I have been shipwrecked three times, I have spent a night and a day as a castaway at sea. What journeys I have undertaken, in danger from rivers, in danger from robbers, in danger from

---

[34] Phil. 2:8
[35] 1 Cor. 1:23
[36] Gal. 3:1
[37] Gal. 6:17
[38] Col. 1:24
[39] Phil. 3:10
[40] 1 Cor. 1:22
[41] Gal. 6:14

my own people, in danger from the Gentiles, danger in cities; danger in the wilderness, danger in the sea, danger among false brethren! I have met with toil and weariness, so often been sleepless, hungry and thirsty; so often denied myself food, gone cold and naked. And all this, over and above everything else which I do not count; I mean the burden I carry every day, my anxious care for all the churches.[42]

The apostle's motives for thus detailing his life with pride mixed with sorrow was no doubt to appeal to people whose hearts were upright and sympathetic, but who did not stop to think. But his sufferings, along with his weaknesses and failures, also enable him to share in the mystery of Christ on the cross, where God's glory is shown forth in the failure and helplessness of Christ crucified. When Paul writes 'I will all the more gladly boast of my weaknesses, that the power of Christ may rest upon me',[43] it is the echo of our Lord proclaiming 'Now is the Son of man glorified, and in him God is glorified.'[44]

Paul was not without experience of God's power, triumphing in his own distress. He had realized how, by some mysterious alchemy, all his sufferings were changed into strength: 'We are being hampered everywhere, yet we still have room to breathe, are hard put to it, but never at a loss; persecution does not leave us unbefriended, nor crushing blows destroy us.'[45] Strength is born of weakness. The apostle's strength goes on working when all reserves of physical and nervous energy are exhausted; he is amazed, in the midst of anxieties and disappointments and failures, and in spite of powers failing with age, to see God's work growing, Christian communities springing up everywhere, the gospel spreading throughout the world, the Christians suffering but remaining staunch in the faith. 'So death makes itself felt in us, and life in you.'[46]

This life is the life of the risen Christ. St Paul's experience of this is second to none in keenness and clarity. All the apostles, from the first early days of the Church, felt that

[42] 2 Cor. 11:23–28   [43] 2 Cor. 12:9   [44] John 13:31
[45] 2 Cor. 4:8–9   [46] 2 Cor. 4:12

suffering endured for Christ brought them into communion with the passion, and they were filled thereupon with strange and wonderful joy. St Paul identified what this joy consisted of, the radiance of the glory of the risen Christ in his heart. The powers of death were attacking him and often threatened to lay him low, overwhelming him with a burden that grew heavier day by day, fixing him to the cross of Christ. And yet how explain that, at every moment, life seemed to emerge more vigorous than ever from these trials! The reason was that, by clinging to Christ crucified, Paul was united to him in his resurrection, living and triumphant. This communion with the risen Christ was just as close as his communion with the suffering Christ: 'We carry about continually in our bodies the dying state of Jesus, so that the living power of Jesus may be manifested in our bodies too. Always we, alive as we are, are being given up to death for Jesus' sake, so that the living power of Jesus may be manifested in this mortal nature of ours.'[47] It was almost as though the apostle were reproducing the apparitions of Jesus in the risen life.

The apostle's joy in communion with the risen Jesus was essentially apostolic, the joy of seeing the growth of the work of Jesus, his Church. 'I rejoice in my sufferings for your sake, and in my flesh I complete what is lacking in Christ's afflictions for the sake of his body, that is, the Church.'[48] Suffering for the Church and rejoicing over her growth is one and the same thing as suffering for Christ and rejoicing over his conquest of death. Such is the mystery whose unfathomable riches unfolded to St Paul as he saw the visible organism of the Church born and taking shape, thanks to his own and the other apostles' work. The more he saw of this unfolding, the more their conquests became consolidated everywhere, the more did St Paul see the inner dimensions of the Church in depth. He summed this up when he said the Church is the Body of Christ. In this comparison, with which we are now so familiar, people often think of a vigorous organism, building itself into an imposing structure, gathering together the divine forces at work in the world. St Paul was well aware of that aspect.[49] But it was perhaps not the most vital aspect of

[47] 2 Cor. 4:10-11   [48] Col. 1:24   [49] Cf. Eph. 2:20-22

the Church. In this Body that he found growing constantly wherever he went, from one end of the Mediterranean to the other, following and fostering its close links and currents of life, St Paul at heart only looked for one thing and fastened on to that, namely the action and presence of his Lord Jesus Christ. This body of men would not have had any interest for St Paul if it had not been the Body of Christ, a Body given by God to his risen Son. This was the secret of his heart and his apostolic life. He had behind him a lifetime of labours, he had established so many centres of Christianity, he had had to confront so many controversies and settle so many problems of the age, he had so many friends and people to write to in all the communities of Asia Minor, Greece and Rome, he had been so interminably travelling from place to place, for ever obsessed by the cares of all the churches everywhere— and yet when he looked back on all these labours, wherein he had shed so much blood and tears, nothing mattered at all, apart from the presence of the living Christ, his Lord.

How did St Paul see this living Christ? He could given no exact description, since it was a presence vaster even than the world. His glory filled the universe and surpassed all creation, animating the whole Church for all time. But however exalted, however inaccessible in glory, Christ was always seen by St Paul with the face of a man and the features of him 'who loved him and gave himself for him'.[50] Paul's response to the love that enfolded him retained to the end the eagerness of the simplest and most direct kind of love in return. The person he loved was always none other than the man Jesus whom the apostles proclaimed at Pentecost. His thanksgiving and admiration for the unfathomable riches of Christ are akin to the joy of the apostles rejoicing to suffer the scourging for the sake of Jesus. In the thirty years between, Christian experience had grown in depth and extent, but it had not changed in character, for the Christian man gets to know our Lord in the measure in which he carries the witness of Christ into the world.

This experience, of which we have seen these glimpses in the apostolic writings, was not limited to the early Church.

[50] Gal. 2 : 20

The Church will always live on this experience until the end of time, for it is the making of real Christians. But to get to know Christ and live on him, they must set aside any illusions and not seek him in the satisfaction of any sentimental contact, they must not reduce him to the scale of human causes. They will come to know him aright if they follow the guidance of the Holy Spirit and recognize his face in the present moment, in the service of their brethren and of the poor, in the service of the gospel and the Church. The more complete their service is, the more intimately they will know him, and if, as they may well expect, this service leads to suffering and persecution, happy indeed they will be. Then they will realize how close to them, in the depth of their heart and the fibre of their being, our Lord is, both in his passion and in the glory of his resurrection.

XVI

Christ's Prayer and Ours

LIKE THE REST of the Christian life, our prayer is 'in Christ Jesus'. We might be inclined to think that this is just a convenient way of saying that whatever we do as Christians is through the merits of Christ and owes its value to him. At that rate, praying in Christ Jesus would mean uniting our prayer to his, as it were just tacking on our poor prayer to his unique and sovereign intercession, hiding our mediocrity behind his magnanimity, keeping our distance, leaving to him the power and the glory, and contenting ourselves with our own petty insignificance.

There is some truth in this, and it is one way of putting the attitude we should have in prayer to God. But it is inadequate and might lead us to think that our prayer has somehow to be added to Christ's. This might be because we hoped thereby to dissolve anything selfish or impure in our prayer; or we might be seeking to attune our own feeble note to his, the only prayer the Father delights to hear. But we should still be keeping a sort of dualism between our prayer and our Lord's, and the objection would remain: what is the use of our contributing anything in addition to his prayer which is already perfect?

Some people, reacting against this difficulty, give up trying to add anything themselves to our Lord's prayer, which alone merits the name of true prayer. They hasten to explain that we must rightly understand our Lord's prayer in a contemporary

211

setting. Our Lord is no longer living in his mortal flesh with its one-time limitations of place and race and culture. Our Lord is now the head of the Church, and his prayer is the prayer of his Mystical Body. Hence it would seem there can be no other prayer for Christians than the prayer of the Church as expressed in the liturgy, partly because only the Spouse of Christ knows how to address God, but still more because all Christ's prayer is concentrated in his sacrifice, the sacrifice now entrusted to the Church for all time in the Mass. Could anyone be so bold as to venture to improve on the inexhaustible splendour of the liturgy?

This is all very well said, and the sentiments are irreproachable. However, there can be an element of illusion underlying this enthusiastic point of view. Are we really to believe that our Lord's prayer, as formulated in and by the Church, dispenses the individual Christian from praying personally, or from seeking anything else in his prayer than the closest possible adherence to the words of the Church? There are too many examples in Christian tradition of the highest order to believe such a conclusion. St John, St Paul, St Ignatius of Antioch, St Francis of Assisi, all gave expression to the spontaneous outpourings of their hearts in prayer. To suggest that personal and direct communion with God is only an inferior, if not a mistaken kind of prayer, would be to frustrate an essential religious aspiration of man and would run counter to something quite certainly given in the gospel.

The way to reconcile these ideas is to give the fullest meaning and development to what is undoubtedly true, the basic principle that the prayer of Christ as the head of the Church is the only absolutely authentic prayer. This principle implies the unique nature of our Lord's prayer, but it implies also the individual contribution we Christians can make. It is all one prayer, our Lord's, because for God there is no other; but that very prayer also wells up in all hearts moved by the Holy Spirit. We can all say with St Paul, and we can say it of our prayer as of all else that springs from the Holy Spirit: 'I am praying; or rather, not I, it is Christ that is praying in me.'[1] Thanks to the Spirit of life and holiness in us, a mysterious

[1] Cf. Gal. 2:20

communication takes place; our Lord's prayer really becomes ours, not just as a model or replica we imitate: it is a personal communion of Christ's own prayer welling up in us. We do not just pray as our Lord did, like him and at his side, inspired by his example and strength. We do all this, and rightly, as the normal way of learning to pray with him. It is our own prayer, not just a current passing through; it springs up from our own heart, with its most personal and secret feelings of joy or love or distress. But at the same time it is, by its very nature and origin, our Lord's own prayer, the stirring of his own heart in its eager aspiration to the Father.

How can this be? It is the mysterious presence of the Holy Spirit, more unaccountable than the wind that 'bloweth where it listeth'. But it is a truth that God reveals to little ones a truth that our Lord and the apostles, by word and example, bring home to us in its fullness. The better to understand how the Spirit leads us along this road, and the better to follow it faithfully, an excellent way he shows us is to contemplate, in the New Testament, how our Lord's prayer did indeed well up more abundantly as time went on in the hearts of his disciples, visibly enlightening and strengthening them, becoming present to them from within and putting them into prayer before God in the service of his Church.

1. The prayer of the Son in the gospel

'When you pray, go into your room and shut the door and pray to your Father who is (there) in secret; and your Father who sees in secret will reward you.'[2] The first thing our Lord says about prayer in the sermon on the Mount is to remind us of its objective, the Father. He does not need to tell us to pray, he takes it for granted, so obvious is the need to his way of thinking. Significantly he says to the disciples not 'Pray . . .' but 'When you pray . . .', 'When you put yourself in prayer. . . .' No new formula is prescribed, no particular method; he leaves them to the framework of prayer in which, as Jews, they had been brought up. The important point is not so much what to pray for. The gospel sometimes suggests we can ask God anything we like, such as moving a mountain.

[2] Matt. 6:6

Sometimes it seems to want us to forget all our own concerns
and think only of the kingdom of God. For our Lord the one
essential is that prayer should put us in the presence of the
Father. 'When you pray . . . pray to your Father who is
there', and because he is there, and hears and sees and knows
our prayer, this is bound to be a secret thing between him and
us, a silent surrender of ourselves to him.

That God is a Father to us, for anyone with any religious
sense, is self-evident. All this seems simple and natural to us.
Jesus, coming from the Father, could not but stress this basic
truth with sovereign authority. He lays down from the first
the ultimate truth that all religions have sensed and tried to
express. But notice: Jesus did not content himself with telling
us that God is our Father. In saying so he was answering a deep
need of the human heart, but he says it with the stress on
something further and even more important: the Father is
there, though in secret: he sees, he hears, he knows. The
Father is there, of course, as he is everywhere; but the point
our Lord makes is that the Father is there present to him, and
so: 'I know whom I am talking to you about (he seems to say),
I see him watching you, listening to you, recognizing you.'
Without our Lord's teaching men might know God is a
Father to them, might have some idea what fatherhood means
in dignity, responsibility and intimacy, realizing what it can
mean between father and son, especially when lost or missing.
We might well realize that there is no name more fitting for
God. But in the Our Father there is far more than this. There
is the realization and feeling that we are God's children, in the
presence of the Father, experiencing this vital natural bond
between Father and children. It would not be enough to know
God is a father, unless we realize we are his children. What
would be the use of gathering in his presence, if we did not
feel that, with him, we are in our own home? Jesus alone could
invite us to his Father's home and bring us into his presence
there, and it is by his own prayer that he ensured this would
really happen.

To believe this, it is enough for our Lord to tell us so, in
the natural way he does. Such simple words, that our children
recite every day, have a naturalness about them which is

characteristic of true prayer. Our Lord's way of telling us about
the Father, putting us in his presence, suggesting what to say
to him but with full freedom in his sight, is not just incom-
parable pedagogy or an exceptional influence at work on us,
it is the very revelation of his own soul, a soul always in prayer.
He who speaks to us of the Father in this way, and who would
have us speak to him likewise, is the same who in his own joy
and sorrow, to express his own needs or thanksgiving, so constantly turned to his Father in trust, 'Abba, Father'.[3]

Because he himself was in prayer in the presence of the
Father, our Lord could also let us know the response his soul
received from him. For prayer means listening as well as speaking, receiving as well as offering. It is noticeable in the teaching of the sermon on the Mount about prayer that the Father
is always portrayed as welcoming the prayers of his children
and responding to them: 'Your Father who sees you';[4] 'Your
Father who is there' to hear you;[5] 'Your Father knows what
you need before you ask him';[6] 'Your heavenly Father also will
forgive you';[7] 'Your heavenly Father knows that you need
them all';[8] 'How much more will your Father give. . . .'[9]
Jesus sees the Father as attentive to the needs of his children,
foreseeing their requests, on the look-out for them to look to
him, so that he can see himself reflected in their eyes.

Our Lord's own prayer both puts us in the presence of the
Father and assures us of his response. It shows us the Father
forestalling our response, and in fact takes the form of a
response itself, whether he fell into admiration or grief,
whether jubilant or suppliant, it is always a response to the
Father's decision or initiative: 'Yea, Father, for such was thy
gracious will';[10] 'Thy will be done';[11] 'Father, I thank thee
that thou hast heard me';[12] 'I glorified thee on earth, having
accomplished the work thou gavest me to do; and now, Father,
glorify thou me. . . .'[13] Thus the dialogue between Father
and son, as between the disciples and his Father, is one of

[3] Cf. Matt. 11:25; Mark 14:36; John 11:41; 17:1
[4] Matt. 6:4; 6:18   [5] Matt. 6:6; 6:18
[6] Matt. 6:8   [7] Matt. 6:32
[8] Matt. 6:32   [9] Matt. 7:11
[10] Matt. 11:26   [11] Luke 22:42
[12] John 11:41   [13] John 17:4-5

H

mutual confidence and compassion, admiration and magnanimity, generosity and gratitude; something wonderful and sacred, yet homely and familiar, an intimate exchange as between members of the same family.

Our Lord's teaching on prayer in the sermon on the Mount is summed up in the Our Father, which also forms a summary of our Lord's own prayer. Quite naturally, and with no effort to conform to it, every time our Lord momentarily lets us glimpse his own prayer, we find him absorbed in one or other of the petitions of the Our Father. 'Father, glorify thy name';[14] 'Holy Father, keep them in thy name';[15] 'Thy will be done'; [16] 'Father forgive them'.[17] He says to Peter, 'Satan demanded to have you, that he might sift you like wheat, but I have prayed for you that your faith may not fail';[18] and for them all he prays, 'Keep them from the evil one'.[19] These correspondences are striking. In giving us the Our Father it was not just a convenient and suitable form of words, it was the substance of his own prayer. So he cannot merely mean us to repeat the formula faithfully and meditate on it conscientiously; he expects us to give it the strength he gave it, with something of the dedication he put into it. In order to realize what the Our Father means, we should do well on occasion to recall, at each petition, our Lord's fulfilment:

Our Father who art in heaven—Father of Christ our Lord; Hallowed be thy name—as he dedicated himself to its glory; Thy kingdom come—as he looked forward to it; Thy will be done—as he wished to achieve it; Give us this day our daily bread—as he accepted it from thy hands; Forgive us our trespasses—as he prayed to thee to forgive us; Lead us not into temptation—as he warned us and prayed for us; Deliver us from the evil one—as he prayed we might be.

This is not artificial; it is just a way of raising our mind and heart to the Father as our Lord did, giving the well-worn phrases their true significance, that expressed by our Lord,

[14] John 12:28
[16] Luke 22:42
[18] Luke 22:31–32

[15] John 17:11
[17] Luke 23:34
[19] John 17:15

whether in the desert confronting Satan, at the supper, in the garden, or on Calvary. If these petitions had not been expressed by our Lord, with all the ardour of the Son at prayer, we could never have made them our own.

2. Our Lord's prayer a source of strength to the apostles

The Our Father is God-given: it is not just something to be said; God insists on its being taken seriously, and this involves decisions, committing one's life to the service of the Father and his kingdom. 'Thy will be done. . . . Forgive us our trespasses, as we forgive them that trespass against us.' The first time the apostles heard these words, they were delighted, no doubt thinking that all this was automatically fulfilled and that it was enough to say the words for them to be achieved in real life. They had a lot to learn. They would need a long apprenticeship, prolonged contact with our Lord to learn what the kingdom of God was to involve, how its adversaries would show their hatred for it, how the evil one would afflict it to the full extent of his power. All the time our Lord spent with them he was forming them in depth to make the Our Father their way of life as well as the substance of their prayer.

What was the force that kept these men together, simple and willing men, but subject to human respect and ambition and jealousy? It was our Lord, the strength of his personality, of his example and of his prayer for them. This latter strength would not strike them at first, so much as the power of his words and looks. What first filled them with wonder was how he spoke of God 'as one having authority', how he enabled them to hear the voice of their own conscience, how he thwarted the forces of evil, disease, demons, death, and yet how he upset he was at the sight of suffering. But other people besides the twelve saw all these things, and some may have been even more deeply struck and impressed. How was it that the apostles alone were so grouped about him, involved in the same fate and committed to the same task? Because he chose them, sure enough, but also because he prayed for them, and the two things must go together. The gospels quietly but insistently show us both how the apostles were called and followed our Lord, and how our Lord prayed for them. Before choosing the twelve 'he continued all night in prayer to God'.[20] After the feeding of the five thousand he shipped them off again to be away from the crowds clamouring to proclaim him as king, and he went up the mountainside; then, while they were at the mercy of the storm, as well as disappointed over the triumph that might have been, he prayed through the night for their loyalty to prevail over their inability to see and the bitterness of their disappointment.[21] Just before putting them the decisive question that would call forth Peter's profession of faith on which the Church would be founded, St Luke tells us he was praying alone.[22] Before the passion came on, he had prayed for Peter that, in spite of his fall and denial, his faith should not fail.[23] These are no coincidences: in the choosing and training of the apostolic group, as in their loyalty and perseverance and unity, we see our Lord's prayer at work. Throughout his time with them his prayer was their support, preserving them from harm and leading them on to the Father.

But the hour was to come when Jesus had to leave them, and it was then that his prayer came into full force. Its intention remained the same, continuing to ask the Father to let the disciples keep up their faithfulness, their perseverance and their unity. 'Keep them true to thy name, thy gift to me';[24] 'Keep them holy, through the truth';[25] 'That they all may be one';[26] 'So that the love thou hast bestowed on me may dwell in them'.[27] Our Lord's prayer had now become more urgent, it was for all time. In his priestly prayer as he went out to meet his passion he prayed for all those whom he wanted to follow him—the apostles and all who accepted their message. All that the Church would ever receive from Christ stems from his prayer the evening of the last supper, truly a priestly prayer, inseparable from the sacrifice whose meaning and force it served to express. As he was going to sacrifice for us all the powers of body and soul and every drop of his blood, all of which had been expended for us day by day throughout his

[20] Luke 6:12
[21] Matt. 14:22
[22] Luke 9:18
[23] Luke 22:32
[24] John 17:11
[25] Ibid. 17:17
[26] Ibid. 17:21
[27] Ibid. 17:26

life, so he gathered together in one supreme effort all the in-
cessant stream of prayer he had poured out for us all his life
on earth.

The fruits of our Lord's prayer were seen at Pentecost with
the founding of the Church, far richer fruits than the modest
results obtained by his prayer during his lifetime with the
apostles. Left without him to guide them and lead them and
keep them together, the apostles, once so sluggish, so quarrel-
some, so slow to see the ways of God, became forthwith full of
courage and assurance, all of one mind, endowed with power
to raise up a Christian community sharing all things in common, one in heart and soul. These were the fruits of our Lord's
prayer, signs that it had been heard by the Father and that it
continued to be at work helping and sustaining the Church.
Among these fruits one of the most noteworthy is the disciples'
prayer. We saw that our Lord took for granted that they
needed to pray, and yet the gospel never shows them actually
doing so, and in spite of his teaching on the subject our Lord
did not seem to oblige them to put it into practice yet. The
only occasion when he did actually call upon them to pray,
in the garden of Gethsemani, their inability became only too
painfully obvious: 'So could you not watch with me one
hour?'[28]

But scarcely had he gone from their midst when we find
them in prayer, as if they had always been used to it, as if they
knew exactly what God wanted them to be doing. Coming
down from the Mount of Olives after the ascension, 'they
went back full of joy to Jerusalem, where they spent their
time continually in the temple, praising and blessing God';[29]
'they went up into the upper room where they dwelt . . . all
these with one mind, gave themselves up to prayer, together
with Mary the mother of Jesus, and the rest of the women and
his brethren'.[30] The content of their prayer is not stated, but
it is clear it was about the Master and his work. What should
they praise God for after the ascension, if not for the wonders
they had seen accomplished in Jesus? What motive could
gather together with one mind the apostles, the disciples and
the holy women, if not the very same force that drew them

[28] Matt. 26:40   [29] Luke 24:53   [30] Acts 1:13–14

together while he was with them, the fascination of his personality and the power of his prayer? We see here the Church, gathered in prayer, beginning the ceaseless vigil she maintains down the centuries and for which she derives the strength and the secret from the prayer of her divine spouse.

With the visible gift of the Holy Spirit and the assurance of his presence in the Church from Pentecost onwards, the place of our Lord's prayer in the prayer of the Church grew in strength and in extent. When the Church gathered for the breaking of bread to celebrate the eucharist,[31] she was imitating our Lord's thanksgiving offering of his body and blood to God for the salvation of his brethren. When threatened by persecutors, the Church called upon God 'to enable thy servants to preach thy word confidently', as the Son had done, and even 'to let signs and miracles be performed in the name of Jesus'.[32] When the Church at Antioch was consecrating, for their mission as apostles, the disciples called by the Holy Spirit, Saul and Barnabas, they fell to prayer, as Jesus had done before calling the twelve. Instinctively the Church does as he had done and prays as he prayed. There was no question of adding anything to his prayer, or to his unique sacrifice, as if there could be any other way to the Father than through the prayer of the Incarnate Word, as if the Father would listen to any other voice than that of his Son. Precisely because the Church was conscious of expressing our Lord's own prayer, she knew she could pray; because she held in her hands the sacrifice of her master, she knew she had the right and the power to offer God his body and blood, and with it the labours of her sons and the death of her martyrs. Knowing as she does the heart of the Bridegroom, she knows what to pray for to the Father and how God fills her with blessing.

Taking its rise from the prayer of our Lord, the Church's prayer knows no other intentions than those of the master. With him, the Church prays for God's kingdom to come, for his children to learn to live according to their Father's will, to forgive and to share, and finally that God may use his strength to restrain the power of the evil one. It was to 'devote themselves to prayer' and the ministry of preaching that the

---

[31] Acts 2:42   [32] Acts 4:30

apostles gave up attending to administrative details and the provision of food for their communities.[33] St Paul, day and night, prayed before God, thanking him for the work of Christ being accomplished at Thessalonica, Corinth, and Philippi, begging him to carry it forward with ever-increasing fruit.[34] But in return he calls upon them: 'Pray, too, for us . . .' for him to have the strength he needs to proclaim the gospel and 'the right utterance to make it known'.[35]

The prayer of the Church, the prayer of our Lord giving rise to it, and the prayer of every member of the Church, is all summed up in the Mass. A perfect prayer, the expression of perfect sacrifice down to the last drop of his blood; a unique prayer, the only prayer that can gather up the whole Church and enter into contact with God, even about the humblest altar; a prayer for ever new, each time the Church offers it, and always fresh, constantly arousing in the Church new expressions of prayer and sacrifice, whether it be the prayer of a priest in an empty church or of Chinese Christians in prison for the faith. Each time the prayer of our Lord bears fruit, it presents to the Father new faces wherein he delights to find the inexhaustible love of his Son reflected in their eyes.

No form of distress or joy is foreign to Christian prayer, for nothing in life was outside our Lord's prayer. No human need escaped him, any more than the lilies of the field; no shadow on men's faces or sentiment in the heart went unnoticed. In it all our Lord saw the Father, his will, his generosity, his kingdom and his glory. Of the whole world around him, to which he belonged in mind as well as in the flesh, and of every element of sin or grace it contained, our Lord made the inexhaustible material for prayer and sacrifice to the Father, in thanksgiving for grace and remedy for sin. Now in his risen glorified flesh he is in contact with all humanity, and his prayer is of infinite extent; it springs up in all hearts that turn to him in faith, making them pray too in the interests of the Father's work and concern for the well-being of his kingdom, seeking only his glory.

[33] Acts 6:4
[34] 1 Thess. 1:2; 2 Thess. 2:12; 1 Cor. 1:4; Phil. 1:3; 1:9
[35] Col. 4:3-4

We saw in the Our Father the Son in prayer before the Father, inviting us to join with him. 'He was heard', for this prayer was his very life, expressing his appointed task. For this prayer to take on its total efficacy, for it to become *Our* Father, Jesus had to fulfil it; he had to do the forgiving and the accomplishing of the Father's will. Then it became the prayer of sacrifice, the prayer of the Church, in the Mass. The Mass is the Our Father lived by Christ in each of his members, and prayed by him in every Christian.

3. *Praying as sons in the Spirit of the Son*

At the source of this mysterious extension of our Lord's prayer and sacrifice to the Church and all her members there is the Holy Spirit. Naturally, we cannot perceive his presence, nor can we represent it or grasp it in any tangible way. He is not present before us, but in us; his task is not to tell us things, but to enable us to remember what we have heard and communicate what we have learned about our Lord; he does not have to bring himself to our notice for us to visualize him in any way, but he does make us conscious of the Father and sensitive, as the Son is, to the Father and his word. As we do not feel our own soul, and yet it is our soul that lives in us and keeps us alive; so the Holy Spirit is the soul of the Church, the living soul of our own souls, giving us the life of the Father's children. The clearest sign he is living in us and we have his life in us, is that he makes the very prayer of the Son well up in our soul, and creates in us the sentiments and reactions of the Son towards the Father.

These mysteries do not need long explanations. Difficult as they may be to express, they spring spontaneously in any Christian who is really in communion with God. We do not need to explain the working of the Holy Spirit any more than we need to teach a child to breathe or what it means to be at home with his parents: heart and lungs find it out for themselves. By the working of the Holy Spirit we know how to see God as our Father and Jesus as our Lord. No human effort or striving of the mind could do this otherwise. But though we cannot grasp the Holy Spirit, faith teaches us to recognize he is there and to respond to him. Here again the experience of the early Church throws a great deal of light.

When he sent his disciples out to proclaim the gospel, Jesus promised them the Holy Spirit. The promises at first seemed limited to urgent circumstances, persecutions under which the disciples were to bear witness to the Lord before tribunals. 'Do not consider anxiously what you have to say or how you are to say it; words will be given to you when the time comes; it is not you who speak, it is the Spirit of your Father that speaks in you.'[36] When about to leave them and enter on the passion, he widens the scope of his promise: 'The Holy Spirit . . . will in his turn make everything plain and recall to your minds everything I have said to you';[37] 'The truth-giving Spirit . . . will guide you into all truth'.[38] However, as long as the Holy Spirit was still only a promise, he could only be thought of as some 'other to befriend you', external to them as Jesus was, and separate from them. True, the Holy Spirit could not be separate from them, and all our Lord said really only took on meaning for them once the disciples experienced the interior coming of the Spirit. Till then, he was bound to seem a stranger.

Pentecost was the Church's experience of his coming. Even then there was no vision or feeling of the Holy Spirit himself, but the Church felt transformed, endowed with strength to proclaim Christ and his passion and glory, braced to imitate him, directed like him to the achievement of the kingdom, inspired by his prayer. The greater the crisis, the more daring the witness needed to be, the more did this identity between the Church's prayer and our Lord's become manifest. Stephen, when being stoned, could repeat the words of Jesus: 'Lord, do not count this sin against them',[39] 'Lord, receive my spirit'.[40] We have seen, too, how St Paul went up to Jerusalem knowing he was to suffer, perhaps to die; and to the Christians of Caesarea restraining him all he could say was: 'The Lord's will be done.'[41] Our Lord's promises were being fulfilled beyond expectation: not only did the disciples find the exact

[36] Matt. 10:19
[37] John 14:26
[38] John 16:13
[39] Acts 7:59; cf. Luke 23:34
[40] Acts 7:59; cf. Luke 23:46
[41] Acts 21:14

words to confound their enemies, but they found themselves
praying the same prayers as their Master in the same situations.
As they confessed the Lord before men, they were united in
the prayer of him who stood for them in the presence of God.
Here we see unity between prayer and action, between suffering and apostolate. We see how well the Spirit of Christ had
taught his disciples.

The ordinary Christian is in the same position in regard to
prayer:

> The Spirit you have now received is not, as of old, a
> spirit of slavery, to govern you by fear; it is the spirit of
> adoption, which makes us cry out, Abba, Father. The
> Spirit himself thus assures our spirit that we are children of
> God; and if we are his children, then we are his heirs too;
> heirs of God, sharing the inheritance of Christ; only we
> must share his sufferings if we are to share his glory.[42]

All Christian prayer is governed by this rule; prayer spontaneously finding the Father, putting itself in his presence
with the naturalness of a son, in union with Jesus. Only with
him can this be done, identifying ourselves with his dispositions and way of speaking to God. But it can be done, with
full success, enabling us to share our Lord's most intimate
prayer, that of absolute obedience, the secret of his life and
death. This requires of the soul radical abnegation of self
when we are 'sharing his sufferings'. To measure how truly
we are God's sons, how truly God is our father, we must be
willing to lean only on him, to leap into the unknown. Our
earthly hearts are incapable of this, but the Holy Spirit works
it in us. How, St Paul does not undertake to explain. The
work of the Spirit of God on the spirit of man escapes us;
but we are assured of its reality by the assurance wherewith
the Spirit enables us, overcoming our own fears and defying
all dangers, to stand before God as his sons.

As we cannot sound the depths where the prayer of the
Spirit wells up in us, so we cannot fix its direction or limits.
It is the prayer of our Lord and has the scope of his boundless
vision, so it must transcend any human horizons. Yet the

[42] Rom. 8:15–17

prayer in us is our own, and we know this only too well, by reason of the restlessness we feel, the urge towards a purer and deeper kind of prayer. This ever-restless need we feel so painfully in our prayer is a sign of the Holy Spirit, and we can only put up with it peacefully:

> The Spirit comes to the aid of our weakness; when we do not know what prayer to offer, to pray as we ought, the Spirit himself intercedes for us, with groans beyond all utterance; and God, who can read our hearts, knows well what the Spirit's intent is; for indeed it is according to the mind of God that he makes intercession for the saints.[43]

We need not be surprised then if we do not feel that our prayer is the prayer of Christ. We must not imagine that, to become so, it must change its character and acquire a facility or purity of intention we could never achieve. Every time we address the Father, every time we say the Our Father and mean it, the Lord is uttering his prayer within us. We must not be surprised either if this prayer is often difficult and apparently sterile. To 'confess the Father' means renouncing all else besides his will to satisfy us and his kingdom to hope for. When our prayer, however prolonged, seems to bring no relish and bear no fruit, we must recognize the finger of God and allow him to work out his prayer in us.

[43] Rom. 8 : 26–7

XVII

Our Work in Life and the Expectation of God's Kingdom

EEK FIRST his kingdom . . . and all these things shall be
yours as well.'[1] It would seem that our Lord did not attach
a great deal of importance to the demands of what we call
'duties of state'. These, for the vast majority of men, mean
their work, their responsibilities as citizens; if grown up, their
responsibilities at home and at business; as children, the
duties of obedience and readiness to learn. On all these points
the gospel shows a reserve which, in view of the place these
preoccupations hold in our lives, seems deliberate and intended by our Lord. He condemned adultery, but he never
depicted what we nowadays call a Christian home. As for
work, too, if we want to base it on the gospel, we are reduced
to a commentary on the very slight indications on the life at
Nazareth. Even so we have to read between the lines, for there
is no mention of the word work, and none of the episodes of
our Lord's early life would seem to refer to it explicitly. We
do know that when he began to appear in public, those who
knew him were quite surprised: 'Is not this the carpenter?'[2]
During the public life the gospels continue to tell us little
about work; they do not contain a single explicit exhortation
to work. The only use of the word is to designate the kind of
works we should undertake, and the reference is to 'the works
of God';[3] or else we are given the example of the birds of the

---

[1] Matt. 6 : 33   [2] Mark 6 : 3   [3] John 6 : 28; cf. 5 : 17

air that 'neither sow nor reap',[4] or the lilies of the field that 'neither toil nor spin'.[5] To be honest, duties of state would not seem to have the almost sacred value for our Lord that we so often attribute to them.

The only thing that matters, in our Lord's teaching, was the kingdom of God. It is there for the asking, and he who will not sell all he has cannot acquire it. If a man wants time to think about it, to put his affairs in order, 'to bury his father', it will be too late, Jesus will have passed on and the kingdom is not for him. If a man wants to go and take possession of a farm he has bought, to try out a yoke of oxen from the market, even the time to bring home the wife he has married, it is too late, the banqueting hall is full and the door closed on him. And yet none of these errands, that Jesus seems to condemn, are wrong in any way; they are not contrary to any commandment, they are simply obligations naturally involved in the duties of state: a husband owes himself to his wife, a father must see to the well-being of his dependents. Yet it was just such preoccupations Jesus seemed to want to wean people from. Pagans could worry themselves what to eat and drink, for they know nothing of the Father who is in heaven. But his children, who know he has them in his hand and see him feeding the birds of the air and clothing the lilies of the field, are failing in trust towards God if they live in anxiety. Let the children of God allow their Father to prove himself a father, as he is so anxious to; let them allow him to take upon himself all their worries and take care of their life. Is not that the heart of the gospel? But would it not lead us away from our duties of state?

However, there are in St Paul many exhortations that give to duties of state the importance we normally attribute to them: 'Husbands, love your wives';[6] 'Children, obey your parents';[7] 'Keep away from any brother who is living in idleness';[8] 'If anyone will not work, let him not eat';[9] 'Be submissive . . . magistrates are in God's service. Pay every man

[4] Matt. 6:26
[5] Matt. 6:28
[6] Eph. 5:25
[7] Eph. 6:1
[8] 2 Thess. 3:6
[9] Ibid. 3:10

his due; taxes, if it be taxes; customs, if it be customs'.[10] Here we seem to be back in real life again.

To try to find opposition between St Paul and the gospel would be a sure way of misunderstanding both; for, being both inspired by the same Spirit, they both convey the single truth that is the word of God. But it would be equally wrong to claim to reconcile them by whittling them down, for this would imply we still consider them somehow contradictory to each other. So we must, with the light God gives us, endeavour to go fully into the teaching of Christ as well as the ideas of St Paul.

1. 'Stay as you are'

To begin with St Paul. Here the doctrine is more worked out, as it is an answer to actual difficulties in practice. St Paul does speak of what we call duties of state, but they are not the only ones, and he allots them their place in the general setting of Christian life. In this the supreme value remains attachment to Christ, and the only hope we must absolutely cling to is the kingdom of the Lord and his coming. The First Epistle to the Corinthians, Chapter 7, puts forward a series of counsels concerning married life and professional life. They have the particular advantage of envisaging, on the one hand, the different conditions a Christian might be in, married or single, free or slave; and on the other hand, the attitude of mind, quite new and typically Christian, aroused by the conviction that 'the form of this world is passing, and that the only thing that matters is 'to secure your undivided devotion to the Lord'.[11] In this passage we see duties of state and the expectation of the kingdom explicitly presented side by side.

How they are related is not altogether simple, we must admit, in fact it cannot be. For there is such diversity of situations, and of callings within the same situations. There is also, varying with different situations and callings but always paramount, the priority to be given to the Lord. Also two factors act and interact: the state of life you are in, and the call of the Lord. These two factors are not opposed. The state of life I am in does not cut me off from the Lord, of course, otherwise

[10] Rom. 13:5–7   [11] 1 Cor. 7:31, 35

the question would not arise. But in itself it is not identified
with the call of the Lord; it does not bring with it all that I
hope for from the Lord, nor does it contain for me all that
the Lord wants of me. So between these two factors there is an
interplay, between God's initiative and man's response, in
the freedom of his choices and the generosity of his love.
Whatever the state of life you are in, it matters little, only
the Lord is important, but while awaiting his coming stay
with this state of life. St Paul envisages the basic conditions a
Christian might be in, circumcised or uncircumcised, single
or married, slave or free, three times over; he does not lay down
any law, but is clearly insisting on a principle that seems
important to him: 'Remain in the condition in which you are
called.'

The part which God has assigned, the vocation which
God has bestowed, is to be the rule in each case. That is the
direction I am giving all through the churches. If a man is
already circumcised when he is called, he is not to disguise it;
if he is uncircumcised, he is not to undergo circumcision.
There is no virtue either in circumcision or in the want of
it; it is keeping the commandments of God that signifies.
. . . Hast thou been called a slave? Do not let it trouble
thee; and (even) if thou hast the means to become free, make
all the more use of thy opportunity (as a slave). If a slave
is called to enter Christ's service, he is Christ's freedman;
just as the free man, when he is called, becomes the slave
of Christ. A price was paid to redeem you; do not enslave
yourselves to human masters. Each of you is to remain,
brethren, in the condition in which he was called.[12]

The meaning is quite clear, but the attitude St Paul presupposes implies several finer points worth bringing out. The
spirit that conditions all else is absolute detachment, and in
this we have an exact echo of the sermon on the Mount.
Nothing in the world is of any importance in itself, only God
matters, his will, his call, his redemption. Circumcised or not,
slavery or freedom, what do such human concerns and temporal conditions matter compared with God? He alone is

[12] 1 Cor. 7:17–24

eternal, he alone merits allegiance and honour. With St Paul
this is a fundamental principle that comes up several times in
similar, if not identical, terms: 'Once we are in Christ,
circumcision means nothing, and the want of it means
nothing; the faith that finds expression in love is all that
matters.'[13] 'It is not what we eat that gives us standing in God's
sight; we gain nothing by eating, lose nothing by abstain-
ing.'[14] 'There is neither Jew nor Greek, there is neither slave
nor free, there is neither male nor female; for you are all one
in Christ Jesus.'[15] This absolute priority given to redemption
links St Paul with the most abrupt sayings of our Lord: 'No
one is good but God alone';[16] 'If your eye causes you to sin,
pluck it out'.[17] St Paul had heard this imperious voice, and
'in order that I may gain Christ', he says, he has chosen to lose
everything, 'counting everything as loss', all the advantages of
birth and religion and zeal hitherto.[18] All the treasures of the
earth are nothing when we seek to purchase the one pearl of
great price.

But St Paul does not infer that nothing in this world has
any value. If that were so, if all situations were equally point-
less, if everything we did were only going through the motions,
what would our choices matter at all? The Christian would
then be free to behave as he liked, to be a Jew and act as a
Gentile, to heed only his own inclinations to achieve freedom,
or even to give free rein to his passions. This has been, down
the centuries, the sequence of ideas of so many pseudo-spiritual
'enthusiasts' who condemned all flesh as impure and reckoned
any use of it immaterial. Not so St Paul: given that all ways
of life are 'nothing', he does not draw the conclusion, 'Do as
you like'; on the contrary he persists in saying, 'Stay in your
way of life.' What is the idea behind this?

From the confrontation of human situations and the call of
the Lord, two sets of consequences can be drawn, not contradictory, but complementary to each other, and St Paul draws
them both. He can infer, negatively, that 'there is no virtue
in circumcision or in the want of it', for neither means anything; but he can reach a positive conclusion; have no fear of

[13] Gal. 5:6

[14] 1 Cor. 8:8

[15] Gal. 3:28

[16] Mark 10:18

[17] Mark 9:47

[18] Cf. Phil. 3:4-9

either, both are all right, any condition can be the setting of
a Christian life. In fact, the positive line normally seems more
familiar to St Paul than the other. It reappears constantly, at
important stages in his teaching, crystallizing major points:

> God has not destined us for wrath, but to obtain salvation
> through our Lord Jesus Christ, so that whether we wake or
> sleep we might live through him.[19]

> Nobody should repose his confidence in man. Everything
> is for you, whether it be Paul or Apollo or Caphas, or the
> world, or life, or death, or the present, or the future; it is
> all for you, and you for Christ, and Christ for God.[20]

> Whether you eat or drink . . . do all for the glory of
> God.[21]

> Who will separate us from the love of Christ? . . .
> neither death, nor life, no angels or principalities or powers
> neither what is present nor what is to come, no force what-
> ever neither the height above us nor the depth beneath us,
> nor any other created thing, will be able to separate us from
> the love of God, which comes to us in Christ Jesus our
> Lord.[22]

> Now as always Christ will be honoured in my body,
> whether by life or by death.[23]

> In any and all circumstances I have learned the secret of
> facing plenty and hunger, abundance and want. I can do all
> things in him who strengthens me.[24]

St Paul's way of expressing himself varies with the situations
envisaged, and many shades of meaning can be discerned in
the above texts. Some 'creatures', as we say, spontaneously
attract us, some situations help us to go forward, while others
fill us with repugnance; St Paul is no less sensitive than we
are to such reactions, and so his language varies accordingly,
whether it be attractive circumstances or obstacles in our way.
All the former can be permissible, all can be profitable, all

---

[19] 1 Thess. 5:9–10   [20] 1 Cor. 3:21–23   [21] 1 Cor. 10:31
[22] Rom. 8:35–38   [23] Phil. 1:20   [24] Phil. 4:12–13

is good, in Christ Jesus. *None* of the latter need be bad, none need be dangerous, none need be insurmountable to those who belong to Christ. Whether he says *all* or *nothing*, St Paul's meaning is ultimately the same.

All situations have a positive value, though in a relative way, and this explains why, after stressing the insignificance of 'circumcised or not, slave or free', St Paul could conclude, with an apparent lack of logic: 'stay the way you are'. If a man must stay the way he was on becoming a Christian, if this could be called the condition assigned to him by the Lord, the point was that this condition was neutral in theory but contained a real value that might be lost by quitting it hastily. Not only can any state of life be compatible with the Christian life and so be lived with a clear conscience; but moreover the grace of Christ has the power to operate in any human situation and bring out strictly Christian values even under the most unfavourable conditions. Why then should a slave not seek to escape from slavery? Perhaps on the ordinary principle of resignation, we would say, so as to entrust himself to God's providence. But St Paul has a higher idea of this providence, God's wisdom that confounds human wisdom, and the motive he gives to the slave labouring under an inhuman system is that nowhere more than in the person of a slave does God show what the freedom of Christ can do for a man who is a victim of injustice. St Paul goes on to give the converse to this paradox. In the case of the free man, Christianity should produce responses of submission and dependence, it should take the form of acting as 'the slave of Christ'.[25]

[25] True as it is, the explanation given by Père Huby: 'Christian slaves can accept their social condition as a disposition of Providence that will turn to their spiritual good' (cf. *Saint Paul, Verbum Salutis, XIII*, Paris, 1946, p. 170) does not quite give the literally triumphant note of St Paul recognizing in a slave 'the freedman of the Lord'. Still less is it right to infer from this passage that 'Jesus serenely admits differences of condition subsisting between masters and slaves' (cf. M. Scheler, *L'Homme du Ressentiment*, French translation, Paris, 1936, p. 102). Père Montcheuil (*Mélanges théologiques*, Paris, 1946, pp. 206ff) rightly showed that, though Christ did not preach political, economic or social reforms, it was not that such reforms are a matter of indifference to the gospel message. Charity that did not take the form of 'a constant effort to raise people up and bring relief and peace' would be quite unreal, like an artist's dream that he never took the trouble to paint. But Christ

2. *Duties as a man and duties as a Christian*

In all the examples we have considered, it is a matter of being faithful to a given situation and so to one of our duties of state, but not quite 'the duty of state' normally referred to. The duty of state usually means being faithful to everyday tasks, conscientiously carrying out our jobs in the home or at work. Such tasks do have their value, and fidelity to them is precious. St Paul does appreciate them, since he expects people to remain attached to them. 'The man who makes no provision for those nearest to him, above all his own family, has contradicted the teaching of the faith, and indeed does worse than the unbelievers do.'[26] However, such fidelity in itself does not carry membership of the kingdom. An unbeliever is capable of it; a most devoted mother and a most conscientious worker may remain far from the faith. What faith gives the Christian is a new way of adhering to his condition in life, a light from God to see God's guidance in it. It is normal, it is written into the nature of a woman to lean on her husband and refer her life to him, as it is normal and in the nature of things that a husband should love his wife and protect her. But Christian spouses receive from the sacrament of marriage the grace to live their union on another plane and in greater depth. In devoting herself to her husband the Christian wife, because her faith makes her a 'handmaid of the Lord', finds in this service an inexhaustible source of devotedness and tenderness and self-sacrifice, in a way that transforms her love. So too the Christian husband, if he has entered into the spirit of Christ and realized how our Lord loves him; when he gives his heart, he gives a heart conscious of God's own love, and it is not just natural generosity that makes him devoted to his wife, it is a love that makes him capable of sacrificing himself for her, as our Lord did for the Church.[27]

---

in preaching the religious element, the heart of his message, was creating the only climate wherein the implications of his teaching (in a domain where it is easy to go astray) could develop on the right lines. This was not a case of indifference to concrete applications of charity, but insistence on first revealing the true nature of charity.

[26] 1 Tim. 5:8   [27] Cf. Eph. 5:21–33

Duties of state have their proper human value, but they have their Christian value as well, and the latter value, though based on the former, gives it an original character. It is a duty for every man to work, to undertake his share of humanity's common need to earn their bread by the sweat of their brow.[28] On occasion, St Paul reminds idlers that this applies to them: 'If anyone will not work, let him not eat';[29] 'We did not eat any one's bread without paying (he says), but with toil and labour we worked night and day, that we might not burden any of you'.[30] So he warned the faithful no one had any right to live at the expense of others and not pay their debts. But rising beyond these mundane considerations, he adds: 'Owe no one anything, except to love one another.'[31] 'The man who was a thief must be a thief no longer; let him work instead, and earn by his own labour the blessings he will be able to share with those who are in need.'[32] By doing his job wherever it is, being careful not to exploit anyone else's work or deprive them of their rights, the Christian as a man among men is to secure the balance and soundness of the social body, but he has, besides all that, a special witness to bear, that of charity. On being converted, the idler and the crook who lived hitherto on other people do not just become useful members of society, they contribute something new. The chronic debtor, who was for ever dodging people as creditors, now as a Christian man will find himself drawn to people and will never have finished his payments of charity to his brethren. Likewise the thief, on being converted, does not just take up a job to earn an honest living, but as a means of helping his brethren in their needs.

This new value in the duties of state as practised by the Christian is none other than charity. If situations that are in themselves neutral and indifferent may create special duties for a Christian, it is because they can be made the channels of charity. The Christian who takes his task in this world seriously does so primarily because, as a man among men, he must not evade his duty of solidarity with them. But above all it is because, being a son of God, he owes it to his fellow men to reflect on to them the love God surrounds him with. This

[28] Gen. 3:19   [29] 2 Thess. 3:10   [30] Ibid. 8
[31] Rom. 13:8   [32] Eph. 4:27

latter obligation provides the highest justification for the former. Wherever his duty as a man and as a citizen places him, the Christian welcomes his situation in the world and is quick to see in it his special duty of state as a Christian, his special vocation as a member of the Church, which is charity. Just as God alone must be sought in any and every situation, so charity is the only duty of state which is an absolute obligation in all circumstances. It is always possible, it allows of no dispensation from its demands, and it is always in force.

The language of St Paul verifies remarkably this correlation of the sovereign priority of God with the primacy of charity. The basic point outlined above, that situations matter little and only the Lord really matters, carries two parallel implications: one that the only consideration that counts is God and his love; the other, that the only conduct that is always right is the love of other people. This second response, so close to the gospel, works infallibly. Along with the key passages: 'whether we wake or sleep we live through him'; 'whether you eat or drink, do all for the glory of God'; 'all is for you, you are for Christ, and Christ for God', we also have, equally categorical and similarly expressed, the declarations that closely correspond to them: 'Circumcision means nothing, nor the want of it; the faith that finds its expression in charity is all that matters';[33] 'That is my own rule, to satisfy all alike, studying the general welfare rather than my own, so as to win their salvation';[34] 'I may speak with every tongue that men and angels use . . . I may have the powers of prophecy . . . if I lack charity, it goes for nothing'.[35] Compared with charity, all God's gifts are relatively unimportant and all human duties take second place.

3. 'As though . . .'

This combination of ordinary fidelity to our duties as men and the Christian fidelity to the love of God and neighbour is not always easy. Often, it is true, ordinary fidelity and Christian allegiance do go together and reinforce each other, though Christians may too easily take themselves for models of family, civic and professional virtues. But normally those who are

[33] Gal. 5:6   [34] 1 Cor. 10:33   [35] 1 Cor. 13:1–3

most conscious of their duties do find in their allegiance to our Lord the strength to be faithful to the duties of their state with self-sacrifice. However, it does also happen that one senses in Christians, even in most conscientious and enlightened people, a lack of genuine interest in their task as men. They may practise the virtue of being conscientious in their work, but it is not a vital reflex in their make-up; it may be a strict obligation, but it always requires an effort. The scandal that the children of this generation take at the casualness of the children of light, at the surprising mixture of assurance and indifference that they assume with regard to the problems of humanity, is not always ill founded. And the Christian who really thinks finds himself at times affected by a disturbing thought—what value can there be in his efforts on this earth, if eternity is the only future that matters?

The same seventh chapter of the Epistle to the Corinthians where St Paul urges the faithful to remain in the same state as the Lord's call found them in contains a little further on the most definite and trenchant expressions of this Christian indifference to the world, which nowadays shock the unbeliever and may easily disturb a believer whose faith is not too sure:

> From now on, let those who have wives live as though they had none; and those who mourn as though they were not mourning, and those who rejoice as though they were not rejoicing, and those who buy as though they had no goods, and those who deal with the world as though they had no dealings with it. For the form of this world is passing away.[36]

To understand these words which sound harsh to our ears we must accept them with respect, allowing for the shock they give us. Yet we must take care not to travesty them by over-simplifying them, for they only become clear for single-minded souls who are detached enough to meet the two-fold demands they make. It is of course an elementary point in the Christian faith that the end of our time on earth is not far off. Not only because with the Lord a thousand years are

[36] 1 Cor. 7 : 29–31

as a day, but because here and now the Lord stands at our door and knocks, and his presence there changes the meaning of our life. It may be that the world will go on for many thousands of years, but it remains true, just as true for us as for the first Christians and for our furthest descendants living in a world we could not recognize, that only a matter of time separates us from the Lord's coming. It is also true that, on leaving this world, we hope to find ourselves in a world that will be for all eternity the world of redeemed humanity, a world which will be ours, the world for which we have laboured and loved and grieved, but transformed by the visible presence of God and radiant with his joy, the world of the kingdom of God. Compared with this kingdom and its life, the most successful achievements of this earthly life not only fade into insignificance, they are dark and insubstantial shadows. Every Christian hopes to enter this kingdom. A man most passionately devoted to this world and men's achievements in it, Pierre Teilhard de Chardin, throughout his life and increasingly as time went on, was buoyed up by the expectation of the time when he should see the whole universe transfigured and consummated in the fullness of the incarnate Word.

From this basic Christian conviction there may result either of two attitudes, and St Paul's 'as though' lessons can be taken in two quite different ways, almost diametrically opposed. The lesson can be taken in the disillusioned frame of mind of one never satisfied with anything, the peevishness of a spoiled child who does not care for any present he is given. Seen in this way, this world, in the eyes of many Christians and others, because it offers countless occasions of suffering compared with the few fleeting compensations, seems one vast failure. In view of the disappointments involved in this miserable world, the 'as though' lessons might suggest a reaction which might seem to be wisdom: not to take anything unduly seriously, never to have any great expectations, not to get too deeply involved in anything or too deeply committed to anybody. Such an attitude would only produce a form of paganism, considering the world evil and at the mercy of conflicting divine caprices. Such an attitude has affected many Christians, in more or less gross or subtle forms, not in the

name of their Christian hope, but because something in them
has still been immersed in darkness and despair.

The lesson St Paul recommended to the Corinthians and
carried out in his own life was radically different. In no way
did it arise from a heart that was sophisticated and dissatisfied
with everything. St Paul was most ready to welcome every
form of beauty, open to every kind of sympathy. He recommended the Philippians to appreciate 'all that rings true, all
that commands reverence, and all that makes for right; all that
is pure, all that is lovely, all that is gracious in the telling;
virtue and merit, wherever virtue and merit are found'.[37] In
wanting to live 'as though . . .' he was not inspired by contempt for this world, but by concern for a higher liberty,
determined 'not to abdicate my own liberty'.[38]

In their reactions to love and riches, in their response to
the joys and goods of this world, as also with regard to their
sorrows and griefs, men are always tempted to attribute an
absolute reality to their experiences in unreserved pursuit of
happiness or preoccupation with their own grief. There is a
sort of idolatry in this morbid need to clutch at this life God
gives us, refusing to believe in God's generosity as soon as it
makes demands on our faith, and incapable of letting God
take care of our lives. Nothing in this life is a unique object
of love or hatred: everything must be welcomed and appreciated with gratitude and respect for God's work. There is a
certain reserve to be kept in all joy as in all grief, a restraint to
be observed, not out of prudence or fear, but from veneration
for something mysterious and divine dwelling in all creation.
Such was the courteous and brotherly attitude of St Francis of
Assisi towards the Lord Sun and Sister Death. The Christian's
response to the 'as though' aspect of life is not a bitter compensation for illusions unmasked; it is the serene conviction
of a man who takes the world and all its tasks seriously, without
cursing them or worshipping them, but realizing that they are
giving birth to a new world whose glory he cannot even
imagine.

So St Paul's attitude had nothing to do with laziness or
wanting to avoid useless commitments in view of the little

[37] Phil. 4:8   [38] 1 Cor. 6:12

time we have to live, it represents an act of faith. Wanting to
change one's state would mean a lack of trust in the power of
the redemption. The time is short, it is true, but the time
allotted is not expendable, time to kill in any way we like: on
the contrary, it is rich in opportunities for the fulfilment that
is to come. This time is a 'dawning day' with the light of a sun
we do not yet see, but it enables us to live as 'sons of light
and sons of the day'[39] and work 'as men of the daylight'.[40] So
the Christian slave who could seek his freedom, as he is entitled
to and others in his place would, has something even better to
do: he can remain a slave and live as 'Christ's freedman'.[41] He
is not merely accepting his slavery with patience, because
time is short and the end is not far off—this is only a secondary
consideration. He welcomes his condition with the freedom
of spirit of the man redeemed by Christ, the man of faith who
knows that sin and injustice, though ravaging humanity till
the end, have been overcome once and for all on the cross. The
Lord's freedman, like Christ himself, bears on his person and
in his heart the traces of human injustice and sin, but with
the strength of Christ he responds to this violence with forgiveness and love. In the midst of injustice the Christian slave
bears witness to the redemption: that is his 'duty of state' of
the highest order, a duty freely binding him to his state and
transfiguring it with the radiant dawn of the risen Christ.

The free man has his own kind of witness to contribute, a
duty of state with its freedom of action. We might be inclined
to think straight off that his duty is to be efficient in his activi-
ties, determined to take full advantage of his powers to benefit
men as much as possible, representing in this world generous-
handed authority, the magnanimity and liberality of God. This
ideal has a lot to be said for it, and a Christian is not unfaithful
to the gospel in professing it. But it does not rise to the essentially Christian idea of the cross, and St Paul would invite such
a man to look higher: 'You are a free man; use your freedom
to show what you are in the sight of God, his servant.' He
would tell the Christian in a prominent position with considerable influence that it is well that he puts all this to the
service of men. That he puts all his powers and resources at

---

[39] 1 Thess. 5:5   [40] Ibid.   [41] 1 Cor. 7:22

the disposal of the Church too, may be very well. But the sign that he personally is first seeking the kingdom is that he sheds in spirit the reflexes of power; accustomed as he is to having his orders obeyed, he puts himself at the disposal of others, willing if necessary to be at the mercy of the poor, with real simplicity towards men and absolute trust in God. Then he will be making the most of the condition allotted to him by God, then he will have found his true vocation and his place for ever in the joy of the Lord.

4. *Duties of state in the gospel*

The outlook of St Paul brings us back precisely to that of the gospel, which we should now be in a better position to understand. For St Paul as for our Lord, the thing that matters first and foremost, the treasure for which we must sell all we possess, is the kingdom of God; and the obligation that allows of no exceptions, the great commandment, is that of loving God and our neighbour. This ever-present obligation, this paramount preoccupation, though reducing any particular duties of state to a subordinate position and diminishing the halo we sometimes surround them with, really raises them to a new dignity and throws on them the light of charity and the glory of the kingdom that is to come. We have seen this was St Paul's teaching, but our Lord gave us the same lesson, not so closely reasoned, but spontaneously implied. To Martha, 'distracted by waiting on many needs', he said: 'Martha, how many cares and troubles thou hast! But only one thing is necessary.'[42] The one thing necessary is to devote all one's attention, as Mary did, to our Lord and to let his words sink deep into our souls. It was not because he had no time for household cares or for civilized usages. To Simon the pharisee, who had gone to no trouble to receive him properly, he pointed out the sinful woman weeping at his feet and showed the lack of courtesy on Simon's part: 'Thou gavest me no water for my feet. . . . Thou gavest me no kiss of greeting . . .; thou didst not pour oil on my head. . . .'[43] The only thing necessary here below is to keep our gaze fixed on our Lord in the expectation of his coming, but if we do this aright we shall

[42] Luke 10:40–2   [43] Luke 7:44–6

discover that there is nothing superfluous in our duties of
state and their unending demands, and that every present
moment calls for more care and patience and courage.

We need not be surprised that our Lord is so reticent on
duties of state. It is not that he condemns them or does not rate
them highly. On the contrary he presupposes them as normal
conditions of human life, as he presupposes the legitimacy of
the state, with its civil service officials and armed forces. It
was not his task to proclaim these duties that rise from human
nature and not from his coming into the world. It was sufficient
for him to recognize their validity and confirm their obligation,
but in doing so he gave them a new dimension. 'Render unto
Caesar' is a convenient summing-up, and it might seem to
meet only one set of circumstances. But actually it is characteristic of him who, being the Son of God, is always and wholly
'about his Father's business'; and though it is a 'quick answer'
it does not brush the issue aside as of little consequence. By
distinguishing once and for all the scope of the kingdom of
God and the proper objectives of the state, by showing that
they are different from each other but both equally operative,
our Lord gave the state its definitive standing in God's eyes and
assured for it its indisputable claims on the Christian conscience. In the same way his judgment on marriage: 'What
God has joined together, let not man put asunder'[44] is a straight
answer to a question put to him, and does not claim to be an
innovation coming in with the gospel, but only the confirmation of the original intention of the Creator. But this simple
statement, restoring the true position of women and demanding from man the mastery of their passions, was enough to
establish among human beings the basis of genuine married
love and give it its place in the coming of God's kingdom.

One way of being sure that the sovereignty of God's kingdom
does not involve any lack of appreciation for duties of state,
but gives them full scope in the single-minded service of the
Lord, is to listen to our Lord's message. He speaks only of the
kingdom, but always starting from our duties of state, as a
man who knows by experience their importance and value in
life. The concern of the vine-grower for his harvest, the house-

[44] Matt. 19:6

wife for the housekeeping money, the shepherd's care for his flock, the patient endurance of the ploughman or the fisher-man, the importance of due hospitality for guests and good arrangements for a wedding reception—he knew all these things from the inside, and while he used them as images of the kingdom and its priority, he also first appreciated them for their own sake.

To get to know all our tasks from the inside, our Lord took the surest way, that of experience. No doubt he could have done without; being the man he was, with his power of sym-pathy and insight, with his human heart wholly possessed by divine charity, he could, in any state of life himself, have assimilated our own way of life and been close to us. However, he chose the common way, that of experience, experience so prolonged as to be second nature. The way he portrays things in the gospel springs from his own memories. For thirty years he lived in this world without the slightest trace of not belonging to it or being out of keeping with it; and when he began to speak to men, this upbringing came out in him. That is the real point of the life at Nazareth that the gospel brings home to us; it does not so much draw attention to a life of piety and family affection, but rather to an ordinary life and a man so well adapted to it that, even in a village where everyone knows everything about everybody else, no one ever spotted anything in Jesus other than the son of a working man. Even his parents, when for once he departed from this role, did not understand, so accustomed were they to their son being like anyone else. This was certainly no pretence on his part: we need not imagine him taking precautions so that the secret would not slip out. Spontaneously and without the slightest embarrassment, Jesus lived this human condition, absorbed from morning till night by the duties of his state. He lived it as Son of God, as he was to live his life, when the time came and with the same naturalness, as a prophet in Israel. But this would only be two or three years, as against thirty. This was the Father's plan; this was how he revealed his Son, and himself through him; such was the character he was forming for him during these thirty years of work and submission to the duties we all have. This must mean that our ordinary way of life and our daily duties are capable of being lived in a fully Christian way, in the pure spirit of the gospel, as the children of the Father, and so, lived in this way, they take on considerable dimensions and a value that we cannot imagine in the coming of the kingdom of God.

For those who have chosen to seek first the kingdom of God and his righteousness, duties of state do not need to be made a devouring preoccupation or an overwhelming burden —they just are the way by which the kingdom comes among us.